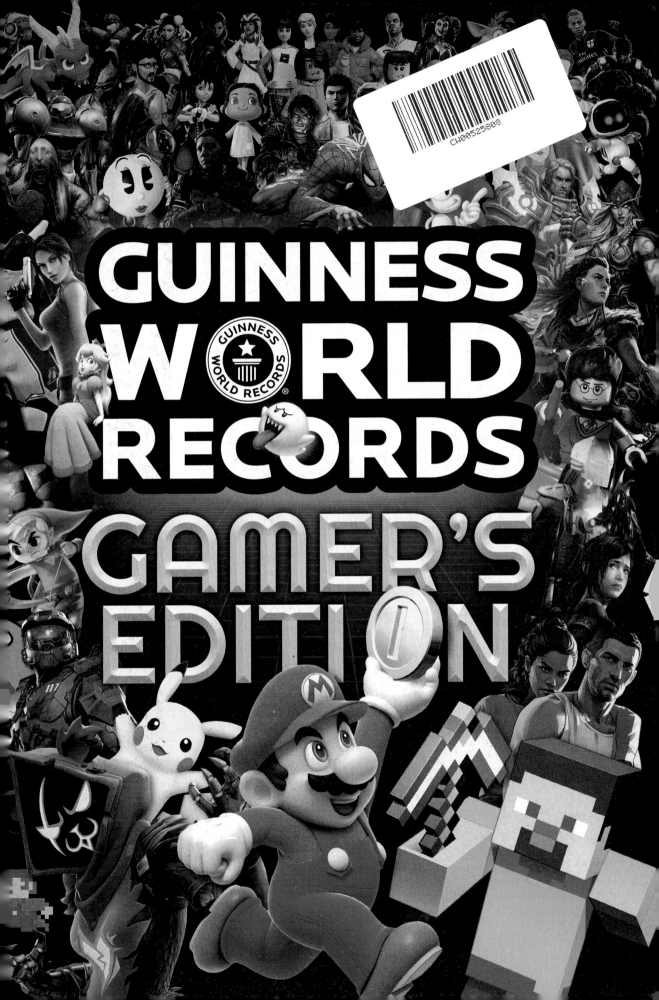

GUINNESS W🏛RLD RECORDS

GUINNESS WORLD RECORDS®

GAMER'S EDITION

SVP Global Publishing
Nadine Causey

Editor-in-Chief
Craig Glenday

Layout Editors
Chris Bryans, Eddie de Oliveira

Managing Editor
Adam Millward

Senior Editors
Tom Beckerlegge, Ben Hollingum

Junior Editor
Caitlin Hyem

Proofreading & Fact-Checking
Matthew White

Picture Editors
Lucy Talavera, Abby Taylor

Layout Design
Ryan Gale

Cover Design
Paul Wylie-Deacon at
55design.co.uk

Indexer
Marie Lorimer

**Director of Publishing
& Book Production**
Jane Boatfield

Production & Distribution Director
Patricia Magill

Production & Distribution Manager
Thomas McCurdy

Talent Researcher
Charlie Anderson

Head of Commissioned Content
Michael Whitty

Original Photography
Paul Michael Hughes

Production Consultants
Yannick Laag, Astrid Renders,
Kevin Sarney, Maximilian Schonlau,
Dennis Thon

Printing & Binding
Mohn Media Mohndruck GmbH,
Gütersloh, Germany

Global Marketing Director
Nicholas Brookes

**Head of Publishing & Brand
Communications
(UK & International)**
Amber-Georgina Maskell

PR Manager (UK & International)
Madalyn Bielfeld

PR Executive (UK & International)
Alina Polianskaya

**Marketing Executive
(UK & International)**
Nicole Dyer-Rainford

**Senior Content Manager
(UK & International)**
Eleonora Pilastro

Senior PR Manager (Americas)
Amanda Marcus

**Senior PR Executive
(Americas)**
Kylie Galloway

CRM Marketing Manager
Jody Ho

Global Sales Director
Joel Smith

Senior Key Account Manager
Mavis Sarfo

International Sales Manager
Aliona Ladus

Reprographics
Resmiye Kahraman and Louise
Pinnock at Born Group

British Library Cataloguing-in-publication data: a catalogue record for this book is available from the British Library

UK: 978-1-913484-52-1
US: 978-1-913484-53-8
CAN: 978-1-913484-59-0

Records are made to be broken – indeed, it is one of the key criteria for a record category – so if you find a record that you think you can beat, tell us about it by making a record claim. Always contact us before making a record attempt.

Sustainability

At Guinness World Records, we continue to run our business in the most sustainable, environmentally conscious way we can. As part of that commitment, the pages of this book are printed on a fully recycled paper, made of 100% reclaimed paper and post-consumer de-inked pulp. No chlorine bleaching is used in the paper production process. It has been awarded the Blue Angel and EU Ecolabel recognition.

This paper is produced at the Steinbeis Papier mill in Germany, which is one of the most energy-efficient and low-emission paper mills in Europe. The mill is focused on ecological balance throughout the production process – from the regional procurement of reclaimed paper as a raw material, to production with an almost entirely closed energy and water cycle.

GWR is committed to ethical and responsible sourcing of paper, as well as ink. We also work to ensure that all our supply-chain partners meet the highest international standards for sustainable production and energy management. For more information, please contact us.

GWR has a very thorough accreditation system for records verification. However, while every effort is made to ensure accuracy, GWR cannot be held responsible for any errors contained in this work. Feedback from our readers on any point of accuracy is always welcomed.

GWR uses metric and imperial measurements. Exceptions are made for some scientific data where metric measurements are universally accepted, and some sports data. Where a specific date is given, the exchange rate is calculated according to the currency values at the time. Where only a year date is given, the exchange rate is calculated from 31 Dec of that year.

Appropriate advice should always be taken when attempting to break or set records. Participants undertake records entirely at their own risk. GWR has complete discretion over whether or not to include a record attempt in any of its publications. Being a GWR record holder does not guarantee you a place in any Guinness World Records publication.

Printed in Germany by Mohn Media
Guinness World Records Limited's authorized representative in the European Union is Mohn Media Mohndruck GmbH, Carl-Bertelsmann-Straße 161M, 33311 Gütersloh, Germany
www.mohnmedia.de

Registered address: Ground Floor,
The Rookery, 2 Dyott Street,
London, WC1A 1DE

OFFICIALLY AMAZING

Global President
Alistair Richards

Governance
Alison Ozanne

Global Finance
Elizabeth Bishop, Jess Blake, Arianna Cracco, Lisa Gibbs, Kimberley Jones, Jacob Moss, Bhavik Patel, Ysanne Rogers

Business Partnering: Sian Bhari, Lorenzo Di Sciullo, Thomas Jones, Maryana Lovell

eCommerce
Sara Kali, Athina Kontopoulou, Scott Shore

Global Legal
Mathew Alderson, Greyson Huang, Matthew Knight, Maria Popo, Jiayi Teng

IT & Global Operations
Rob Howe

Project Management:
Caroline Brouwer, Vivian Peter

Digital Technology & IT:
Anita Casari, Mohamed Hanad Abukar, Oliver Hickie, Veronica Irons, Joshua Jinadu, Apon Majumder, Sohail Malik, Benjamin McLean, Ajoke Oritu, Cenk Selim, Gerry Sweeny, Roelien Viljoen, Alex Waldu

Central Records Services
Mark McKinley

Record Content Support:
Lewis Blakeman, Amelis Escalante, Clea Lime, Will Munford, Mariana Sinotti, Dave Wilson, Melissa Wooton

Records Curation Team: Nana Asante, Erin Branney, Megan Bruce, Dominic Heater, Esther Mann, Thomas Marshall, William Sinden

Global People & Culture
Stephanie Lunn

London: Eleonora Angelova, Jackie Angus, Gurpreet Kaur, Monika Tilani

Americas: Jennifer Olson, Mariama Sesay

China: Crystal Xu, Nina Zhou

Japan: Emiko Yamamoto

UAE: Monisha Bimal

Brand & Digital
Katie Forde

Brand Strategy & Communications
Jack Brockbank, Juliet Dawson, Lucy Hunter, Doug Male

TV & Digital
Karen Gilchrist

Social Media: Josephine Boye, Dominic Punt, Dan Thorne

Website Content: Sanj Atwal, Vassiliki Bakogianni, Vicki Newman

Commissioned Content:
Michael Whitty

Video Production & Design:
Callum Dean, Rebecca Fisher, Jessica Hargrave, Rikesh Mistry, Fran Morales, Matthew Musson, Joseph O'Neil, Catherine Pearce, Aaron Quinn, Emma Salt

Content Licensing: Kirsty Clark, Kathryn Hubbard, Kate Stevenson

GWR Entertainment
Alexia Argeros, Fiona Gruchy-Craven, Paul O'Neill, Alan Pixsley

Global Consultancies
Marco Frigatti

Global Demand Generation:
Angelique Begarin, Melissa Brown

Global Product Marketing:
Catherine Blyth, Aled Mann, Rebecca Ward

Americas Consultancy
Carlos Martinez

Commercial Account Services: Isabella Barbosa, Mackenzie Berry, Brittany Carpenter, Carolina Guanabara, Ralph Hannah, Kim Partrick, Michelle Santucci, Joana Weiss

Commercial Marketing: Nicole Pando, Ana Rahlves

Records Management: Raquel Assis, Lianett C. Fernandez, Maddison Kulish, Alba (Niky) Pauli, Callie Smith, Carlos Tapia Rojas

Beijing Consultancy
Charles Wharton

Content Licensing: Chloe Liu

Editorial: Angela Wu

Commercial Account Services: Catherine Gao, Linda Li, Xiaona Liu, Tina Ran, Amelia Wang, Elaine Wang

Commercial Marketing: Theresa Gao, Nicole Kang

Events Production: Fay Jiang

Brand Comms: Echo Zhan, Yvonne Zhang

Records Management: Vanessa Tao, Kaia Wang, Richard Xie, Alicia Zhao

Dubai Consultancy
Talal Omar

Commercial Account Services: Sara Abu-Saad, Khalaf Badi, Naser Batat, Danny Hickson, Mohammad Kiswani, Kamel Yassin

Commercial Marketing: Shaddy Gaad

Brand & Content Marketing: Mohamad Kaddoura, Alaa Omari

PR: Hassan Alibrahim

Records Management: Reem Al Ghussain, Sarah Alkholb, Dina Charafeddine, Hani Gharamah, Karen Hamzeh

London Consultancy
Sam Prosser

Commercial Account Services: Nick Adams, Monika Drobina, Sirali Gandhi, Shanaye Howe, Nick Hume, Spoorthy Prakash, Nikhil Shukla, Lucia Sinigagliesi, Nataliia Solovei

Commercial Marketing: Amina Addow, William Baxter-Hughes

Records Management: Muhammad Ahmed, Shreya Bahuguna, Andrew Fanning, Apekshita Kadam, Ted Li, Francesca Raggi

Tokyo Consultancy
Kaoru Ishikawa

Commercial Account Services: Saif Alamannaei, Minami Ito, Takuro Maruyama, Yumiko Nakagawa, Nana Nguyen, Yuki Sakamoto, Wei Watanabe, Masamichi Yazaki

Commercial Marketing: Momoko Cunneen, Hiroyuki Tanaka, Eri Yuhira

Event Production: Yuki Uebo

Brand Comms: Kazami Kamioka, Masakazu Senda

Records Management: Aki Makijima, Mai McMillan, Momoko Omori, Naomi-Emily Sakai, Lala Teranishi

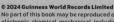

FOREWORD BY BLUE SCUTI

THE BOY WHO BROKE *TETRIS*!

Hi, Willis "Blue Scuti" Gibson here, welcoming you to the latest release of the *Guinness World Records Gamer's Edition*!

The Editors at the GWR Gaming HQ in London have asked me to introduce you to this cool new book – the 14th edition of the world's **best-selling gaming annual**... So, hello, nice to meet you!

I'm really excited to get my hands on this compendium of news, stats, facts and figures – not just because I'm in it (find out how I smashed the NES *Tetris* record on p.83) but because it's packed with the Top 100 Greatest Gaming World Records, as chosen by a team of GWR gaming geeks from around the planet. I'm sure you'll find all your favourite games in here, from arcade classics like *Space Invaders* right through to the latest console blockbusters such as *Mario vs. Donkey Kong*. Oh, and *Tetris*, of course! And it's not just the biggest blockbusting games – you'll also find the richest esports athletes, the most creative games designers and the fastest speedrunners.

I couldn't believe it when I became the first person to "beat" *Tetris*. I nearly passed out and I couldn't feel my hands by the end of it! But I wasn't the only one excited by it – there was so much interest around the world about the record that I ended up on TV news stations everywhere! There was me, a 13-year-old from Oklahoma, on TV channels from Tokyo to London. That's when the team at Guinness World Records reached out to me, and here I am now, an official record breaker!

If, like me, you're passionate about games, then you, too, can earn one of those GWR certificates – it looks great on my bedroom wall! According to Tom Marshall – he's the new Gaming Records Manager at GWR – there is a record in everyone, so I hope you'll be inspired by reading this book to attempt a record of your own. Maybe see you in the 2026 edition?! Good luck!

So, why are you called Blue Scuti?
My handle comes from the supergiant star UY Scuti – it's one of the biggest stars in the universe, about five billion times bigger than our own Sun!

You've become a big star yourself! How does that feel?
I'm just a regular kid doing regular kid things – I go bowling and stuff – but I just happen to be pretty good at an old videogame. My next goal is to win the Classic Tetris World Championship!

Any tips for wannabe record breakers?
If you set your mind to something and you put work into it, most likely you will get it if you try hard enough.

Blue Scuti
Willis Gibson

CONTENTS

Welcome to this countdown of our Top 100 gaming records, hand-picked by GWR's videogames experts.

	Title	Page
	Foreword by Blue Scuti	3
	Introduction	6
	How to Be a Record-Breaker	8
	Year in Gaming	10
	Awards Round-up	14
	GWR Gaming Awards	16

Rank	Title	Page
100	First dog to hold a speedrun record	18
99	Tallest videogame cosplay costume	19
98	Most wins of the LEC	20
97	Best-selling PS5 exclusive	21
96	Most viewed game on Twitch	22
95	Most Golden Joysticks won in a single year	23
94	Best-selling MMO	24
93	Longest-running gaming comic character	25
92	Most PlayStation trophies won	26
91	Highest-earning female esports player	27

Rank	Title	Page
90	Largest esports team for people with disabilities	28
89	Fastest-growing non-mobile game	29
88	Most concurrent players on Steam	30
87	Largest collection of *Tomb Raider* memorabilia	31
86	Best-selling PS4 exclusive	32
85	Largest playable Game & Watch device	33
84	Largest mobile game prize pool	34
83	Best-selling instrument game	35
82	Best-selling game starring a solo female protagonist	40
81	Best-selling racing series	41

Rank	Title	Page
80	Best-selling American sports game	42
79	Best-selling fighting game series	43
78	First console gamepad	44
77	Best-selling 9th-generation console	45
76	First HD videogame console	46
75	Highest-grossing biographical movie based on a videogame	47
74	Longest-running flight sim series	48
73	Best-selling 1st-generation game console	49
72	Most critically acclaimed *Star Wars* videogame	50
71	Longest-running arcade series	51

Rank	Title	Page
70	Best-selling Nintendo home console	54
69	Best-selling game based on a movie	55
68	Largest gaming acquisition	56
67	Most Emmy wins for a game adaptation	57
66	Best-selling videogame soundtrack	58
65	Most critically acclaimed survival-horror game	59
64	Largest human image of a Pokémon	60
63	Best-selling Nintendo game	61
62	Longest-running gaming podcast	62
61	Highest-earning esports player	63

Rank	Title	Page
60	Longest-running esports game	64
59	Most money raised by a speedrunning event	65
58	Largest third-party Game Pass launch	66
57	Largest Game Boy Color	67
56	Best-selling game for Nintendo Switch	70
55	Rarest Nintendo Game	71
54	Fastest-selling Nintendo game	72
53	Longest videogame campaign/story	73
52	Largest arcade cabinet	74
51	Most-funded videogame on Kickstarter	75

Rank	Title	Page
50	Most Platinumed PlayStation game	76
49	Most popular game (by monthly active users)	77
48	Most viewers for a debut stream on Twitch	78
47	Best-selling farm-life sim	79
46	Largest gaming collection	80
45	Most planets in a videogame universe	81
44	Most popular virtual pet app	82
43	First player to reach the kill screen in *Tetris* (NES)	83
42	First multi-platform videogame	86
41	Largest game-streaming service	87

40	Best-selling PC exclusive	88
39	Highest peak viewership on Twitch	89
38	Longest single game of *Football Manager*	90
37	Largest playable area in a handcrafted open-world videogame	91
36	Most viewed videogame trailer in 24 hours	92
35	First interactive videogame documentary	93
34	Oldest streamer	94
33	Most concurrent players for a debut on Steam	95
32	Most popular social simulation	96
31	Most viewed single-player videogame on Twitch	97

30	Largest Xbox Studio launch	98
29	Fastest-selling PlayStation exclusive	99
28	Largest first-person shooter battle	102
27	Most Game of the Year awards	103
26	Longest-running videogame series	104
25	Largest multiplayer PvP battle	105
24	Most critically acclaimed superhero game	106
23	Most critically acclaimed MMORPG	107
22	Largest cast for a videogame	108
21	Highest-earning esports team	109

20	Most downloaded mobile exclusive	110
19	Largest videogame convention	112
18	Most concurrent views for an esports event	114
17	Best-selling first-person shooter series	118
16	Longest videogame marathon	122
15	Longest-running soccer series	126
14	Longest-running fighter series	130
13	Most pre-orders for a PC game	134
12	Largest gathering of people dressed as videogame characters	136
11	Best-selling console	138

10	Best-selling videogame heroine	140
9	Most ported videogame	142
8	Most followers on Twitch	144
7	Largest user-generated content platform	146
6	Fastest entertainment property to gross $1 billion	150
5	Best-selling RPG series	152
4	Most critically acclaimed videogame	156
3	Most concurrently played videogame	164
2	Most ubiquitous videogame character	170
1	Best-selling videogame	176

Round-Up	182
Index	184
Acknowledgements and Country Codes	189
Meet the Team	190

FEATURES

LEGO® blockbusters	36
LEGO MOCs	38
Top 25 most-played videogames	52
Gaming at the movies	68
Videogame spaceships	84
Most streamed videogame soundtracks	100
Accessibility in gaming	116
Longest videogame marathons	124
Game the Record	132
Greatest *Gamer's Edition* photo shoots	148
Metaverse gaming	162

THE XP ICONS

The record holders listed in the Top 100 are categorized under one of the following headings. You'll find the icons in the XP panel – and as you'll see, they range from genres and events to people and, erm, dogs... a reminder of how varied the world of records can be!

 Action-Adventure

 Adventure RPG

 RPG

 Shooter

 MMORPG

 Open World

 Strategy & Simulation

 Sport

 Racing

 Arcade

 Fighting

 MOBA

 Sandbox

 Casual & Mobile

 Party & Rhythm

 Social & Deduction

 Battle Royale

 Survival Horror

 Person

 Technology & Hardware

 Gaming Community

 Movies, TV & Streaming

 Competition & Events

 Music & Soundtracks

 Business

 Trophies

 Comics & Books

 Dog

INTRODUCTION

Welcome to the *Guinness World Records Gamer's Edition 2025* – the latest book in the world's best-selling gaming reference series! I'm Tom, the newest recruit to the Records Curation Team, and I've got the best job in the company: I get to look after the gaming records!

Find out how YOU can get your name on that official GWR certificate!

This year's *Gamer's Edition* is built around 100 of the greatest gaming world record titles of all time. This list has been compiled with the help of our chief gaming consultant, Wesley Yin-Poole (you can read more about him on p.190), as well as the editorial staff here at GWR HQ in London, and an international team of gaming enthusiasts drawn from GWR offices around the world.

Will you agree with what's in our Top 100? Maybe not! Is your favourite game in here? Most likely, if you're a fan of the most popular titles! In creating this list, we've been lucky enough to play dozens of the biggest gaming franchises, so expect to find records involving legends like Mario and Pikachu, as well as relative newcomers such as Aloy and Miles Morales.

World of gaming

But it's not just about the games. Of course, we cover the best-selling and the most critically acclaimed, but as my *Tetris*-playing buddy Blue Scuti alluded to in his Foreword, our Top 100 includes everything from the highest-earning esports athletes and the most popular gaming influencers to the fastest speedrunners and the most creative builders. (You can check out a couple of my epic *Minecraft* builds below!)

You'll also find feature articles dotted throughout the book. These include a celebration of the biggest LEGO® gaming

My 20-hr recreation of the gothic Bath Abbey in Somerset, UK, using 24,453 blocks

My 101,384-block *Minecraft* village inspired by the real-life Rochester in Kent

Find out about the highest earners, best sellers and most fun record breakers.

Discover the records set by all your favourite games, genres and franchises

sets (pp.36–37) and MOCs (pp.38–39); a selection of some iconic videogame movies, comparing their box-office figures with their critical acclaim (pp.68–69); and a rundown of the most popular gaming soundtracks (pp.100–01).

Game the Record

It's my job here at GWR to assess (and hopefully approve!) all the gaming applications that we receive, so I'm always on the lookout for new ideas and challenges. That's why we've introduced gaming records specially created for under-16-year-olds. We want as many people attempting gaming records as we can! In the "Game the Record" feature on pp.132–33, you'll find a selection of challenges created specially for under-16s, so if you've always wanted to see your name in the record books, and you think you've got what it takes, then this is the best place to start. On pp.8–9, you'll also find a step-by-step

guide to making an official application, whatever age you are (check out some of the oldest gamers on p.94!)

Finally, I'm excited to announce the first-ever *Guinness World Records Gamer's Edition* Awards. The team here has been voting on their favourite games, soundtracks, developers and streamers, looking to celebrate the best in gaming from the past year. See how our list on pp.16–17 compares with the Awards Round-Up on pp.14–15.

So, I hope you enjoy reading about our Top 100 greatest gaming records as much as we've enjoyed compiling them. And who knows, if you're inspired by what you read here and think that you could break a record of your own, you might even make it into the next edition! Good luck!

Thomas Marshall
Thomas Marshall
Gaming Records Curator

XP
Date: 2016
Developer: Hello Games
Publisher: Hello Games

Start exploring each record with the XP: The need-to-know basics for each record holder

INORITE!

Minecraft's annual convention, Minecraft Live, now takes place entirely online. But the first gathering of fans was a spontaneous event held in Bellevue, Washington, USA, in 2010. Around 30 people showed up – including the game's creator, Markus Persson. A year later, more than 5,000 people attended the first official convention in Las Vegas, USA.

INORITE!: Fun facts and trivia helping to tell the stories behind the record-breaking games

RNG
4,483,253
Average number of hours of WoW content watched weekly on Twitch, as of Mar 2024, attesting to its ongoing popularity.

RNG: Highlights the most amazing stats and facts to put the records into perspective

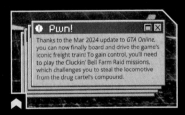

Pwn!
Thanks to the Mar 2024 update to *GTA Online*, you can now finally board and drive the game's iconic freight train! To gain control, you'll need to play the Cluckin' Bell Farm Raid missions, which challenges you to steal the locomotive from the drug cartel's compound.

PWN!: Hints and tips to improve your gameplay and maybe help you become a record breaker

"I have an air-con unit just for my collection room. Climate control is a must."

Antonio Romero Monteiro

QUOTE: Hear from the record holders in their own words

HOW TO BE A RECORD BREAKER

Whether you're a speedrun specialist, an esports pro, a devoted collector or just an inspired newcomer keen to make your mark, there's sure to be a GWR title with your name on it. Here, we walk you through the process of making an official attempt. If you're keen to have a go, then scan this QR code for more details on registering your claim. If you're successful, that framed certificate will soon make you the envy of your friends!

Start

1

You're probably keen to get on with your record attempt, but there are some things you need to do first. Every record breaker's journey starts on our website – **guinnessworldrecords.com**. Head for the "Records" section to see how the process works and how to create an account. It's a quick task that will open up a world of records.

2

Have a good look through the *Gamer's Edition* (we're sure you're already doing that every day!) It will give you plenty of ideas for which record to aim for, as will the website. When you get in touch, tell us which record you'd like to attempt and we'll send you the guidelines. We've already set up two pages of records specially created for under-16 gamers – see pp.132–33.

3

Did none of our existing titles catch your eye? Perhaps you want to make an attempt in one of the latest gaming releases, or you've thought of some unique challenge in an old game that you love. In that case, get in touch and tell us your idea – if we like it, and it meets with our rules, then we can help you shape your outline into a proper record attempt.

4

Official attempts at a GWR title have a lot in common with a sports competition – you need to train hard and often to make sure you are in peak condition for the big day. So keep telling yourself to practise, practise, practise. Good preparation is always a vital part of success. Think of the reward that might be waiting for you and how proud of yourself you'll feel!

5

When you're certain your gaming skills are in prime condition, it's time to take on the record. But first make sure you have everything in place to meet the GWR guidelines. No one wants to see all that effort going to waste! We're talking witnesses, photo/video evidence and anything we have specified for a valid claim. It might be a good idea to make a checklist.

6

Finally, send us all of your evidence. We'll review everything to make sure it conforms to the guidelines. If you've followed the rules correctly and beaten the record, then congratulations! You'll receive email confirmation and – drum roll! – your authentic GWR certificate. You are now Officially Amazing! Welcome to the Guinness World Records family!

Finish

Your name here!

YEAR IN GAMING

PART 1

From huge corporate takeovers to iconic trailer launches, a lot of big things happened in the world of gaming in the past year. This is just half of the story – turn over for part 2.

MICROSOFT GET THEIR WAY

A judge in San Francisco, USA, denied the Federal Trade Commission's request for a preliminary injunction against Microsoft's $69-bn (£55-bn) acquisition of *Call of Duty* maker Activision Blizzard. Judge Jacqueline Scott Corley's decision paved the way for the biggest takeover in tech history (see p.56). The dramatic ruling came after a four-day trial packed with behind-the-scenes revelations.

BALDUR'S GATE 3 BLOWS UP

This epic story-driven RPG, with its focus on faithfully adapting the *Dungeons & Dragons* tabletop role-playing experience, sold more than 10 million copies and achieved a clean sweep of Game of the Year gongs at the big awards ceremonies (see pp.14–15). *Baldur's Gate 3* wowed players and critics alike with its complex story and brilliant cast of characters – including the vampire rogue Astarion and Tiefling barbarian Karlach.

MARTINET IS MARIO NO MORE

Nintendo confirmed that Charles Martinet (USA), the original voice actor of Mario and several other roles since 1991 (see p.168), would be "stepping back from recording character voices for our games". Instead, Martinet now serves as a "Mario Ambassador". Switch exclusive *Super Mario Bros. Wonder* marked the debut of voice actor Kevin Afghani (USA) as Mario, Luigi and Wario.

STARFIELD FINALLY ENTERS THE UNIVERSE

After several delays, Bethesda finally released *Starfield*, the next big game from the team behind *Fallout* and *The Elder Scrolls*, on PC and Xbox. *Starfield* also went straight into the Game Pass subscription service. The game enjoyed a huge launch, with over 12 million players securing it a spot in the top 10 most-played titles from Xbox studios.

A NEW ERA IN SOCCER GAMES

The release of *EA Sports FC 24* marked the first mainline soccer game from EA since the company's 30-year licensing partnership with FIFA ended. *FC 24* included more than 19,000 players, over 700 teams and dozens of national leagues, including England's Premier League and Women's Super League, the USA's MLS and NWSL, and Spain's La Liga.

SPIDEY VS MARIO VS SONIC

Friday 20 Oct 2023 was a big day for gamers, with two huge releases – *Marvel's Spider-Man 2* (Insomniac Games; see p.21) and *Super Mario Bros. Wonder* (Nintendo; see p.169). Spare a thought for poor *Sonic Superstars*, which came out three days before. Sega admitted sales were impacted by the combined might of Mario and Spider-Man!

[PS] PORTAL TO A NEW WORLD

Sony released the PlayStation Portal, a handheld gaming accessory for the PS5 that streams games from a PS5 over Wi-Fi using Remote Play. It's not quite the PS Vita 2 some had hoped for, but is an indication, perhaps, of where PlayStation may head in the future.

LIVE-ACTION LEGEND ON ITS WAY

After years of speculation, Nintendo and Sony Pictures announced a live-action *Legend of Zelda* film. Nintendo's Shigeru Miyamoto – creator of *Mario*, *Zelda*, *Donkey Kong* and more – is working on the movie with film producer Avi Arad, the founder and ex-CEO of Marvel Studios. (See p.175.)

GTA FEVER GOES VIRAL

Rockstar released the first trailer for *Grand Theft Auto VI*, the most anticipated game of 2025. The trailer revealed dual protagonists Lucia and Jason (left), and the game's sun-soaked setting inspired by Miami, Florida. The trailer broke viewing records (see p.92), and some analysts are already saying that *GTA VI* might become the biggest game of all time.

GAME OVER FOR E3

After 29 years, the Entertainment Software Association announced the end of the long-running and much-loved videogame trade event E3. The first edition, in 1995, was the site for Sony's announcement of the PlayStation. E3 had already skipped 2020 and held an online-only event in 2021 due to the COVID-19 pandemic, before shows in 2022 and 2023 were cancelled.

YEAR IN GAMING

PART 2

Picking up from where we left off, there is the long-awaited conquest of a gaming classic, the passing of a manga legend and a new game that is proving to be as controversial as it is wildly successful...

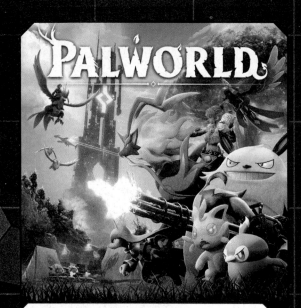

"POKÉMON WITH GUNS"?

After its trailer went viral in 2021, it was clear that *Palworld* was going to be a hit. However, the scale of its success was a surprise to even its developers, Pocket Pair. The game rocketed to the top of the Steam "concurrently played" list (see p.95), despite an initial hiccup when hordes of players struggled to get on to the servers. But its success has not come without controversy. Some players have accused the studio of "ripping off" *Pokémon* in the creation of the Pals.

THE TEEN WHO KILLED *TETRIS*

Willis Gibson, 13, became the first person to "beat" the NES version of *Tetris* by reaching its killscreen (p.83). Gibson, aka Blue Scuti, broke world records for **total number of lines**, **level achieved** and **overall score** as he forced the 35-year-old classic to crash. Previously, only AI had broken *Tetris*. Developers didn't think a human would ever make it that far!

SEEING IS BELIEVING

Apple Vision Pro launched in the US priced $3,499 (£2,757). The mixed-reality headset supports multitasking via windows that appear to float within the user's surroundings, as in Tom Cruise's sci-fi movie *Minority Report* (USA, 2002). Since its release, users have been seen wearing Apple Vision Pro while walking city streets and even courtside at a basketball game!

DISNEY'S EPIC DEAL WITH EPIC GAMES

Disney bought an eye-watering $1.5-bn (£1.178-bn) stake in *Fortnite* maker Epic Games and announced plans to develop a persistent social universe to "interoperate" with the world's biggest battle royale. This expansion of the metaverse will let fans play, watch and shop with their favourite characters from the likes of Disney, Pixar, Marvel and Star Wars. See pp.162–63.

HELLDIVERS COMES OUT GUNS BLAZING

Available for PC and PS5, *HELLDIVERS II* made an instant splash. Arrowhead Game Studios' chaotic co-op shooter – inspired by cult classic sci-fi movie *Starship Troopers* (USA, 1997) – sees players dropping on to alien planets to fight monstrous bugs and terrifying robots. *HELLDIVERS II* shot up Steam's most-played games list and is easily **Sony's biggest-ever PC game launch**.

MANGA LEGEND TORIYAMA DIES

Akira Toriyama, legendary creator of manga phenomenon *Dragon Ball*, died aged 68. Toriyama designed characters for a number of videogames, including *Dragon Quest*, *Chrono Trigger* and *Blue Dragon*. *Sand Land*, the game based on Toriyama's manga series of the same name, launched on 25 April 2024.

STAMPEDE FOR STARDEW VALLEY

Stardew Valley developer Eric "ConcernedApe" Barone released update 1.6 for the PC version of the hugely popular farming and life sim. The long-awaited release sparked a huge influx of players on Steam, with more than 130,000 people logging in at the same time. Among the changes added with the patch was the ability to drink mayonnaise. Yuk!

AT LONG LAST...

Capcom released *Dragon's Dogma 2* some 12 years after the first game. The wait proved to be worth it, with the sprawling fantasy role-playing game selling an impressive 2.5 million copies in just 11 days. Players used the powerful character creator to recreate famous faces from the likes of *Game of Thrones*, the movie *Dune: Part Two* (USA, 2024) and the Marvel Cinematic Universe.

AWARDS ROUND-UP

Baldur's Gate 3 swept the 2023–24 awards board with no fewer than six major Game of the Year gongs – as well as scooping lots of other prizes. A diverse roster of games received other accolades from the major ceremonies. Here's our round-up of some of the key prizes from the past year's most prestigious award do's.

— THE 41ST ANNUAL —
GOLDEN JOYSTICK AWARDS

THE GAME AWARDS

GOLDEN JOYSTICK AWARDS
10 November 2023, London, UK

Award	Winner
Ultimate Game of the Year	*Baldur's Gate 3* (Larian Studios)
Best Storytelling	*Baldur's Gate 3*
Best Multiplayer Game	*Mortal Kombat 1* (Warner Bros. Games)
Best Visual Design	*Baldur's Gate 3*
Best Game Expansion	*Cyberpunk 2077: Phantom Liberty* (CD Projekt Red)
Best Audio	*Final Fantasy XVI* (Square Enix)
Best Indie Game	*Sea of Stars* (Sabotage Studio)
Best VR Game	*Horizon Call of the Mountain* (Guerrilla/Firesprite)
Best Streaming Game	*Valorant* (Riot Games)
Still Playing Award	*No Man's Sky* (Hello Games)
Best Gaming Community	*Baldur's Gate 3*
Studio of the Year	Larian Studios
Best Lead Performer	Ben Starr as Clive Rosfield (*Final Fantasy XVI*)
Best Supporting Performer	Neil Newbon as Astarion (*Baldur's Gate 3*)
Breakthrough Award	*Cocoon* (Geometric Interactive)
PC Game of the Year	*Baldur's Gate 3*
Best Gaming Hardware	PlayStation VR2
PlayStation Game of the Year	*Resident Evil 4* (Capcom)
Xbox Game of the Year	*Starfield* (Bethesda)
Nintendo Game of the Year	*The Legend of Zelda: Tears of the Kingdom* (Nintendo)
Best Game Trailer	*Cyberpunk 2077: Phantom Liberty*
Most Wanted Award	*Final Fantasy VII Rebirth* (Square Enix)
Critics' Choice Award	*Alan Wake II* (Remedy Entertainment)

THE GAME AWARDS
7 December 2023, Los Angeles, California, USA

Award	Winner
Game of the Year	*Baldur's Gate 3*
Best Game Direction	*Alan Wake II*
Best Narrative	*Alan Wake II*
Best Art Direction	*Alan Wake II*
Best Score	*Final Fantasy XVI* (Masayoshi Soken)
Best Audio Design	*Hi-Fi Rush* (Tango Gameworks)
Best Performance	Neil Newbon as Astarion (*Baldur's Gate 3*)
Best Independent Game	*Sea of Stars*
Best Ongoing Game	*Cyberpunk 2077* (CD Projekt Red)
Best Mobile Game	*Honkai: Star Rail* (miHoYo)
Best Esports Game	*Valorant*
Best Esports Athlete	Lee "Faker" Sang-Hyeok (T1)
Best Esports Team	JD Gaming (*League of Legends*)

BAFTA GAMES AWARDS
11 April 2024, London, UK

Award	Winner
Best Game	*Baldur's Gate 3*
EE Players' Choice Award	*Baldur's Gate 3*
Best Music	*Baldur's Gate 3*
Best Narrative	*Baldur's Gate 3*
Best British Game	*Viewfinder* (Sad Owl Studios)
Best Animation	*Hi-Fi Rush*
Best Artistic Achievement	*Alan Wake II*
Best Game Design	*Dave the Diver* (Mintrocket)
Best Audio Achievement	*Alan Wake II*
Best Multiplayer Game	*Super Mario Bros. Wonder* (Nintendo)
Best Family Game	*Super Mario Bros. Wonder*

The Steam Awards 2023

GAME DEVELOPERS CHOICE AWARDS

THE STEAM AWARDS
2 January 2024, voted for by Steam users

Award	Winner
Game of the Year	*Baldur's Gate 3*
VR Game of the Year	*Labyrinthine* (Valko Game Studios)
Labor of Love	*Red Dead Redemption 2* (Rockstar)
Better with Friends	*Lethal Company* (Zeekerss)
Outstanding Visual Style	*Atomic Heart* (Mundfish)
Most Innovative Gameplay	*Starfield*
Best Game You Suck At	*Sifu* (Sloclap)
Best Soundtrack	*The Last of Us Part I* (Naughty Dog)
Outstanding Story-Rich Game	*Baldur's Gate 3*
Sit Back and Relax	*Dave the Diver*
Best Game on Steam Deck	*Hogwarts Legacy* (Avalanche Software)

GAME DEVELOPERS CHOICE AWARDS
20 March 2024, San Francisco, California, USA

Award	Winner
Game of the Year	*Baldur's Gate 3*
Best Audio	*Hi-Fi Rush*
Best Debut	*Venba* (Visai Games)
Best Design	*Baldur's Gate 3*
Innovation	*The Legend of Zelda: Tears of the Kingdom*
Best Narrative	*Baldur's Gate 3*
Best Technology	*The Legend of Zelda: Tears of the Kingdom*
Best Visual Art	*Alan Wake II*
Audience Award	*Baldur's Gate 3*
Lifetime Achievement	Yoko Shimomura (composer for various games including the *Kingdom Hearts* series and *Final Fantasy XV*)

D.I.C.E. AWARDS
15 February 2024, Las Vegas, Nevada, USA

Award	Winner
Game of the Year	*Baldur's Gate 3*
Online Game of the Year	*Diablo IV* (Blizzard)
Mobile Game of the Year	*What the Car?* (Triband)
Independent Game	*Cocoon* (Geometric Entertainment)
Immersive Reality Game	*Asgard's Wrath 2* (Sanzaru Games)
Game Direction	*Baldur's Gate 3*
Game Design	*Baldur's Gate 3*
Animation	*Marvel's Spider-Man 2* (Insomniac Games)
Art Direction	*Alan Wake II*
Character	Miles Morales (*Marvel's Spider-Man 2*)
Original Music	*Marvel's Spider-Man 2*

INDEPENDENT GAMES FESTIVAL AWARDS
20 March 2024, San Francisco, California, USA

Award	Winner
Seumas McNally Grand Prize	*Venba*
Excellence in Visual Arts	*Phonopolis* (Amanita Design)
Excellence in Audio	*Rhythm Doctor* (7th Beat Games)
Excellence in Design	*Cryptmaster* (Paul Hart, Lee Williams, Akupara Games)
Excellence in Narrative	*Mediterranea Inferno* (Eyeguys, Lorenzo Redaelli)
Nuovo Award	*Anthology of the Killer* (Thecatamites, Tommy Tone, A. Degen)
Best Student Game	*Once Upon a Jester* (Bonte Avond)
Audience Award	*RAM: Random Access Mayhem* (Xylem Studios)
alt.ctrl.GDC Award	*Chú Mó* (The Chú Mó Team@ArtCenter)

GWR GAMING AWARDS

For the first time ever, we're celebrating the best in gaming with the *GWR Gamer's Edition* Awards, as selected by the team at gaming HQ. Here, the shortlisted finalists are listed below each winner.

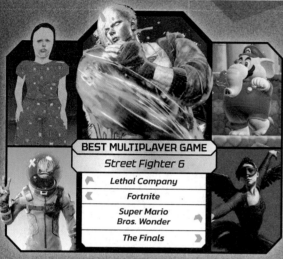

BEST MULTIPLAYER GAME
Street Fighter 6
- Lethal Company
- Fortnite
- Super Mario Bros. Wonder
- The Finals

BEST SINGLE-PLAYER GAME
Baldur's Gate 3
- The Legend of Zelda: Tears of the Kingdom
- Marvel's Spider-Man 2
- Alan Wake II
- Resident Evil 4

BEST NARRATIVE
Baldur's Gate 3
- Alan Wake II
- Cyberpunk 2077: Phantom Liberty
- Final Fantasy XVI
- Marvel's Spider-Man 2

BEST MUSIC
Final Fantasy XVI
- Baldur's Gate 3
- Hi-Fi Rush
- Cyberpunk 2077: Phantom Liberty
- Alan Wake II

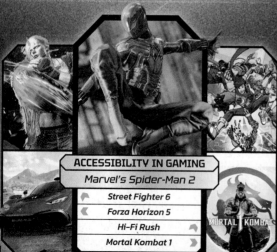

ACCESSIBILITY IN GAMING
Marvel's Spider-Man 2
- Street Fighter 6
- Forza Horizon 5
- Hi-Fi Rush
- Mortal Kombat 1

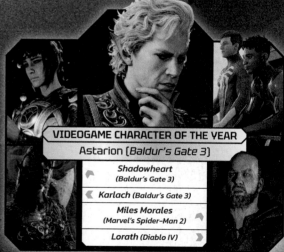

VIDEOGAME CHARACTER OF THE YEAR
Astarion (Baldur's Gate 3)
- Shadowheart (Baldur's Gate 3)
- Karlach (Baldur's Gate 3)
- Miles Morales (Marvel's Spider-Man 2)
- Lorath (Diablo IV)

STREAMER OF THE YEAR
Valkyrae

- grumpygran1948
- Shroud
- MoistCr1TiKaL
- Pokimane

STUDIO OF THE YEAR
Larian Studios

- Nintendo
- Insomniac Games
- Capcom
- Remedy Entertainment

HARDWARE OF THE YEAR
Steam Deck

- Nintendo Switch
- Xbox Series S
- Xbox Series X
- PlayStation 5

GAME OF THE YEAR
Baldur's Gate 3

- Street Fighter 6
- The Legend of Zelda: Tears of the Kingdom
- Marvel's Spider-Man 2
- Super Mario Bros. Wonder

First dog to hold a speedrun record

Peanut Butter

XP

Name: Peanut Butter, aka PB
Born: July 2020
Breed: Shiba Inu

For years, the idea of a dog collaring a speedrun record would have been considered barking mad. But the achievement of a four-year-old Shiba Inu has given the gaming world paws for thought. With some guidance from his owner – speedrunner JSR_ – Peanut Butter finished Nintendo's 1985 puzzle platformer *Gyromite* in 23 min 9 sec in Jan 2024. His owner told *GWR*: "PB broke his own record last night with a nearly PERFECT run." And raised money for charity, too. Good boy!

🔓 *INORITE!*

Gyromite was designed to be played by instructing a robot accessory called *ROB* to press the correct buttons on the controller. For his canine speedrun, PB took on this role, pawing giant, customized buttons made by his owner. Keeping him motivated was his favourite treat: string cheese!

Name: Reinhardt
Creator: Thomas DePetrillo
Debut: 7 Oct 2016

Tallest videogame cosplay costume

99

Thomas DePetrillo's Reinhardt

!

If you think *Overwatch*'s wandering German knight Reinhardt cuts an intimidating figure on screen, just imagine how frightening he'd be in real life! Looming over visitors to New York Comic-Con in Oct 2016 was cosplayer Thomas DePetrillo in his 8-ft 4-in (2.54-m) fully mobile Reinhardt armour. "I've always been drawn to Reinhardt just because he looks so incredibly badass," said DePetrillo, the owner of Extreme Costumes (see below).

Overwatch's armour-plated, rocket-hammer-wielding "tank" Reinhardt

85

Weight of the suit in pounds (38.5 kg). Thomas – who has fitted the outfit with 45 ft (13.7 m) of lights – takes about 10–12 min to put it on.

Thomas's cosplay assistant Qi Ma (aka Quin Mae)

Massive achievements

Reinhardt is not the only creation from Thomas (right) to wow NYC's Comic Con. On the left is his 8-ft-tall (243-cm) Hulkbuster from *Avengers: Age of Ultron* (USA, 2015). To the right is hero autobot Bumblebee of the *Transformers* films – at 9 ft 6 in (2.89 m), the **tallest mobile cosplay costume**.

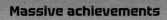

Most wins of the LEC

XP

Team: G2 Esports
DoB: 17 Nov 1999
Nationality: Danish

Rasmus "Caps" Borregaard Winther

The LEC is the *League of Legends* EMEA Championship, a professional *LoL* esports league launched in 2013 by Riot Games. The event started out solely in Europe but, since 2023, it has encompassed the Middle East and Africa, too (aka EMEA). The LEC took place annually in the spring and summer until 2023, when a winter contest was added to the schedule. As of 17 Apr 2024, Caps (DNK) had scooped 12 titles, making him the most successful gamer at the tournament. His team, G2, has won 14 titles – twice the number of its closest competitor, Fnatic – giving them the **most team wins of the LEC**.

G2 celebrate 2024's LEC Winter win

RNG

1

The number of teams from outside Asia to win the Mid-Season Invitational *LoL* tournament. G2 took the title in 2019. As of Apr 2024, the four other champions were all Asian teams.

"I'm proud to be the player with the most trophy wins, and I'm not planning to slow down any time soon."

🔊 Caps talks future plans

Caps was previously a member of the Fnatic team

Most critically acclaimed *Spider-Man* games

1	*Marvel's Spider-Man 2* (2023)	90
=2	*Marvel's Spider-Man* (2018)	87
=2	*Marvel's Spider-Man Remastered* (2022)	87
=2	*Spider-Man* (2000)	87
=5	*Marvel's Spider-Man: Miles Morales* (2020)	85
=5	*Spider-Man Total Mayhem* (2010)	85

Metacritic, as of 24 Apr 2024

XP
Date: 2023
Developer: Insomniac Games
Publisher: Sony Interactive Entertainment

R N G
14
Number of New York neighbourhoods to visit in the game. The action focuses on Manhattan but also includes areas of Queens and Brooklyn.

Best-selling PS5 exclusive

97

Marvel's Spider-Man 2

Swinging into action above New York, Marvel's *Spider-Man 2* (2023) and Marvel's *Spider-Man* (2018) completed a double whammy of domination for the webslinger's adventures. The two games are now the best-selling exclusives on the PS4 (see p.32) and PS5. *Marvel's Spider-Man 2* sold 2.5 million copies on 20 Oct 2023, its first day of sale. That figure had doubled by day 11, and sales of 10 million were confirmed by Sony on 14 Feb 2024. *Spider-Man: Miles Morales* (2020) – an expansion of the original – also added more millions to the total.

96 Most viewed game on Twitch

twitch

! League of Legends

Riot Games' all-conquering MOBA had been watched 65.41 billion times as of 21 Nov 2023. That makes it the most popular game on what is the **most popular gaming-focused broadcasting service**. Millions logged in for Worlds 2023 – a five-week, 22-team tournament that saw South Korea's T1 walk away with the $445,000 (£357,000) first prize (see pp.114–15).

R N G
40
Number of player-controlled champions in the roster of the original 2009 *League*. Today, there are 168, each with their own unique skill sets.

XP
Date: 2009
Developer: Riot Games
Publisher: Riot Games

Most concurrent viewers for a game on Twitch

LoL is, unsurprisingly, also the most popular single title on Twitch when it comes to *peak* viewership, with a record 3.11 million fans tuning in simultaneously for the Worlds finale on 6 Nov 2022. Figures this high are beaten only by special events, such as *Night of the Year 3*, organized by Ibai Llanos (right) – see how it compares on p.89.

Most Golden Joysticks won in a single year

95

Baldur's Gate 3

The annual Golden Joystick Awards have been held in the UK since 1983. The game that's had the best single night in the event's history is the third instalment of Larian's *Dungeons & Dragons*-set *Baldur's Gate* series, with seven wins in 2023.

Most Golden Joysticks won

The game that's taken home more Golden Joysticks than any other is *The Witcher 3: Wild Hunt* (CD Projekt RED, 2015), picking up 11 gongs between 2013 and 2016. This includes two "Most Wanted" awards, a five-trophy sweep of the major categories in 2015, and four wins in 2016 for its final expansion, *Blood and Wine*.

XP

Date: 2023
Developer: Larian Studios
Publisher: Larian Studios

❶ Pwn! □ ☒

Want to chat with the wildlife in Faerûn? Then cast the "Speak with Animals" spell on yourself. This allows you to talk to non-hostile animals – you'll not only learn a lot, it's also a lot of fun!

Best-selling MMO

! World of Warcraft

Blizzard's genre-defining massively multiplayer online RPG celebrates its 20th birthday in Nov 2024. Over the last two decades, *WoW* has seen dozens of rivals come and go, and recorded sales of more than 40.6 million copies, including its various expansions. This total includes 2020's *Shadowlands*, but the figures for the most recent title, *Dragonfight* (2022, below), have not yet been released.

XP

Date: 2004
Developer: Blizzard Entertainment
Publisher: Blizzard Entertainment

Longest marathon playing *WoW*

Drawing on more than a decade of experience battling his way across the wilds of Azeroth, Hungarian gamer Barnabás Vujity-Zsolnay endured a *Warcraft* session that lasted an epic 59 hr 20 min 12 sec. He completed his stint at home in Budapest on 28 Sep 2022.

🔓 INORITE!

With worldwide box-office takings of $438,899,824 (£345.8 m), the game's big-screen version, *Warcraft* (2016), assumed the throne for the **highest-grossing movie based on a game**. And there it stayed for seven years. It needed a certain plumber and his adventures in *The Super Mario Bros. Movie* (2023) to beat back the orcs and the trolls. See pp.68–69 for our look at how films based on games have fared with moviegoers.

fastest completion of *Sonic the Hedgehog 2*

On 25 Sep 2023, speedrunner eandis set a new record on the 1992 *Sonic* sequel. A back-and-forth had been going on with JoeyBaby69 before eandis broke the 13-min mark – and then lowered it further to 12 min 43 sec. The game is more than 30 years old, but there's life in this veteran hedgehog yet.

SCORE 4900
TIME 0:18
RINGS 6

XP

Date: 1993–2016
Publisher: Archie Comics
Issues: 290

Longest-running gaming comic character

93

Sonic the Hedgehog

The Blue Blur has appeared in comic-book form since at least Nov 1992, when he featured in a four-part mini series published by Archie Comics (USA). This was followed by a full launch in Jul 1993 of *Sonic the Hedgehog*, which ran for 290 issues until Dec 2016. Although the series was cancelled, another US firm, IDW Publishing, picked up the license and since 4 Apr 2018 has published a monthly comic under the same title. Artist Tyson Hesse, who has worked on both series, also animated cut scenes for the games *Sonic Mania* (2017) and *Sonic Origin* (2022), and is responsible for the look of our favourite blue hedgehog on the silver screen (see pp.68–69).

Pwn!

The Summer of Sonic convention started on 9 Aug 2008 in London and was the **first official fan event for a single game character**. With its staging in 2016, this magnet for Sonic-inspired artists, musicians and cosplayers became the **longest-running fan convention for a videogame character**.

SUMMER OF SONIC
2012

IDW
ISSUE 1
COVER A
$3.99

SONIC THE HEDGEHOG™

92

Most PlayStation trophies won

ikemenzi

Japanese gamer Kenji "ikemenzi" Ito had won an incredible 287,668 PlayStation trophies as of 12 Apr 2024 – an average of 73.73 trophies each day! That put him 23,740 ahead of his nearest competitor.

ikemenzi also holds the record for winning the **most bronze** trophies (139,410). He previously held the **most gold**, **silver** and **platinum** records – titles since claimed by dav1d_123 (CAN) with 81,174 and 10,123 respectively.

PS Trophy Leaderboard

ikemenzi (JPN)
🏆 287,668

dav1d_123 (CAN)
🏆 264,823

caro3c-gabber9 (FRA)
🏆 253,725

tusman (CHE)
🏆 248,543

MarCCeoN (AUT)
🏆 245,454

PSNProfiles.com, as of 23 Apr 2024

Pwn!

As any PlayStation gamer will know, some platinum trophies are easier to win than others. One of the less tricky paths to platinum is to complete *SpongeBob SquarePants: Battle for Bikini Bottom – Rehydrated* (Purple Lamp Studios, 2020). It only takes about 15 hours and is a whole lot of fun to play! There are 33 trophies in total.

XP

Tag: Ikemenzi
Games played: 18,513
World rank: 3

R N G

18,513

Number of PlayStation games ikemenzi has played. He has scooped 723 Ultra Rare trophies and 2,039 Very Rare ones.

Best-selling strategy game for PC

The enduringly popular real-time strategy *StarCraft* (Blizzard, 1998) has sold more than 11 million copies. The game's three carefully balanced factions and complex gameplay earned it a dedicated multiplayer community, and it remains a staple of esports events to this day.

Highest-earning female esports player

91

Sasha "Scarlett" Hostyn

Sasha "Scarlett" Hostyn (CAN) had earned $465,550 (£371,025) in prize money as of 12 Apr 2024, according to Esports Earnings. The winnings come almost exclusively from *StarCraft II: Wings of Liberty* (Blizzard, 2010), though Scarlett has played a few *StarCraft: Remastered* (Blizzard, 2017) events. Her biggest prize – $50,000 (£35,848) – came in 2018, when she won the Intel Extreme Masters (inset), an international Olympics-affiliated *StarCraft II* competition. (Turn to p.63 to find out who the overall **highest-earning esports player** is.)

XP

Tag: Scarlett
Nickname: Queen of Blades
Team: Shopify Rebellion

2018 INTEL EXTREME MASTERS PyeongChang

Esports influencer

The New Yorker called Scarlett "the most accomplished woman in esports" while *Forbes* magazine placed her at No.24 on their list of "most powerful women in international sports" – and that's not just esports but *all* sports! Scarlett appears to take the fame and adulation in her stride. "Mostly, success for me would be about being happy," she said.

Highest-earning female esports players

Player	Earnings
Sasha "Scarlett" Hostyn (CAN)	$465,550 (£371,025)
Xiao Meng "Liooon" Li (CHN)	$241,510 (£189,404)
Ksenia "vilga" Klyuenkova (RUS)	$122,693 (£96,822)
Katherine "Mystik" Gunn (USA)	$122,550 (£96,719)
Julia "juliano" Kiran (SWE)	$96,304 (£76,018)

EsportsEarnings.com, as of 4 Jan 2024

Largest esports team for people with disabilities

Permastunned Gaming

XP

Founded: 2019
Members: 37
X: PermastunnedG

GUINNESS WORLD RECORDS

CERTIFICATE

The largest eSports team for people with disabilities is Permastunned Gaming, conceived by Alexander Nathan (NLD) in Jan 2019, with a total of 33 members from all around the world as of Nov 2021

OFFICIALLY AMAZING

RECORD HOLDER

PERMASTUNNED

PERMASTUNNED

CRISTA

In Jan 2019, streamer Alexander Nathan (NLD) set out to build a *Dota 2* team of people with disabilities like him. Within days, Nathan had the four teammates he was looking for, but it didn't stop there. Five years later, that *Dota 2* team has evolved into a 37-member esports collective "made from gamers with disabilities, for gamers with disabilities". In addition to competing in tournaments for games as diverse as *Counter-Strike: Global Offensive* (Valve, 2012), *Call of Duty* (Activision, 2003) and *Tekken* (Bandai Namco, 1994), Permastunned advocates for the estimated 400 million disabled gamers worldwide.

"It always bothered me people with disabilities were underrepresented in the professional *Dota 2* scene."

Cristal1337, aka Alexander Nathan

Fastest-growing non-mobile game

89

Mobile battle royale

On 21 Mar 2024 – two years after it was announced – Activision released *Call of Duty: Warzone Mobile*. More than 50 million people pre-registered for this much-anticipated free-to-play FPS, which deployed with the fan-favourite map *Verdansk*. The battle-royale mode supports 120 players, up from the 100 available on the OG console and PC version.

Call of Duty: Warzone

Within three days of its launch on 10 Mar 2020, Activision's free-to-play battle royale had gathered over 15 million gamers. Players, known in-game as Operators, leapt at the chance to take up arms. *Warzone* cut down its rivals on the way to topping 50 million downloads within the month and more than 100 million by Apr 2021. For many people, it was their go-to game during the COVID-19 lockdowns.

R N G

17

Most kills in a *CoD: Warzone* match using a Quadstick mouth-operated joystick, by RockyNoHands, aka Rocky Stoutenburgh (USA), on 18 Nov 2020.

XP

Date: 2020
Developer: Raven Software/ Infinity Ward
Publisher: Activision

88

Most concurrent players on Steam

PUBG: Battlegrounds

The epic battle royale *PUBG: Battlegrounds* recorded an all-time peak of 3,257,248 gamers playing at the same time on 13 Jan 2018. Neither *PUBG* nor any other game has managed to reach that lofty level on the PC gaming platform since, according to tracking website SteamDB. On 9 Sep 2018, *PUBG* became the **first game on Steam to maintain 1 million concurrent players for an entire year**.

🔓 INORITE!

- PlayerUnknown was the gaming tag of Ireland's Brendan Greene, the game's creator.
- Publisher Krafton decided to change the game title from *PlayerUnknown's Battlegrounds* to *PUBG: Battlegrounds* in 2021.
- The game's popular phrase "Winner Winner Chicken Dinner" is thought to have originated among gamblers in the 1930s.

R N G

2,279,084

Number of gamers who played *PUBG: Battlegrounds* at the same time in Oct 2017, making it the **first game to reach 2 million concurrent players on Steam.**

XP

Date: 2017
Developer: PUBG Studios
Publisher: Krafton

All aboard the Steam train

PUBG sits ahead of some formidable competitors on Steam. The game with the second-most-concurrent players as of Feb 2024 is newbie *Palworld* (Pocketpair, 2023, see pp.66 and 95) with a peak of 2.1 million players. First-person shooter *Counter-Strike 2* (Valve, 2023, above right) is next at 1.8 million, ahead of action RPG *Lost Ark* (Smilegate/Tripod Studio, 2019, left) on 1.3 million and MOBA stalwart *Dota 2* (Valve, 2013, right) with 1.2 million. The only other game to top a million is *Cyberpunk 2077* (CD Projekt Red, 2020), which hit 1,054,388 concurrent gamers.

XP

Size: 3,050 items
Location: Spain
Estimated value:
€300,000 (£259,563;
$336,642)

Largest collection of
Tomb Raider memorabilia

87

Rodrigo Martín Santos

!

When the first Lara Croft game dropped in 1996 (*Tomb Raider*, Core Design), it made an instant fan of a nine-year-old Spanish boy who soon began seeking out memorabilia. During an official count two decades later, Rodrigo's collection had grown so large – to 3,050 distinct items – that it had to be split between two sites, in Madrid and Tenerife. Among his most prized possessions is an Arctic coat worn by Angelina Jolie in the 2001 movie, *Lara Croft: Tomb Raider*. "It has been an adventure that has changed my life," says Rodrigo. "It has taken me across the world."

Largest collection of *Sonic* memorabilia

Barry Evans (USA) also has a collection of 3,050 items – but in his case, it's of *Sonic the Hedgehog* memorabilia. After 30 years of collecting, Barry's Blue-Blur hoard is now on display in a room that he's styled to look like "Yesterdays" – his favourite childhood arcade. His first ever item was a Sonic bubblegum container.

Memorabilia Collectormania

Game	Items	Collector
Digimon (left)	24,331	Ng Tze Ying (CHN)
Super Mario	5,441	Mitsugu Kikai (JPN)
Skylanders (right)	4,100	Christopher Desaliza (USA)
Final Fantasy	3,782	Tai-Ting Tseng (CHN)
Sonic the Hedgehog	3,050	Barry Evans (USA, see left)
Street Fighter (below)	2,723	Clarence Lim (CAN)
Silent Hill	342	Whitney Chavis (USA)

86

Best-selling PS4 exclusive

Marvel's Spider-Man (2018)

Everyone's favourite webslinging hero takes on Mister Negative and Doctor Octopus in this original story, set in a fictionalized Manhattan. Insomniac's third-person open-world action-adventure sold 3.3 million copies within three days of the game's launch in 2018. By 2020, the total had rocketed to more than 20 million, propelling the game to the top of the chart for titles available only on the PS4. (See also p.21.)

XP

Date: 2018
Developer: Insomniac Games
Publisher: Sony Interactive Entertainment

R N G

2,500,000

Copies sold of *Marvel's Spider-Man 2* (2023) for the PS5 on the day of release. This figure had doubled to 5 million just 10 days later!

Top 5 fastest-selling PS4 exclusives in first three days

The Last of Us Part II (2020, right)	4.0 million
Final Fantasy VII Remake (2020)	3.5 million
Marvel's Spider-Man (2018)	3.3 million
God of War (2018, above)	3.1 million
Ghost of Tsushima (2020)	2.4 million

Sony Group Corporation Q2 results, 9 Nov 2023

Largest playable Game & Watch device

Thomas' device is about 17 times bigger than the original

Thomas Tilley

This mammoth version of Nintendo's original handheld measures a mighty 1.93 m (6 ft 4 in) wide, 1.16 m (3 ft 9 in) high and 0.14 m (5 in) deep. It was constructed by computer scientist Dr Thomas Tilley (AUS), who unveiled it at the Maker Faire in Adelaide, Australia, on 5 Nov 2017. His Game & Watch runs the title *Octopus* (aka *Mysteries of the Sea* or *Mysteries of the Deep*). The aim is to retrieve treasure from a sunken ship while avoiding a dastardly octopus. The original version of this device was released in Jul 1981 and sold more than 1 million units. Turn to p.44 for more about the *G&W*.

R N G

43.4 million

Number of Nintendo Game & Watch devices sold worldwide during its production run from 1980 to 1991. Some 12.87 million were sold in Japan alone.

Thomas gets into character. The game involves scuba divers searching for hidden treasure

XP

Date: 2017
Width: 1.93 m
Location: Adelaide, Australia

The giant G&W is built from a large LCD TV, wood and some old curtains!

Largest mobile game prize pool

Honor of Kings International Championship (KIC)

Tencent's fast-paced MOBA *Honor of Kings* never made much of a splash in the west (where's it's known as *Arena of Valor*). In China and east Asia, however, the game is a cultural phenomenon, with daily player counts in the tens of millions.

Its popularity makes *Honor of Kings* a big draw for esports pros, who battle it out at the annual Kings International Championship. Since 2022, the total prize pool has totalled 69 m Chinese yuan ($9.7 m; £7.6 m). The final of the 2023 KIC, which took place on 30 Dec, was won by AG Super Play (CHN), who received the first prize of 20 m yuan ($2.8 m; £2.2 m).

XP

Date: 2022/2023
Organizer: Level Infinite, VSPO

Honor of Kings has been a big earner for Tencent, with an income now estimated at over $10 bn (£7.89 bn). The inclusion of characters from China's history and folklore has been a factor in that success. But Tencent has faced criticism for the liberties it has had to take to transform historic figures into magical heroes. The medieval explorer Marco Polo, for example, has become a gunslinger in a top hat and waistcoat, with abilities such as "Gorgeous Revolver" and "Fever Barrage".

RNG 6,460,909

The **most viewers of an** *Honor of Kings* **livestream**, by Sao Bai (CHN) in Hangzhou, China, on 10 Jan 2023.

Best-selling instrument game

Guitar Hero III: Legends of Rock

Building on the runaway success of the first two *Guitar Hero* games, *Legends of Rock* turned everything up to 11, adding more songs, more game modes and a host of cameos from celebrity shredders. It flew to the top of the charts, selling more than 16 million copies across the PS2, PS3, Wii and Xbox 360 versions. Patrick Young (USA) made his own piece of history in Feb 2012 with the **longest marathon playing a *Guitar Hero* game** – a finger-blistering 72 hr 17 min.

INORITE!

Guitar Hero III was the high water mark of the instrument game genre, which you might know only from the dusty plastic guitars that still show up in odd corners. Between this series and its rival, *Rock Band*, a total of 24 play-along games were released between 2007 and 2010 before gamers tired of the idea.

First game to earn $1 billion

Guitar Hero III: Legends of Rock set another phenomenal world record during the 2008 holiday season. Helped in part by the high cost of the accessories bundled with the game, it became the first title to break through the billion-dollar sales barrier. That success rubbed off on the artists featured in the game, too – many reported an unexpected surge in interest, with some claiming that sales of their music increased by over 800%!

XP

Date: 2007
Developer: Neversoft
Publisher: Activision

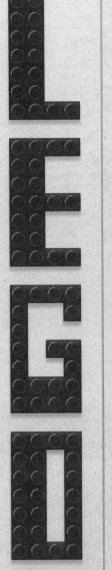

LEGO BLOCKBUSTERS

TOP 10

Largest commercially available LEGO® videogame sets

From clicks to bricks... Get your hands on the 10 biggest real-world official LEGO gaming sets available as of Jan 2023 (excluding expansion sets)

---

10 Sonic's Green Hill Zone Loop Challenge

Inspired by the opening level of Sonic's 1991 debut, this set captures the Blue Blur looping-the-loop in his quest to foil the evil Dr Robotnik's dastardly plans for the animals.

Set #: 76994
Pieces: 802

---

9 The Iron Golem Fortress

Help the Crystal and Golden Knights repel would-be invaders by building an impenetrable fort. Then rebuild this transformable set into a terrifying towering golem with massive moveable arms.

Set #: 21250
Pieces: 868

---

8 Sonic the Hedgehog – Green Hill Zone

Set #: 21331
Pieces: 1,125

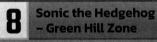

LEGO revisits the *Sonic* scene that sits at No.10 in this list, but this time it's aimed at an older builder (18+). There are close to 50% more pieces.

---

7 Horizon Forbidden West: Tallneck

In its LEGO form, the iconic communication machine from the 2022 *Horizon Zero Dawn* sequel stands more than 34 cm (13.4 in) tall. With its long legs and even longer neck, it dwarfs the Minifigure of Aloy way below.

Set #: 76989
Pieces: 1,222

---

6 The Llama Village

Set #: 21188
Pieces: 1,252

Our second visit to a *Minecraft* community offers a challenging, character-based build. It includes a knight, a herder, a pillager – and a spitting llama that opens up to reveal six changeable rooms inside!

5 Super Mario 64 Question Mark Block

This brick-built cube opens to reveal instantly recognizable levels from 1996's *Super Mario 64*. You'll find Bob-omb Battlefield and Lethal Lava Land, plus some familiar faces, from Mario and Yoshi to Princess Peach.

Set #: 71395
Pieces: 2,064

4 Atari 2600

Build a brick replica of the **best-selling 2nd-generation console** (sales of 27.64 million). It comes with a joystick, three game cartridges – *Asteroids*, *Adventure* and *Centipede* – plus three game scenes to piece together.

Set #: 10306
Pieces: 2,532

3 Nintendo Entertainment System (NES)

Between 1985 and 2003, the **best-selling 3rd-generation console** sold 61.91 million units. Its LEGO counterpart comes with a retro-styled 1980s TV set that features an 8-bit Mario negotiating a side-scrolling landscape.

Set #: 71374
Pieces: 2,646

2 PAC–MAN Arcade

This LEGO take on the **best-selling arcade machine** (over 400,000 units sold) recreates a coin-op classic. It offers a mechanical maze that's operated by a side handle to simulate game play.

Set #: 10323
Pieces: 2,651

Set #: 71411
Pieces: 2,807

1 The Mighty Bowser

The Koopa King, released in 2022, towers over the rest of the Mushroom Kingdom at 32 cm (12.5 in) tall. The Super Mario boss has poseable hands, arms, legs and tail, and boasts a snapping jaw as well as a mouth that launches fireballs. "Bwah hah hah!"

LEGO® MOCs

Thinking outside the box

"Zelda's Hyrule map"

The **largest LEGO-brick game map** is Ian Roosma's (USA) 24,718-piece version of Hyrule, as it appears in the series' 1986 debut. The 218.4-cm-long (7-ft 2-in) map hangs on Ian's wall!

The joy of brick-building is the freedom to make whatever you want – which means gaming LEGO fans aren't limited to the official sets. Here are 10 creative examples of what brick masters call MOCs ("my own creations"). You won't find these on the shelves of the LEGO store!

Horizon's "Tremortusk"

Using 7,957 bricks, Nicola Stocchi (aka SerialBuilder) built a posable model of the Tremortusk from *Horizon Forbidden West* (2022). This human-culling machine stands 39 cm (1 ft 3 in) tall and weighs 4.29 kg (9 lb 7 oz). Attached to the MOC is a brick-built screwdriver that can tilt the Tremortusk's head and deploy its salvo cannons.

"Electric Mouse Life-Sized Sculpture"

This plastic Pikachu was designed by Australian Dave Holder for Bricker Builds in Feb 2021. He used 2,569 bricks to sculpt a 48-cm-tall (1-ft 6-in) replica of Ash's loyal companion from the *Pokémon* series. According to the Pokédex, Pikachu's height is 40 cm (not including ears), making this a life-size model!

"Italian Plumber Life-Sized Sculpture"

This sculpture of Mario Mario (that's apparently his full name) is also the work of former Master Builder and Nintendo fan Dave Holder of Bricker Builds. The platforming plumber was assembled from 4,787 bricks, including the bob-omb and super mushroom.

"Working Fallout Vault"

Treat your Minifigs to a taste of "better living underground" with this blast-proof bunker from Canadian designer MasterBuilderKTC. His 4,260-piece replica of a Vault-Tec shelter from the *Fallout* series features built-in sound effects and an opening, remote-controlled door.

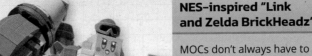

"Kirby: Planet Robobot"

LEGO Ideas user AndeeWow crafted a MOC in honour of his favourite Kirby game, 2016's *Planet Robobot*. The set comes complete with Waddle Dees, Clanky Woods, and the pink defender of Planet Popstar himself, in his somehow-still-cute mecha armour (right).

NES–inspired "Link and Zelda BrickHeadz"

MOCs don't always have to be massive. For example, how about a BrickHeadz-inspired set? You could pick one of your favourite characters and build a mini version of your own. Take these models of Link and Zelda, lovingly crafted by Eric Druon of BaronSat.net – it's amazing to see what can be achieved with less than 180 pieces!

"Sony PlayStation (PS one)", as registered with LEGO Ideas

LEGO has released official sets based on the Atari 2600 and the NES, but not yet the PlayStation. So GoofySwan099 decided to make their own, which meant recreating the console's tricky-to-make circular disk tray, as well as the controller, two memory cards, pushable buttons and even a game disc.

"Among Us: The Skeld"

This 2,998-piece MOC, built by "BrickRealm101", reproduces the interior of *The Skeld* and its doomed crew from *Among Us* (2018). Included are a full set of crewmates (each with optional imposter mouths), the iconic Cafeteria for emergency meetings and the dreaded cable-strewn floor of Electrical.

"Star Wars: The Skywalker Saga – Starkiller Base"

At 7.01 m (23 ft) long and 1.82 m (6 ft) wide, this is the **largest LEGO *Star Wars* build by an individual**. It took YouTuber RichboyJhae (USA) over two years to make from more than 150,000 pieces. It includes Snoke's hologram room (inset) and the trench that Poe Dameron flies through to destroy the base in 2016's *LEGO Star Wars: The Force Awakens*.

Best-selling game starring a solo female protagonist

Horizon Zero Dawn

Sony's vibrant post-apocalyptic adventure owes much of its success to its compelling main character, Aloy. The game follows her from a childhood spent scrabbling among the ruins of a war-ravaged USA to her adventures as the "Seeker" of the Nora tribe. As of Apr 2023, *Horizon Zero Dawn* had sold more than 24.3 million copies, putting Aloy comfortably ahead of her nearest rival, *Tomb Raider*'s Lara Croft, with sales of around 14.5 million (see p.140) for the 2013 reboot.

XP

Debut: 2017
Developer: Guerrilla Games
Publisher: Sony

INORITE!

Aloy is viewed by both fans and critics to be *Horizon Zero Dawn*'s strongest feature – and that's in a game which has building-sized robot dinosaurs! It might be a surprise to learn that she's actually a composite of three different people – she's voiced by Ashly Burch, her appearance is based on Dutch actress Hannah Hoekstra, and her movements are captured by the UK's Amanda Piery.

Way out west

Five years after *Zero Dawn*, Guerrilla released the hotly anticipated sequel *Horizon Forbidden West*. Whereas the first game was set in a 31st-century Colorado, Wyoming and Utah, *Forbidden West* moves the action to California. The series' iconic Tallnecks (left) return to help Aloy map the danger-infested wilderness – see them in blockbusting LEGO® form on p.36.

Best-selling racing series

Need for Speed

Electronic Arts' enormously successful street-racing series began in 1994 on the 3DO console with *The Need for Speed*. Thirty years and 25 main titles later, the franchise has accumulated total sales in excess of 150 million – a racing record if knockabout karting games are excluded (see p.70). The biggest single hitter so far, shifting more than 16 million copies, is the ninth instalment, *Most Wanted* (2005).

Work of c-art

The 2022 release *NFS Unbound* changed gear in terms of the series' graphics, melding the photorealism of previous titles with a flashy graffiti/anime style. The cel-shading aesthetic was a hit with gamers and critics alike, helping the game stand out and giving the series a welcome fuel injection.

Best-selling car-racing franchises

Need for Speed	150 million
Gran Turismo	90 million
Assetto Corsa	28 million
Driver	19 million
Midnight Club	18.5 million
Forza	16 million

XP

Date: 2005
Developer: EA
Publisher: EA

00:26.3
9.2 164 GEAR 3

The Need for Speed, the first game in the series

Best-selling American sports game

NBA 2K20

The 21st instalment in 2K's ever-popular *NBA* series had sold more than 14 million units as of Aug 2020, according to 2K's parent company Take-Two. The game – fronted by cover star and LA Lakers power forward Anthony Davis – was released on multiple platforms, including the PS4 and Xbox One, in Sep 2019. *NBA 2K20* was the first game in the franchise to include WNBA (Women's National Basketball Association) players. All 12 WNBA teams and their players appear.

The Lakers' legendary LeBron James in *NBA 2K20*

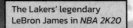

INORITE!

Like most titles in the series, *NBA 2K20* introduced a whole bunch of new features. Customization was taken to the next level in MyPlayer, with the ability to design your own tattoos and place them on the body of your player. The game also added six new classic teams, taking the total number of vintage squads to 68.

XP

Date: 2019
Developer: Visual Concepts
Publisher: 2K

First basketball videogame

Released in 1973 on the **first videogame console**, the Magnavox Odyssey, *Basketball!* required you to cover your TV screen with a plastic overlay depicting static players scattered about the court. The graphics were a small white block that represented the ball and bigger blocks representing the two playable characters. You can read more about 1st-generation consoles on p.49.

Best-selling fighting game series

Mortal Kombat

Flawless victory! The famously gory *Kombat* series had sold more than 83 million units as of Jan 2024. There have been 28 releases in total, excluding bundles and compilations. The most recent title, *Mortal Kombat 1* (NetherRealm Studios) – a second reboot of the franchise – was released in Sep 2023 to largely positive reviews and shifted just under 3 million copies in its first three months on sale.

XP

Debut: 1992
Developer: Midway
Publisher: Midway

R N G
33.6 million

Total sales of *Super Smash Bros. Ultimate* (Bandai Namco, 2018) as of Jan 2024, making it the **best-selling fighting game**.

STREET FIGHTER 6

Top 5 best-selling fighting game franchises

Series	Total sales
Mortal Kombat	83 million
Super Smash Bros.	74.9 million
Dragon Ball	62.5 million
Tekken	57 million
Street Fighter	53 million

TEKKEN 8

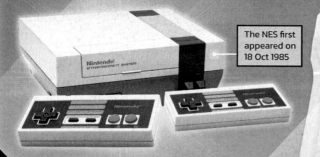
The NES first appeared on 18 Oct 1985

FAMILY COMPUTER™ Nintendo

78 First console gamepad

Famicom/NES

The Famicom was released in Japan on 15 Jul 1983 as part of the third generation of gaming consoles, and was reimagined for an international audience as the Nintendo Entertainment System (NES, above left). The console broke new ground in many ways, and the controller in particular was a game-changer, literally, using buttons rather than a joystick or wheel. The popularity of the NES cemented the D-pad as the primary input device for a generation and turned countless millions of us into a community of button mashers.

Famicom = Family + Computer

XP

Date: 15 Jul 1983
Designer: Gunpei Yokoi (JPN)
Controller ports: 2

The now legendary *Donkey Kong* (Nintendo R&D2) was a launch title

Nintendo engineer Masayuki Uemura created the Famicom

R N G
30%
The proportion of US households that owned an NES, according to *Computer Gaming World* magazine in 1990.

Before the NES...

...there was the button-controlled Game & Watch. The first of Nintendo's series of handheld games was released in Japan in 1980. They weren't consoles as such, as each device only contained one game. The first release – #1 in the "Silver" series – was the juggling-inspired *Toss-Up*. By the time *Donkey Kong* was released in 1982, it had evolved into a two-screen flip unit, helping sales of this game alone to exceed 8 million.

The "New Wide Screen" G&W from 1982

XP

Generation: 9th
Storage: 825 GB
Launch price:
$499 (£449)

Best-selling 9th-gen console

77

Sony PlayStation 5

By Apr 2024, the PS5 had sold an almighty 54.8 million units. While rivals Microsoft haven't announced Xbox Series X and S sales in years, industry analysts estimate that the PS5 outsold its fellow 9th-generation consoles by almost three to one in 2023 alone. (For the **best-selling console**, turn to p.138.)

PS5 owners get a lot of console for their money – at 39 cm high, 26 cm deep and 10 cm wide (15.3 x 10.2 x 4 in), it's the **largest videogames console**. All that graphical prowess means it needs a lot of space for fans and heat sinks.

"Far and away the most flamboyant-looking console I've ever owned."

IGN's Luke Reilly gives his verdict

🔓 INORITE!

Sony released the PS5 in the UK in Nov 2020. To promote the launch, they asked London Underground, the capital's subway system, to transform the signs around Oxford Circus station into PS icons. The traditional London Underground logo is the circle (bottom left). Sadly, as the country was in a COVID-19 lockdown at the time, many Londoners didn't see Sony's branding efforts!

First HD videogame console

FIFA 06 (2005) was one of the first Xbox 360 games

Microsoft Xbox 360

On 21 Nov 2005, people stood in line all night for what was advertised as the beginning of a new era in gaming. Microsoft's new console was to be the first to take advantage of the new High Definition (HD) TV standard, allowing for more than six times the display resolution of older consoles, which could only render about as many pixels as are in the display of a modern smartwatch.

The console had a long life, with two hardware updates (the 360 S and 360 E, below), and opened up access to online gaming with its built-in network connectivity and Xbox Live service. It may not have been the best-selling console of its generation, but it was arguably the most influential.

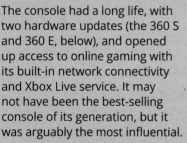

R N G

2,150+

Games released for the Xbox 360. The first titles included *Call of Duty 2* (Infinity Ward, below) and *Need for Speed: Most Wanted* (EA).

XP

Date: 22 Nov 2005
Developer: Microsoft
Units sold: 84.48 million

First million-selling game on the Xbox 360

The World War II-themed *Call of Duty 2* was snapped up by more than two-thirds of 360 owners. The beach-storming title shifted more than 200,000 copies in its first week and marked the beginning of *CoD*'s record-breaking run, with seven successful instalments being released for the console (see pp.118–21).

Highest-grossing biographical movie based on a videogame

Gran Turismo

BASED ON THE INCREDIBLE TRUE STORY OF A GAMER WHO BECAME A RACER

NISSAN

DAVID HARBOUR   ORLANDO BLOOM   ARCHIE MADEKWE

GRAN TURISMO

XP
Release: 2023
Director: Neill Blomkamp

The hit movie *Gran Turismo* (USA, 2023) tells the true story of Jann Mardenborough, a British teenager whose dream of becoming a real-life racing driver is fulfilled thanks to his gaming skills. The biopic follows Jann (played by Archie Madekwe) as he masters the driving sim *Gran Turismo* (Polyphony Digital, 1997). When he comes to the attention of Nissan, he's invited to compete for a place on their GT Academy programme (spoiler alert – he wins, beating 90,000 entrants to become their **youngest winner**!). As of 9 Feb 2024, the movie had grossed a record $117,862,107 (£93.39 m) worldwide.

RNG
19
Age at which Jann (b. 9 Sep 1991) became the **youngest winner of the Nissan GT competition**. He went on to become a stunt driver in the movie about his life!

Most courses in a *Gran Turismo* game

While many other racers – such as *Forza Horizon* (see p.98) – choose to go the open-world route, *GT* remains committed to the purity of a well-designed racetrack. In the series' latest outing, *GT7*, there are 38 unique venues (including 19 real-world circuits) with a total of 116 track variations. More have been added as DLC, too.

🔓 INORITE!

Since 2013's *GT6*, the Vision Gran Turismo project has opened up in-game car design to the world's leading vehicle manufacturers, including Porsche, Jaguar, Lamborghini and Bugatti. Some cars even exist as real-world mock-ups, such as this sleek 2022 Ferrari V6.

Longest-running flight sim series

Flight Simulator

The phenomenon that is *Microsoft Flight Simulator* began its journey in 1979 on an Apple II computer. Back then, it was called *FS1 Flight Simulator*, developed by a start-up called Sublogic. A sequel, *Flight Simulator II*, followed in 1983, though by then Microsoft had already brought the game's creators into the fold to develop 1982's *Microsoft Flight Simulator* for IBM PCs.

There have been a total of 15 releases under Microsoft's stewardship, plus the two original Apple titles, with a 16th game scheduled for 2024.

First flight simulator

Nuts-and-bolts pilot-training simulation devices have been around for 100 years, but the flight-sim gaming genre can be dated to the 1970s. Bruce Artwick – an electrical engineering student at the University of Illinois, USA – worked on a thesis titled *A Versatile Computer-Generated Dynamic Flight Display*. He created a model of the flight of an aircraft on an Apple computer. Realizing its commercial potential, he went on to set up Sublogic, which released *FS1 Flight Simulator* in 1979.

The high-def cockpit of the Aermacchi M-346 in *MFS*

XP

Debut: 1979
Developer: Various
Publisher: Sublogic/Microsoft

INORITE!

More than 37,000 airports feature in 2020's *Microsoft Flight Simulator*, ranging from grass strips for bush pilots in the Alaska wilderness to sprawling complexes such as Hartsfield–Jackson Atlanta International Airport in Georgia (left). The game also includes real-time weather data, allowing pilots to fly through the smoke of a California wildfire or into the eye of a hurricane.

XP

Debut: Jun 1977
Manufacturer: Nintendo
Territory: Japan

In 1977, a small Japanese toy manufacturer called Nintendo released their takes on the home games console: the Color TV-Game 6 and 15. Both systems came installed with just one game: the *Pong*-inspired *Light Tennis*, which at least offered six different modes of gameplay in the first release and 15 in the second, hence the names. The addictive gameplay and the consumer-friendly price tag made the consoles a smash hit in Japan and each sold a record-breaking 1 million units. And crucially, they also paved the way for the Famicom and the NES (see p.44).

Racing ahead

Color TV-Game Racing 112 (1978) was the third in Nintendo's home console series. The machine was hard wired with a top-down racer that offered seven game modes (four single-player and three two-player) and 16 difficulty levels, giving a total of 112 variations. What made the console unique was the casing, which came with a gear shifter and steering wheel. Single-player modes offered "narrow" and "spacious" roads, and the console also came packaged with two paddle controllers for a series of two-player options.

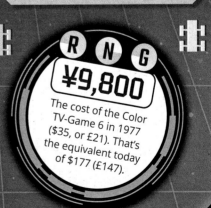

R N G

¥9,800

The cost of the Color TV-Game 6 in 1977 ($35, or £21). That's the equivalent today of $177 (£147).

72

Most critically acclaimed Star Wars game

Star Wars: Knights of the Old Republic

"A remarkable amalgamation of brilliant gameplay elements, jaw-dropping presentation and a huge helping of that special *Star Wars* magic." This glowing assessment was not an isolated example of how the 2003 Xbox version of the BioWare RPG was received by critics. Overall, from 72 reviews, it averaged 94% on Metacritic. What's not to like about a game that features an unhinged assassin droid who calls all non-robots "meatbags"?!

XP

Date: 2003
Developer: BioWare
Publisher: LucasArts

🔓 INORITE!

Numerous figures and events in *Knights of the Old Republic* have been recognized as approved elements of the official *Star Wars* universe. It can be tricky to define a concept that's constantly updating, but Darth Revan has taken his place as a canonical character. Titbits of information also emerge, such as Tatooine being an ocean world before the dustbowl seen in the first film.

Highest-grossing sci-fi movie series

Across 11 live-action films and a 2008 animation, the *Star Wars* series had generated $10,325,452,887 (£8.1 bn) as of 14 Feb 2024. *The Force Awakens* (2015) leads the list with just over $2 bn (£1.5 bn). *Star Wars* is also the **most prolific game licence**. As of 18 Jan 2024, there had been 163 titles across 56 platforms. They include collaborations with *Angry Birds* (left) and LEGO® (above).

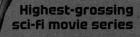

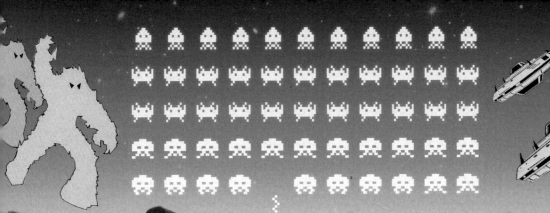

XP

Date: 1978
Developer: Taito
Publisher: Taito

Longest-running arcade series

71

Space Invaders

Taito's *Space Invaders* caused a sensation when it hit the arcades of Tokyo in the spring of 1978. It replaced the silent, methodical gameplay of titles such as *Breakout* (below) with something that felt dynamic and exciting. It was the **first game to include animated enemies** (and **enemies that fired back**), and the first with a **continuous soundtrack**. Its developers could barely keep up with demand – churning out 750,000 cabinets by the end of 1979 – and variations on the game have remained an arcade staple ever since.

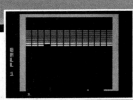

Game that inspired Space Invaders

Atari's block-busting paddle game *Breakout* was one of the biggest hits of 1976. In response, arcade rivals Taito asked developer Tomohiro Nishikado to come up with something similar. The static blocks became an advancing horde of aliens accompanied by ominous music, and the paddle was transformed into a laser gun. Gameplay sped up, too – a fun if unexpected side-effect of the code running faster with every alien sprite removed!

> "I'm proud of the game's huge impact. Even if I still can't clear the first stage!"

Tomohiro Nishikado, *Space Invaders* inventor

TOP 25
MOST-PLAYED VIDEOGAMES

Listed here are the world's most popular games. The chart is based on the number of registered user accounts – one of the few reliable ways of standardizing statistics across the gaming industry. Are your favourite games listed here?

25 **MapleStory** (Wizet, 2003) – 180 million

23= **Club Penguin** (New Horizon Interactive, 2005) – 200 million*

23= **Dragon Nest** (Eyedentity Games, 2010) – 200 million

22 **Roblox** (Roblox Corporation, 2006) – 214 million

21 **Rules of Survival** (NetEase Games, 2018) – 230 million*

20 **Honor of Kings** (TiMi Studio Group, 2015) – 295 million

19 **Runescape** (Jagex, 2001) – 350 million

18 **Crazyracing Kartrider** (Nexon, 2004) – 380 million

15= **Fantasy Westward Journey** (NetEase Games, 2001) – 400 million

15= **Mini World** (Miniplay Inc, 2017) – 400 million

15= **Fortnite** (Epic Games, 2017) – 400 million

14 **Among Us** (Innersloth, 2018) – 500 million

13 **Minecraft** (Mojang Studios, 2011) – 600 million

12 **Call of Duty: Mobile** (TiMi Studio Group, 2019) – 650 million

11 **Pokémon GO** (Niantic, 2016) – 678 million

10 **GKART/QQ Speed** (TiMi Studio Group, 2010) – 700 million

9 **Jetpack Joyride** (Halfbrick Studios, 2011) – 750 million

8 **Dungeon Fighter Online** (Neople, 2005) – 850 million

*Servers now shut down

Minecraft is one of the few games on this list that isn't free-to-play. But that hasn't stopped Mojang's sandbox from attracting an incredible 600 million registered players, 400 million of them in China.

If there's a worthy opponent to *Minecraft* (#13) for the sandbox crown, it's *Roblox* (#22). Over 70 million people play it every day. Some of the games created within its platform – 2017's *ADOPT ME!*, for example, about caring for pets – are among the biggest in the world in their own right.

1

Candy Crush Saga
(King, 2012) – 5 billion

The sweet "match-3" puzzler is the most-played game of all-time. Its broad appeal (the core market is women aged 35 and over) has boosted numbers, as has those attracted to its short-burst gameplay. Maybe because of that plus point, a British Member of Parliament was caught playing it at a committee hearing in 2014!

2

Subway Surfers
(Kiloo/SYBO Games, 2012) – 4 billion

The endless-runner genre was given an underground twist in this Danish runaway success. A set-up of a graffiti artist dodging trains and an inspector made it the most-downloaded mobile game of the previous decade, passing 2.7 billion downloads. A video collage trend on TikTok pushed that to 4 billion.

3

Temple Run
(Imangi Studios, 2011) – 2.5 billion

Who wouldn't want to stay a step or two ahead of a family of demon monkeys for all eternity? *Temple Run*'s simple premise, together with an equal simplicity of use (designed to be played with just a single thumb on a mobile device), has drawn in a remarkable 2.5 billion players. Ruuuun!

As of 23 Apr 2024, there had been 1,025 Pokémon registered in the Pokédex. Bulbasaur was the first and Pecharunt the most recent (pictured below is Togepi at #175). No wonder the critters turn up everywhere!

4

PUBG Mobile
(Lightspeed & Quantum Studios, 2018) – 1.2 billion

This adaptation of game-changer *PUBG: Battlegrounds* has enjoyed huge success, particularly in Asia. It has helped being one of the first games in the battle royale genre to make the jump from PC/console to mobile, blindsiding rivals and nipping in ahead of the likes of *Fortnite*.

5=

Crossfire
(Smilegate Entertainment, 2007) – 1 billion

This online first-person shooter from South Korea initially drew comparisons with Valve's *Counter-Strike*. But since then *Crossfire* has carved out a name and a reputation for itself, reflected in more than one billion registered users to date. It's now one of the biggest entertainment brands across Asia.

5= *Angry Birds* (Rovio Entertainment, 2009) – 1 billion

5= *Fruit Ninja* (Halfbrick Studios, 2010) – 1 billion

Best-selling Nintendo home console

! *Switch*

After the disappointing sales of 2012's Wii U, Nintendo went back to the drawing board. The result was the Switch, a unique handheld/home-console hybrid. Once again, Nintendo gambled everything on an innovative design – as they had before with the Game Boy and the Wii – and were rewarded. As of Dec 2023, the Switch had shifted 139.36 million units, putting it well ahead of Nintendo's previous record holder, the Wii, on 101,630,000. The **best-selling Nintendo console** overall is the handheld DS, which has sold 154.02 million.

XP

Release: Mar 2017
Storage: 32 GB
Weight: 399 g (with Joy-Cons)

6.2–in (15.7–cm) capacitive touch screen

Top-selling Nintendo products

DS (154.02 million)

Switch (139.36 million)

Game Boy (118.69 million)

3DS (75.94 million)

Game Boy Advance (81.51 million)

Wii (101.63 million)

R N G

1.2 billion

Number of games sold for the Switch – the most for a Nintendo console, ahead of 948 million for the DS.

Best-selling game based on a movie

GoldenEye 007

This thrilling FPS, released two years after Pierce Brosnan's first appearance as James Bond in the movie *GoldenEye* (UK/USA, 1995), shifted 8.09 million copies and came to define multiplayer gaming for a generation. Developers Rare avoided the usual retelling of the movie's plot in favour of a globe-trotting single-player campaign that expanded on the film's story and incorporated difficult objectives and stealth gameplay.

GoldenEye was the first Bond movie to gross over $300 m worldwide

Goldeneye was the name of Bond author Ian Fleming's estate in Jamaica

XP

Date: 1997
Developer: Rare
Publisher: Nintendo

Bond switches to Switch

With its release on the Nintendo Switch in 2023, *GoldenEye 007* finally has an online multiplayer option. The vintage 3D graphics are now at a high-definition resolution of 720p, so they're a big improvement on the original game's 240p. However, HD does show up some of the sketchy 90s artwork!

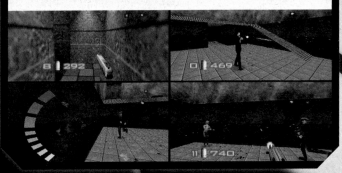

🔓 INORITE!

- This game isn't just about *GoldenEye* the movie: it contains references to all 16 Bond films before it and includes appearances by vintage villains such as Odd Job (above), May Day and Jaws.

- Look out for secret levels set during the events of movies *Moonraker* and *The Man with the Golden Gun*.

Microsoft

ACTIVISION | **BLIZZARD**

XP

Date: 2023
Buyer: Microsoft
Acquisition: Activision Blizzard

68 Largest gaming acquisition

Microsoft/Activision Blizzard

On 13 Oct 2023, Microsoft completed its cash purchase of Activision Blizzard for an eye-watering $68.7 bn (£56 bn). This buy-out gives the giant American corporation ownership of successful franchises such as (pictured left from top) *Spyro*, *Crash Bandicoot*, *Call of Duty*, *Candy Crush* and *Overwatch*. These titles now sit within the multinational Microsoft Gaming division alongside blockbusters like (right from top) *Gears of War*, *Minecraft*, *Psychonauts*, *Fable* and *Halo*.

🔓 INORITE!

In 2020, three years before acquiring Activision Blizzard, free spending Microsoft also coughed up $7.5 bn (£5.42 bn) for ZeniMax Media – the owners of Bethesda, id Software and other developers. The purchase added even more blockbuster titles to their stable, such as *Fallout*, *Starfield*, *The Elder Scrolls*, *Wolfenstein*, *Dishonored*, *DOOM*, *Rage* and *Quake*.

Most Emmy wins for a game adaptation

Storm Reid (Riley): Outstanding Guest Actress in a Drama Series

The creative team: Outstanding Special Visual Effects

Nick Offerman (Bill): Outstanding Guest Actor in a Drama Series

The Last of Us

The history of game-to-screen adaptations isn't all stinkers (see pp.68–69), but it's rare for one to hit the mark as surely as *The Last of Us*. At the 2024 Emmy Awards, this HBO miniseries earned a total of eight trophies from 24 nominations. This wasn't just any game adaptation, but then, *The Last of Us* is not just any game – and one of the key reasons for its success was how little Naughty Dog's critically acclaimed 2013 survival-adventure needed to be changed for a TV audience.

XP

Year: 2023
Channel: HBO Max
Showrunners:
Craig Mazin
Neil Druckmann

Real-world zombies

The Last of Us's global crisis of fungi taking over humans isn't a reality yet, but it exists in nature. Insects have been hosts for a parasitic fungus, *Cordyceps diapheromeriphila*. The **largest fungal "zombie animals"** are 20-cm-long (7.8-in) green-bean stick insects in the Amazon jungle. They become infected – zombified! – by the fungus, which sprouts a spore-making mushroom from its body.

🔓 INORITE!

In the TV adaptation, the roles of combative orphan Ellie and grieving father Joel were portrayed by Bella Ramsey and Pedro Pascal (main image). In the original 2013 game (above), they were played by voice actors Ashley Johnson and Troy Baker. At the time, there were not many award categories for videogame acting, but the two made a clean sweep of the awards available.

Artist's impression

66 Best-selling game soundtrack

Final Fantasy VIII

Nobuo Uematsu (right) penned the score for the eighth instalment of the successful RPG series – all 74 tracks, 249 minutes and four discs of it. It proved such a big hit with fans that within nine months of its release in Mar 1999, the album had sold more than 300,000 copies in Japan alone.

The game's theme song, "Eyes On Me", was also a runaway success, selling 500,000 copies when it was released by famed singer Faye Wong (above). Music from the *Final Fantasy* franchise has been so popular that live orchestral concerts continue to be staged around the world.

XP

Date: 1999
Composer: Nobuo Uematsu
Label: DigiCube/Square EA

Distant Worlds
music from
FINAL FANTASY

A hit for *Halo*

When the orchestral score for *Halo 4* (343 Industries) debuted at No.50 on the *Billboard* 200 on 10 Nov 2012, it became the **highest-charting game score on the US albums chart**. Selling just under 9,000 copies in its first week, it also launched at No.3 on Billboard's Soundtracks chart. *Halo 2: Original Soundtrack and New Music, Volume One* (2004) was the **first game soundtrack on the *Billboard* 200**, entering at No.185 on 27 Nov 2004.

🔓 INORITE!

The frantic gameplay and 1930s-style cartoon visuals of *Cuphead* (Studio MDHR, 2017) were perfectly soundtracked by a big-band extravaganza written by Canadian composer Kristofer Maddigan. In Sep 2019, a double-vinyl album of the game's toe-tapping music became the **first game soundtrack to hit No.1 on Billboard's Jazz Albums chart**.

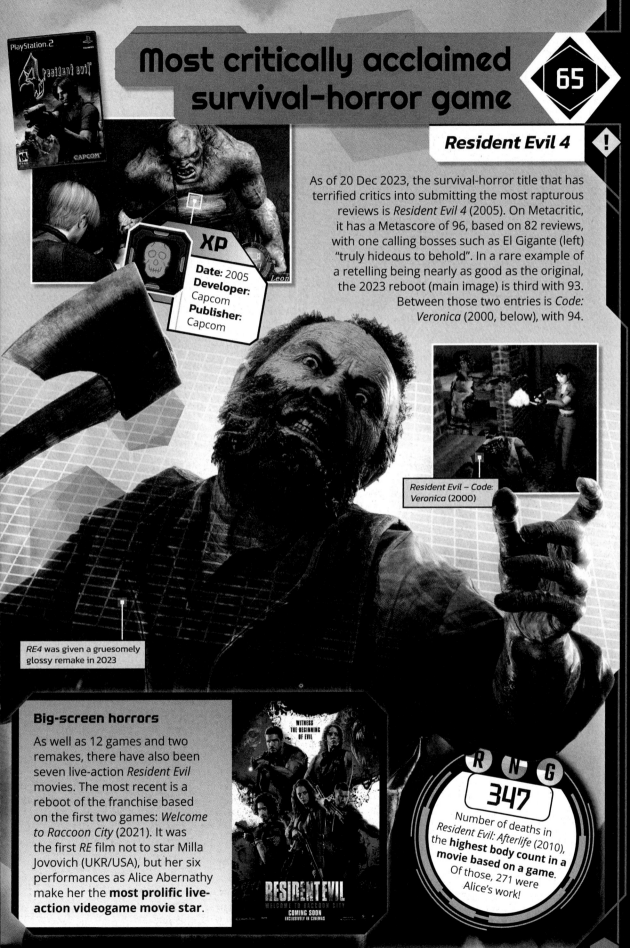

Most critically acclaimed survival-horror game

65

Resident Evil 4

!

As of 20 Dec 2023, the survival-horror title that has terrified critics into submitting the most rapturous reviews is *Resident Evil 4* (2005). On Metacritic, it has a Metascore of 96, based on 82 reviews, with one calling bosses such as El Gigante (left) "truly hideous to behold". In a rare example of a retelling being nearly as good as the original, the 2023 reboot (main image) is third with 93. Between those two entries is *Code: Veronica* (2000, below), with 94.

XP

Leon

Date: 2005
Developer: Capcom
Publisher: Capcom

Resident Evil – Code: Veronica (2000)

RE4 was given a gruesomely glossy remake in 2023

Big-screen horrors

As well as 12 games and two remakes, there have also been seven live-action *Resident Evil* movies. The most recent is a reboot of the franchise based on the first two games: *Welcome to Raccoon City* (2021). It was the first *RE* film not to star Milla Jovovich (UKR/USA), but her six performances as Alice Abernathy make her the **most prolific live-action videogame movie star**.

WITNESS THE BEGINNING OF EVIL

RESIDENT EVIL
WELCOME TO RACCOON CITY
COMING SOON
EXCLUSIVELY IN CINEMAS

R N G

347

Number of deaths in *Resident Evil: Afterlife* (2010), the **highest body count in a movie based on a game**. Of those, 271 were Alice's work!

64 Largest human image of a Pokémon

! **_Pikachu_**

The lovable yellow mascot of the _Pokémon_ franchise was recreated by 994 people in Yoshinogari Historical Park, Saga, Japan, on 26 Nov 2017. The attempt was organized by Shogakukan-Shueisha Productions to celebrate the 1,000th episode of its perennially popular _Pokémon_ anime. Accordingly, the record was supposed to include 1,000 people, but six were disqualified for taking off hats and sitting down! See pp.152–55 for more Poké-records.

XP

Date: 2017
Participants: 994
Location: Japan

R N G
1,280

Number of episodes of the _Pokémon_ anime TV series, as of Apr 2024. The show premiered in Apr 1997 and is the **longest-running videogame TV spinoff**.

Largest human image of PAC-MAN

On 21 May 2015, a giant chomping PAC-MAN materialized in the shadow of the Tokyo Tower in Japan, formed by 351 volunteers wearing yellow hooded overalls. The stunt was organized to mark the 35th anniversary of the original arcade release of _PAC-MAN_ (Namco, 1980); with 293,822 units sold, it remains the **most successful arcade game**.

XP

Date: 2006
Developer: Nintendo
Publisher: Nintendo

Best-selling Nintendo game

63

Wii Sports

With its fun gameplay and friendly visuals, *Wii Sports* was the undisputed star of the Nintendo Wii's 2006 launch line-up. Its minigames showcased the unique motion controls of the Wii –translating a swing of a Wii-mote into the drive of a golf club or the throw of a bowling ball – and appealed to gamers and non-gamers alike. Including copies that were bundled with the console in many territories, *Wii Sports* sold an incredible 82.9 million copies.

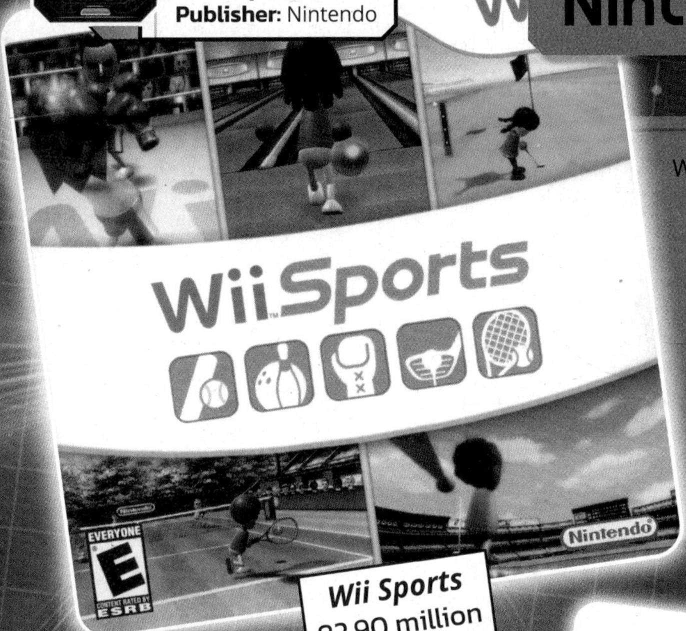

Wii Sports 82.90 million

Mario Kart 8 65.47 million

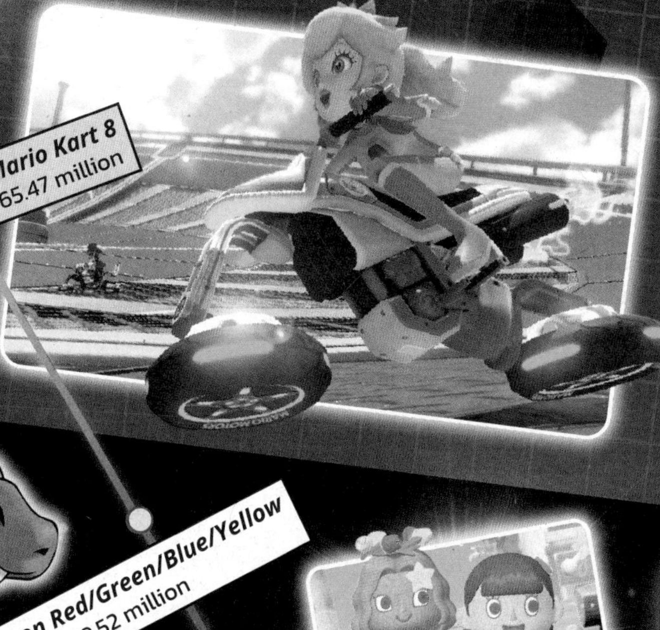

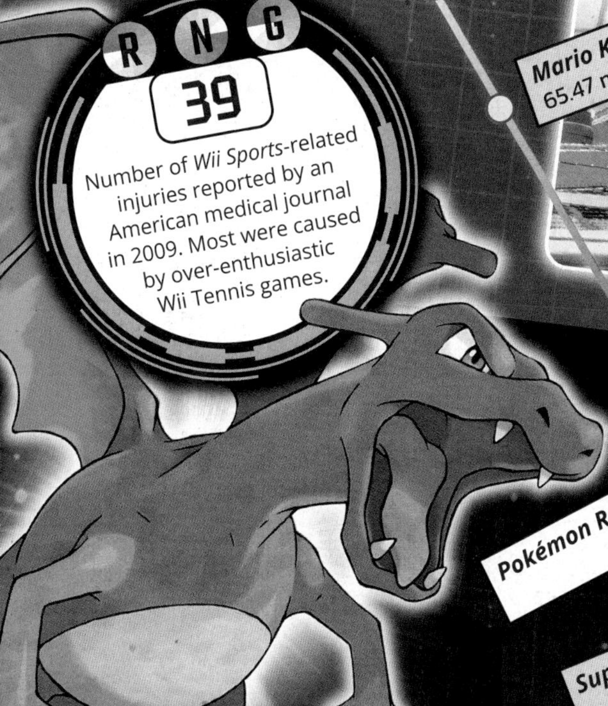

RNG

39

Number of *Wii Sports*-related injuries reported by an American medical journal in 2009. Most were caused by over-enthusiastic Wii Tennis games.

Pokémon Red/Green/Blue/Yellow 59.52 million

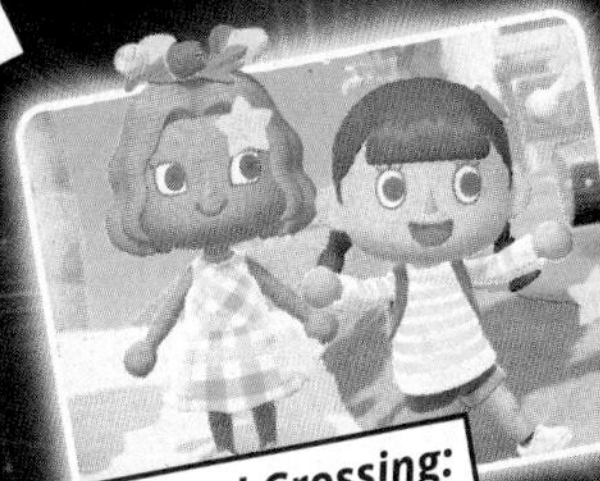

Super Mario Bros. 48.24 million

Animal Crossing: New Horizons 43.38 million

Pokémon Gold/Silver/Crystal – 42.21 million

Pokémon Diamond/Pearl/Platinum – 40.34 million

Pokémon Ruby/Sapphire/Emerald – 37.88 million

Mario Kart Wii – 37.38 million

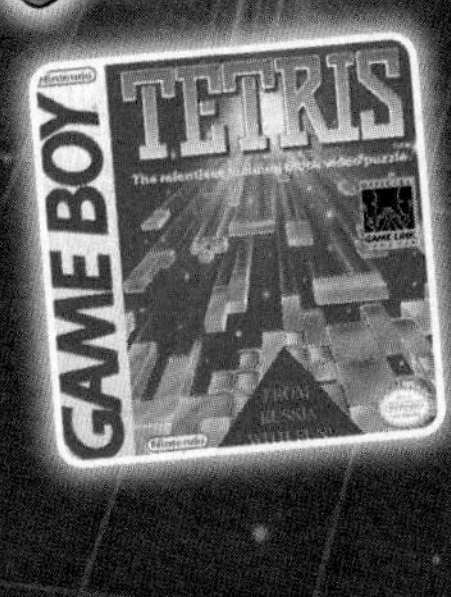

Tetris – 35.84 million

XP

Country: Spain
Established: 1999
Podcasts: 800+

GAME OVER

62 Longest-running gaming podcast

Game Over

Way back in 1999, a gang of Spanish gaming fans – including David Cordovilla, Albert González and Isaac Viana – began discussing all things gaming on their radio show *Game Over*. What started off on Ràdio Despí then became "one of the first radio shows to post shows online before all the podcast stuff". Contrary to its name, there is no sign of *Game Over* stopping any time soon.

INORITE!

On one of the earliest *Game Over* episodes (30 Dec 2000), the game *Jet Set Radio* (Smilebit) was chosen as its pick of the week. Focusing on a young graffiti gang, this Dreamcast title was the **first game to use cel-shading** (making 3D computer graphics appear hand-drawn).

Longest-running gaming podcast in English

For more than 20 years, Jamie Summers, Matt Whiteman and Rob Roberts have been broadcasting their Orange Lounge Radio show "like friends at a diner after a long night of gaming". Starting on internet radio on 23 Jun 2002, the trio set up their podcast in Jan 2005 and in that first year, won a Podcast award in the Games & Hobbies category. On 14 Apr 2024, OLR celebrated its 1,000th podcast!

Orange Lounge Radio
where Every Gamer Has a Voice
twitch.tv/vognetwork

OLR's Rob "V" Roberts, Jamie "DarkSakura" Summers and Matt "LOKI" Whiteman

Largest prize pool for a single esports tournament

At The International 2021 – staged at the Arena Națională in Bucharest, Romania – the staggering sum of $40,018,195 (£29 m) was on offer to the 18 competing teams. The prize pool was raised by in-game purchases from players of *Dota 2*.

Highest-earning esports player

Johan "N0tail" Sundstein

No stranger to the winner's podium, N0tail (DNK) heads up the list of gaming's top earners. As verified by eSportsEarnings.com on 24 Apr 2024, he's taken home a whopping $7,184,163 (£5.6 m) from 130 tournaments. This is despite being retired – unofficially – since late 2021. The vast majority of his hoard was earned playing the MOBA *Dota 2* (Valve, 2013), as a member of the OG team.

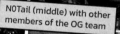

N0Tail (middle) with other members of the OG team

N0tail holds aloft the trophy at The International 2019, where OG won $15.6 m (£12.7 m)

XP

Name: Johan Sundstein
Team: OG
Years active: 2011–2021

R N G

25

N0tail's age when he won The International 2019, making him a "veteran"! The **oldest winner**, though, is Sneyking, aka Wu Jingjun (USA), at 27 years 180 days in 2022.

Longest-running esports game

StarCraft

This iconic sci-fi strategy focuses on a battle for control of the planets of the Koprulu Sector, pitting humans against the psychic Protoss and the insectoid Zerg. The rock-paper-scissors balance of the three factions' strengths and weaknesses made for exciting multiplayer battles, and a fiercely competitive fan community soon emerged, especially in South Korea. The game made its esports debut in the Pro Gamers' League on 12 Nov 1998, and has remained popular ever since. The scene kept going even after the release of a sequel, *StarCraft II*, in 2010, and is still going strong today, more than 25 years later.

StarCraft 1998 (left) compared with the 2017 remaster (right)

RNG

6,116,000

Kilometres (3.8 million mi) travelled by a copy of *StarCraft* taken to the *International Space Station* by gaming astronaut Daniel Barry (USA).

XP
Debut: 1998
Developer: Blizzard
Publisher: Blizzard

Top-earning *StarCraft II* esports player

Since making his competitive esports debut in Jul 2012, Joona Sotala (FIN), aka Serral, has earned $1,483,291 (£1.17 m) exclusively playing Blizzard's 2010 sequel. Of that total, $280,000 (£215,510) came from victory at the *StarCraft II* World Championship Series Global Finals at BlizzCon 2018 (Serral is pictured above with the trophy). He became the first – and only – non-Korean to win the title.

Zerg rush!

StarCraft is a game where victory is won through carefully considered moves and finely balanced tactical choices. Or sometimes it's won by the Zerg player who can build basic units the fastest. The "Zerg rush" strategy – in which you overwhelm your enemy with basic units before they've found their bearings – has since entered gaming infamy.

Most money raised by a speedrunning event

GDQ !

Most money raised from a single speedrun

A 100% completion of *Chrono Trigger* (Square, 1995, left) by puwexil at SGDQ 2019 raised a record $885,456 (£696,946). Other lucrative GDQ hauls include $794,339 (£651,680) from a run through *Super Metroid* (Nintendo, 1994, top left) at AGDQ in 2017 and $507,930 (£371,093) from *Deltarune* (Toby Fox, 2018, left) at AGDQ 2022.

Fastest blindfolded completion of the "child dungeons" in *Ocarina of Time*

One of the highlights of 2015's AGDQ was blindfolded gamer Runnerguy2489 (USA) successfully stumbling through the first three dungeons of this 1998 Nintendo classic (see pp.156–61). With a mix of glitches, sound cues, and carefully counted side-hops and backflips – as well as the raucous support of a live audience – he completed the challenge in 1 hr 26 min 56.66 sec.

Games Done Quick is a twice-yearly, week-long series of livestreams and events that showcase quirky, record-breaking speedruns and raise money for charities in the process. GDQ's big events are Awesome GDQ, which raises money for the Prevent Cancer Foundation, and Summer GDQ, which supports Doctors without Borders. At the end of AGDQ 2022 Online, it was revealed that $3,442,033 (£2.51 m) had been raised in charitable donations. As well as that, the same event hit $1 million in donations in the shortest time in GDQ history, during the event's third day.

GDQ
GAMES DONE QUICK

XP

Debut: 2010
Total raised: $50 m+ (£39 m+)

58

Largest third-party Game Pass launch

GAME PASS

Palworld

Microsoft launched the Xbox Game Pass in 2017 to give players access to a selection of games for a monthly fee. While Microsoft's *Minecraft* remains the **most played game** on the service (as of Apr 2024), Xbox Live announced on 31 Jan 2024 that Pocket Pair's open-world, animal-taming action-adventure phenomenon had made a record-breaking splash when it debuted. The Twitch-stream blockbuster, dubbed "Pokémon with guns", had been played on Xbox and PC by over 7 million people within 10 days (find out more on p.95).

The Pals of Palpagos Islands

Much of the game's popularity is down to the imaginative, quirky, cute-but-potentially-lethal Pals themselves. The islands of *Palworld* are home to more than 100 Pals, including the heavily armed sheep below, known as Lamballs. They're cute, fluffy and harmless enough... until armed with machine guns!

XP

Date: 2024
Developer: Pocket Pair
Publisher: Pocket Pair

INORITE!

Critics have noted that *Palworld* has more than a little in common with some familiar best-selling games. In particular, the cute critters pricked up the ears of The Pokémon Company. In Jan 2024, the publisher pledged to "investigate" any possible copycat claims.

Zelda + *Fortnite* + *Pokémon* =

> "It's all powered by a large gaming PC that I loaded Game Boy emulators on to."

Jake Carlini explains how his behemoth works.

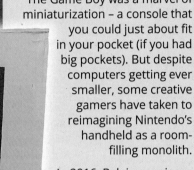

The PC connects to a very heavy plasma–screen TV!

Created by Jake Carlini

The Game Boy was a marvel of miniaturization – a console that you could just about fit in your pocket (if you had big pockets). But despite computers getting ever smaller, some creative gamers have taken to reimagining Nintendo's handheld as a room-filling monolith.

In 2016, Belgian engineer Ilhan Ünal (below) made the **largest Game Boy**, standing 1.01 m (3 ft 3 in) tall. And in 2022, YouTuber Jake Carlini (USA) went even bigger, building the **largest Game Boy Color** – a 2.23-m (7-ft 4-in) giant... ideal for the 28-m-tall (91-ft) gamer on the go!

XP

Height: 2.23 m
Width: 1.24 m
Depth: 0.61 m

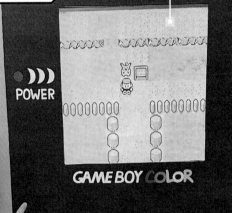

POWER

GAME BOY COLOR

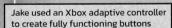

Jake used an Xbox adaptive controller to create fully functioning buttons

ACTUAL SIZE

Small yet perfectly formed

The **smallest Game Boy** is just 54 mm (2.12 in) long, fits on a key chain and boasts an impressive selection of original Game Boy titles. Creator Jeroen Domburg (NLD) was meticulous in his selection of minuscule components to fit inside the tiny compartment.

GAMING AT THE MOVIES

From 1993 flop *Super Mario Bros.* to 2023 hit *The Super Mario Bros. Movie*, videogame films have attracted millions of gamers eager to check out big-screen adaptations of their favourite virtual worlds. Here, GWR's gaming expert Wesley Yin-Poole plots the critical reception of 10 iconic game-inspired movies, using box office sales from The Numbers and ratings from Rotten Tomatoes. After years of erratic quality from Hollywood, are we now experiencing a golden age of gaming blockbusters? Hmm, let's see...

THE **NUMBERS**®

$21 M (£14 M)	$99 M (£63 M)	$104 M (£70 M)	$273 M (£188 M)	$297 M (£238 M)

SUPER MARIO BROS. (1993)

Hollywood's first stab at a *Super Mario Bros.* movie lives in infamy for its stilted performances and terrible plot. The late Bob Hoskins, who played Mario, once called *Super Mario Bros.* a "nightmare" and the worst movie he had ever made.

STREET FIGHTER (1994)

Considered one of the worst videogame movies ever, the ill-fated *Street Fighter* saw Jean-Claude Van Damme's Guile go up against dictator M. Bison. Given that the original is a fighting game with no real story, it's perhaps not surprising this one bombed!

RESIDENT EVIL (2002)

Written and directed by Paul Anderson and starring Milla Jovovich as heroine Alice, *Resident Evil* was a stinker with critics but has achieved a cult status with fans. The six *Resident Evil* films that Anderson directed and/or wrote have grossed a combined $1.2 bn (£950 m) worldwide.

LARA CROFT: TOMB RAIDER (2001)

Before Alicia Vikander played Lara Croft in the 2018 reboot, Angelina Jolie broke Hollywood records as the original Tomb Raider. Jolie was perfectly cast as the all-action Croft in this cheesy adventure based on the famous British-made videogame franchise.

FIVE NIGHTS AT FREDDY'S (2023)

Emma Tammi's adaptation of the horror indie game failed to impress critics, but it proved a hit with audiences. Just like the game, the movie sees a night security guard fight for his life in an abandoned pizzeria packed with creepy animatronic characters who come alive at night.

 29%   11% 35%   20%   32%

Rotten Tomatoes
As of 17/1/24
All films USA

PEACH OF A SONG

Bowser's love song from *The Super Mario Bros. Movie*, "Peaches", was a hit in its own right, peaking at No.56 on the Billboard Hot 100. "Peaches" was also the first-ever solo single by Bowser voice-actor Jack Black (left) to chart. Turns out the Koopa King is quite the crooner, but we doubt Princess Peach would be impressed.

$302 M (£223 M)	$400 M (£332 M)	$428 M (£327 M)	$438 M (£356 M)	$1.3 BN (£1 BN)

SONIC THE HEDGEHOG (2020)

Sega credits the *Sonic the Hedgehog* movie for reviving its famous video-game mascot. Mad scientist Dr Robotnik, gleefully played by Jim Carrey, proved the perfect foil for the cheeky CGI Sonic (Ben Schwartz), who delighted veteran fans after an initial backlash.

UNCHARTED (2022)

While Tom Holland as Nathan Drake and Mark Wahlberg as Victor Sullivan were hotly debated casting choices, the *Uncharted* movie did an admirable job emulating Naughty Dog's critically acclaimed cinematic adventure. It even mirrored the superb cargo plane scene in *Uncharted 3: Drake's Deception* (2011).

POKÉMON: DETECTIVE PIKACHU (2019)

The first-ever live-action Pokémon movie saw Ryan Reynolds' wise-cracking super-sleuth Pikachu solve a mystery in a hyper-realistic world. *Pokémon GO* (Niantic, 2016) even had a limited edition "detective" version of Pikachu!

WARCRAFT (2016)

The much-hyped *Warcraft* movie, directed by Brit Duncan Jones, was a CGI-fest that hoped to capitalize on the huge success of Blizzard's *World of Warcraft* (2004). But a plodding plot and some mediocre battles failed to capture the sense of wonder the virtual world of Azeroth is famous for.

THE SUPER MARIO BROS. MOVIE (2023)

The huge success of the latest Mario film even surprised Nintendo! With Chris Pratt as Mario and Jack Black as the lovelorn Bowser, *The Super Mario Bros. Movie* went on to become the **highest-grossing film adaptation of a videogame**.

 40%

 63%

 68%

 29%

 59%

56 Best-selling game for Nintendo Switch

⚠ Mario Kart 8 Deluxe

Sales of 60.58 million as of 1 Jan 2024 make *Mario Kart 8 Deluxe* both the Switch's best-seller and the **best-selling kart racing game** on any platform. *Deluxe* is a souped-up version of the original *Mario Kart 8* for the Wii U. In 2022–23, the *Booster Course Pass* DLC added 48 extra race tracks and eight more characters. The franchise, which began with 1992's *Super Mario Kart* on the SNES, is the **best-selling kart racing series**, with total sales of 182.15 million.

XP

Date: 2017
Developer: Nintendo
Publisher: Nintendo

❗ Pwn! ☐ ✕

The Super Horn is super useful in *Deluxe*. You can use it to form a shockwave that flips the other racers, but, more importantly, it will protect you from the powerful Spiny (Blue) Shell, which targets the racer in first place. Activate the Super Horn while the Shell is lurking above you and you'll destroy it. Shell yeah!

Best-selling Switch games	
Game	**Units sold**
Mario Kart 8 Deluxe	60.58 million
Animal Crossing: New Horizons	44.79 million
Super Smash Bros. Ultimate	33.67 million
The Legend of Zelda: Breath of the Wild	31.61 million
Super Mario Odyssey	27.65 million
Nintendo, as of 1 Jan 2024	

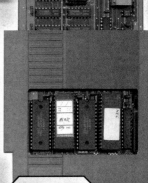

XP

Date: 1991
Developer: Nintendo
Publisher: Nintendo

Rarest Nintendo game

55

Nintendo Campus Challenge

!

Steven Lucas (left), winner of the 1991 Campus Challenge

In 1991, Nintendo made a limited run of cartridges for a competition that was held at colleges across the US. Each copy was loaded with a level from *Super Mario Bros. 3* (1988), *Pin Bot* (1990) and *Dr. Mario* (1990), and students competed to get the highest score in each. When the tournament was over, all of the custom cartridges were destroyed. All, that is, except one, which was kept by a Nintendo employee and sold to collector JJ Hendricks at a yard sale in 2006. It last changed hands in 2009 for $20,100 (£12,350) and hasn't been seen since.

Rarest arcade game

Around the time that *Donkey Kong* hit arcades in 1981, Nintendo was working on *Sky Skipper*, another game involving giant apes. A handful of cabinets were produced for testing in Japanese and American arcades, but the game was not well received. As a result, it was never officially released. The only known *Sky Skipper* cabinet still in existence is kept in storage by Nintendo of America, but, in 2017, a group of arcade collectors in the USA did build one using original *Sky Skipper* circuit boards.

Fastest-selling Nintendo game

The Legend of Zelda: Tears of the Kingdom

As *Tears of the Kingdom* was to be a direct sequel to 2017's critically acclaimed *Breath of the Wild*, the anticipation for a new Hyrulean adventure was even higher than usual. This resulted in *Tears* – a game set at the end of the *Zelda* timeline – shifting 10,000,000 copies in its first three days on sale during May 2023. The previous year's *Pokémon Scarlet* and *Violet* sold more copies on launch, but these numbers are inflated by the dual-release format of main-line *Pokémon* titles. For more on the Zelda universe, head over to pp.156–61.

One of 10 million sales in the game's first 72 hours

The midnight NYC launch included a Zelda-themed bus

XP
Date: 2023
Developer: Nintendo
Publisher: Nintendo

! Pwn!

It's important to tool up before exploring too much of the vast open world of Hyrule and beyond, so make the main quest your first priority. This means you'll also get your hands on the paraglider, which comes into its own later in the game. And be sure to activate all the shrines you come across, to help speed up your travels.

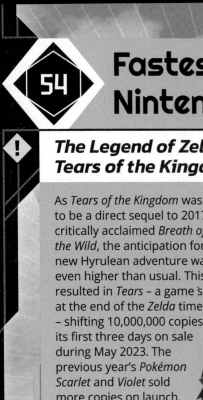
Link battles a Zonai Soldier Construct III

Smashing superstar

Link appears (more than once!) in another of Nintendo's fast-selling games: the crossover cartoon brawler *Super Smash Bros. Ultimate* (2018). This Switch favourite, in which an incredible line-up of Mario, Luigi, Pikachu, Kirby, Link and many others slug it out in a series of fights, sold more than 12 million copies in just 24 days.

Goro Akechi, aka Crow, cutting a dashing figure in his Prince regalia

354 191   306 203   375 153   342 163

Persona 5 Royal

The *Persona* series is famous for telling huge stories that combine epic high-fantasy adventure with emotionally charged high-school drama. In 2019, developers Atlus took the already massive *Persona 5* (2016) and added even more content to make the Royal edition. Just breezing through this game, ignoring the romances and side-quests, and never once pausing to enjoy the amazing soundtrack, takes players 101 hr on average. Get lured off the path of the main story, however, and that total rises to 142 hr – nearly six solid days of gaming!

Another *Monster*

It's not as long as *Persona 5 Royal*, but RPG *Monster Hunter Freedom Unite* (Capcom, 2008) still weighs in with a story lasting 98 hr. In fact, four *MH* games feature in the top 10 longest games. For completionists who like to visit every nook and cranny of games, the quartet gobble up precisely 87 days. Tracking gigantic, ferocious beasts is clearly not a quick process!

PSP

MONSTER HUNTER FREEDOM UNITE

CAPCOM

RNG

13

Number of moves needed to complete *Jack in the Dark* (Infogrames, 1993) – the **shortest action-adventure game** – in stark contrast to the gaming epics above.

XP

Date: 2019
Developer: Atlus
Publisher: Sega

Largest arcade cabinet

Donkey Kong

With a height of 19 ft 4 in (5.89 m) and width of 7 ft 5 in (2.26 m), this version of *Donkey Kong* (Nintendo, 1981) is so big that it's suspended between two floors of The Strong National Museum of Play in Rochester, New York, USA. It was built with help from Nintendo of America and plays the original *Donkey Kong* motherboard. The cabinet is 372% larger than the 1980s original!

Largest *PAC-Man* arcade cabinet

In 2016, Bandai Namco and arcade company Raw Thrills created a giant *PAC-MAN* video billboard screen. It stands at a mighty 2.67 m (8 ft 9 in) tall and 1.71 m (5 ft 7 in) wide, with a total surface area of 4.5 m² (48.4 sq ft). It's played using a console unit attached to the screen.

XP

Date: 2023
Screen: 5 ft (1.52 m)
Location: USA

Largest *Tetris* cabinet

This titanic *Tetris* arcade machine stands 4.90 m (16 ft) tall and 1.98 m (6 ft 6 in) wide. It was constructed by entertainment venue MadLab (ESP) and is located in the La Torre Outlet shopping centre in Zaragoza. To play, visitors need to buy a giant coin and roll it into the giant slot, then climb steps to reach the giant working buttons.

Top 5 most-funded games on Kickstarter

Shenmue III	$6,333,295
Bloodstained: Ritual of the Night	$5,545,991
Eiyuden Chronicle: Hundred Heroes	$4,673,143
Torment: Tides of Numenera	$4,188,927
Pillars of Eternity	$3,986,929

Kickstarter, as of 26 Jan 2024

Most-funded game on Kickstarter

51

Shenmue III

!

K

The first two *Shenmue* action-adventure games were cult classics in the early 2000s, but poor sales meant that further sequels were cancelled. In 2015, unable to get publishers interested, series director Yu Suzuki appealed directly to the games' devoted fans. A campaign on crowd-funding site Kickstarter went on to set the record for the **fastest $1 m pledged for a videogame** and eventually brought in the $6.33 m (£4.05 m) needed to continue the story.

Backers were tempted with various items of merch

MIRRORS double sided Phoenix/Dragon Mirror

GAME a copy of the game

PATCHES iron-on authentic designs from the series

STICKERS classic iconography from the game

LIGHT BOX Shoji Door styled desk lamp

(M) Violence

shenmue3.deepsilver.com

XP
Date: 2019
Developer: Ys Net
Publisher: Deep Silver

R N G
69,320

Number of people who supported *Shenmue III* on Kickstarter. Rewards included an in-game phone card to call characters from *Shenmue I* and *II*.

Most Platinumed PlayStation game

Marvel's Spider-Man: "Be Greater"

PlayStation awards in-game trophies to players who meet certain targets or reach significant milestones. And if you win every trophy in a game, you earn a Platinum award. Insomniac Games' 2018 Spidey adventure sits at the No.1 spot on the chart of games with the most Platinum trophies won (right) – as of 24 Apr 2024, its "Be Greater" trophy was tackled successfully by 379,725 players. For the **most trophies won**, see p.26.

10
9
Assassin's Creed II
"Master Assassin"
170,843

Ghost of Tsushima
"Living Legend"
172,111

8

7
Bloodborne
"Bloodborne"
209,210

Batman:
The Telltale Series
"I'm Batman"
180,737

inFAMOUS: Second Son
"Enjoy Your Powers"
239,059

6
Astro's Playroom
"You've Only
Done Everything"
220,454

5

God of War
"Father and Son"
273,027

4
Rocket League
"Virtuoso"
242,712

3

R N G
35,494,331
Number of *Spider-Man* trophies earned by players, as of 24 Apr 2024. It includes 651,015 for *End Game*, awarded for finishing the story element.

2
Horizon Zero Dawn
" All Trophies"
288,044

1
Marvel's Spider-Man
"Be Greater"
379,725

XP
Trophy: Be Greater
Developer: Insomniac Games
Publisher: Sony

For more *Spider-Man* records, sling yourself over to pp.21 and 32

Among Us

This space-themed social deduction phenomenon launched for free on Android and iOS in 2018, but attracted little attention until the COVID-19 pandemic hit. In 2020, as many countries locked down, the game's popularity surged. In November of that year, *Among Us* was being played by half a billion people, and also inspired more than 1.22 billion viewing sessions on Twitch. Turn the page for more *Among Us* records and trivia.

🔒 INORITE!

A Chicken McNugget that supposedly looked a bit like one of the *Among Us* crewmates sold for a whopping $99,997 (£70,709) on eBay in 2021. Bidding began at just 99¢ (70p) before things escalated. In all, 184 bids were placed. According to seller Tavian S Herrera, the nugget was sent frozen and air sealed in order to "ensure freshness".

Impostors get animated

CBS Studios and Innersloth have teamed up to work on an *Among Us* animated series. Just like the game, the show is all about rooting out the impostor among the crew of a spaceship. The show's creator is Owen Dennis, who was behind Cartoon Network's critically acclaimed hit *Infinity Train* (2019–21).

INCOMING. .

Simple threads

The ultra-simple look and style of the *Among Us* crew has inspired cosplayers worldwide – such as Instagram star ThatJessiWills, who got together with her colourful friends in Nov 2020 (above, with Jessi in orange). There are even official inflatable costumes available from KAP Toys (above right).

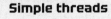

XP

Date: 2018
Developer: Innersloth
Publisher: Innersloth

XP

Date: 20 Oct 2020
Game: *Among Us*
Twitch name: AOC

48 Most viewers for a debut stream on Twitch

Alexandria Ocasio-Cortez

In Oct 2020, congresswoman Alexandria Ocasio-Cortez (USA) took to Twitch to play *Among Us* (see p.77) as a means of encouraging people to get out and vote in the forthcoming US presidential election. She reached 439,000 concurrent viewers at the stream's peak, playing alongside various well-known streamers and a fellow politician, Ilhan Omar. In the opening round of her first-ever game, AOC was picked as the impostor!

"Anyone want to play *Among Us* with me...? (I've never played but it looks like a lot of fun)"

AOC tweets as part of her drive to get people voting.

Trump twitched off

A few months before AOC was backing Joe Biden and imploring her Twitch viewers to vote, then-president Donald Trump was suspended from the streaming service. The temporary ban in 2020, for streaming "hateful conduct", was later turned into an "indefinite" block following the attack on the Capitol Building in Washington, D.C. in Jan 2021.

This channel is currently unavailable due to a violation of Twitch's Community Guidelines or Terms of Service.

Best-selling farm-life sim

47

Animal Crossing: New Horizons

A new title in the famously calming *Animal Crossing* series was just what everyone needed in the stressful first months of the COVID-19 pandemic. Switches flew off the shelves as people retreated to pristine desert islands to build their own neighbourhood of animal pals. *New Horizons* proved to be a huge hit, with monster sales of 44.79 million, as of 1 Jan 2024. This makes the charming community-builder the second-best-selling game on the Nintendo Switch – behind only 2017's *Mario Kart 8 Deluxe* (see p.70).

XP

Date: 2020
Developer: Nintendo
Publisher: Nintendo

R N G

11,200,000

Sales of *New Horizons* in Japan, according to the Game Data Library (as of Feb 2022). This makes it Japan's best-selling game.

Fastest 100% completion of *Animal Crossing* (solo)

On 9 Apr 2023, Mp16 (USA) finished Nintendo's social-sim game in 16 hr 28 min 19 sec. He called it: "16 hours of focus. 5 hours of town resets. 2 weeks of preparation. 1 attempt. What a journey." He also holds speed records for **obtaining the Golden Rod** (53 min 58 sec) and **Golden Net** (39 min 6 sec), and for clearing **All Debts** (33 min 34 sec).

Animal Crossing: 100% Speedrun in 16:28:19 [WR]
BrianMp16

Highest-rated sim on Steam

With sales in excess of 20 million units, the endearing *Stardew Valley* (ConcernedApe, 2016) is the second-best-selling farm sim. With a Steam rating of 97.36%, though, it's not only the most popular sim on the platform, it's the third-highest-rated game overall, with over 685,000 positive reviews.

> "I have an air-con unit just for my collection room. Climate control is a must."
>
> Antonio Romero Monteiro

XP

First game:
Golden Axe (Sega, 1989)
Collection value:
$2.1 m (£1.7 m)

46

Largest gaming collection

Antonio Romero Monteiro

At the last count in 2021, game enthusiast Antonio (USA) owned an incredible 24,268 cartridges, floppy disks, CD-ROMs and DVDs, all catalogued and displayed at his climate-controlled home in Texas. He also has separate records for the **largest collection of games for Xbox, PlayStation, Nintendo** and **Sega systems**. "My collection has grown so much that space has become a premium. At times, it has become a real-life game of *Tetris*."

SCORE 000003600   BLOCK B-3
PLAYER   ♥=06 P=02
ENEMY   TIME 603

super
Castlevania IV

"My most beloved game is *Super Castlevania IV* for the SNES"

SUPER NINTENDO

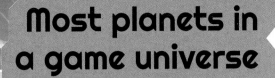

Most planets in a game universe

45

No Man's Sky

Epic really means epic when it comes to *No Man's Sky*. The space saga offers players a mind-boggling 18,446,744,073,709,551,616 planets to discover – that's 18 quintillion unique locations! Hello Games's cosmos is procedurally generated, which means every solar system – including the alien flora and fauna on every life-sustaining planet – is put together on the fly using a toolkit of random elements. In this game, the sky's not the limit – it's just the beginning...

Inspiration from the past

How *No Man's Sky* looks on screen has been influenced by the works of American sci-fi writer Isaac Asimov and the cover art for his books. Sean Murray, director of *NMS*, said before its release: "I hope we're going to get at least one person to look some of those books up who might not otherwise have."

R N G

585 billion

Number of years it would take you to find all the planets in *No Man's Sky*, even if you discovered a new world every single second!

XP

Date: 2016
Developer: Hello Games
Publisher: Hello Games

44

Most popular virtual pet app

Talking Tom & Friends

Talking Tom is not your regular virtual pet – he's like a best friend you can keep in your pocket! He can talk (of course) and he pilots a plane from time to time when he wants to get away. And as he grows up, he and his friends need help with various fun tasks.

What began as a novelty mobile game – in which Tom repeated back everything fans said into the mic – quickly went viral. New friends were introduced, and there are now more than 20 games under the *Talking Tom & Friends* banner, with up to 470 million monthly active users across the series. Tom has also made a big splash on YouTube: one of his original trailers has been seen 343 million times as of Apr 2024, making it the **most-viewed app trailer** ever.

XP

Launch: 2010 (*Talking Tom Cat*)
Developer: Outfit7
Publisher: Outfit7

Most times to poke Talking Tom

Poking Talking Tom is a *very* regular event in the games. One player did it a record 130,534 times in one year (around 15 pokes per hour every hour!) "I wish I could poke you back," says a weary Tom... A warming way to let off steam is to have Tom eat chillies. But 2.7 million of them? Every day? Make sure the bathroom is free!

🔓 INORITE!

- Talking Tom expanded his audience with five seasons of animated adventures in *Talking Tom & Friends*. Between 2014 and 2021, fans watched 156 episodes on YouTube and on TV channels around the world.

- In 2023, over 49 million fans joined in with *My Talking Tom*'s 10th birthday celebrations, making it the franchise's largest digital celebration to date.

First player to reach the killscreen in *Tetris* (NES)

43

Willis "Blue Scuti" Gibson !

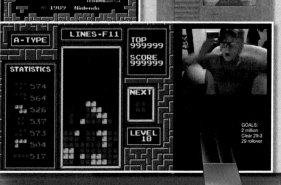

In the decades since the first versions of *Tetris* appeared from behind the iron curtain (see pp.142–43), one thing has remained consistent – the game always wins. Even the best players would inevitably be overwhelmed by the torrent of falling blocks. That was until 21 Dec 2023, when 13-year-old Willis "Blue Scuti" Gibson played his way to level 157 and racked up so many points that the game crashed. It had been assumed for years that no one could play past level 29, the point at which the blocks start falling faster than the controls can move them across the screen. But competitive players developed techniques to push through the barrier (see below).

Start the ball rolling

Willis used a technique pioneered by gamer Christopher "CheeZ" Martinez called "rolling". This method calls for fast reflexes and nimble fingers, partially depressing the face buttons on the back of the gamepad to register hundreds of button presses a second. Willis also wears a glove on his right hand to reduce friction.

XP

Name: Willis Gibson
DoB: 27 Jan 2010
Location: Stillwater, Oklahoma, USA

VIDEOGAME SPACESHIPS

The **first videogame to feature a spaceship** was *Spacewar!* back in 1962 (inset, right). Across the six decades since, technological progress has inspired many different game designs, and just as many different ships to populate them. Here, Pierre Salard, aka @TheSpaceshipper, takes a look at 10 iconic gaming spacecraft.

1
GALAXIP
***Galaxian* (1979)**

A distant cousin of the Y-wing from *Star Wars* (1977), the Galaxip made its mark because it was the first videogame ship to be rendered in colour. The game was also notable for the scrolling effect that was applied to background stars, creating an impression of speed even though the ship wasn't moving.

2
EBON HAWK
***Star Wars: Knights of the Old Republic* (2003)**

Bioware's RPG fulfils an age-old fan wish by offering players a transport ship that is also a home. This asymmetrical *Dynamic*-class light freighter features deployable turrets, a galaxy map, a smuggling compartment and room to carry a small vehicle.

3
COBRA MK.III
***Elite* (1984)**

This iconic starter ship featured prominently on promotional material and the menu screen of Acornsoft's 1980s spacefaring classic. A flying wing of sleek design, the multi-purpose *Cobra* has not aged. And *Elite*'s open-world, wire-frame 3D graphics left their mark on a generation of space explorers.

4
REAVER
***Planetside 2* (2012)**

Affectionately dubbed the "flying brick" by seasoned pilots, this anti-gravity ground-attack aircraft is the New Conglomerate's fastest superiority fighter. The *Reaver*'s massive firepower, high speed and great mobility counter the machine's major drawback: its large profile can make it a vulnerable target.

5
KUSHAN MOTHERSHIP
***Homeworld* (1999)**

Built across several decades, and controlled by cybernetic tech, the *Mothership* became the last refuge of survivors from the planet Hiigara. It serves as a home, military HQ and giant factory. Its vertical design stands out like a gleaming lighthouse in the infinite expanse of space.

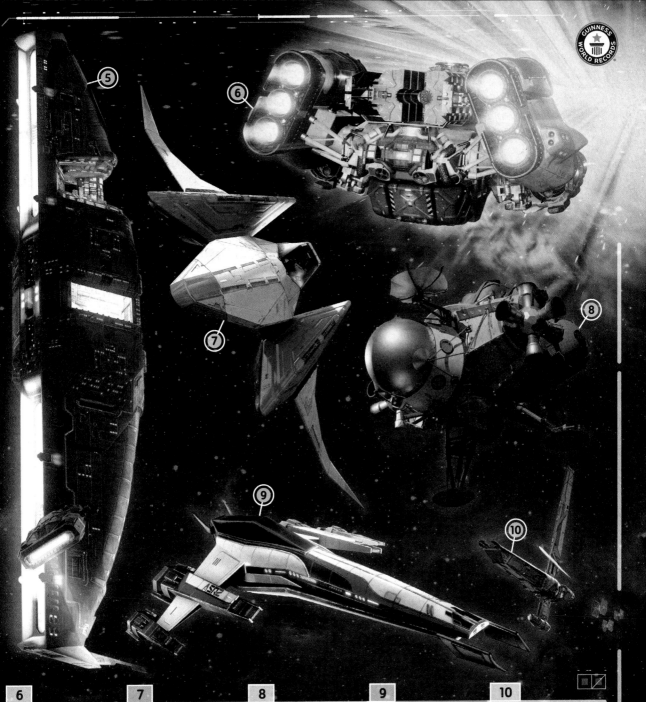

6	7	8	9	10
THE FRONTIER	**ARWING**	**THE SPACESHIP**	**ALLIANCE SCOUT FRIGATE**	**STINGER MANTIS**
Starfield (2023)	*Star Fox* (1993)	*Outer Wilds* (2019)	*Destiny* (2014)	*Star Wars: Jedi Fallen Order* (2019)
The Frontier is the emblematic starter ship of Bethesda's RPG. Built by Nova Galactic, this fully modular old *Discovery*-class ship is a sort of mobile home for players. The designers drew inspiration from *Star Wars*' obsolete *Millennium Falcon* and more elegant ships from other movies.	With its sleek design, the *Arwing* delighted SNES gamers, who were just discovering the appeal of 3D. The ship is extremely manoeuvrable, with instant acceleration and deceleration. The *Arwing*, whose name is inspired by its triangular "A" shape, remains one of the most accomplished ships in terms of acrobatics.	A ship doesn't have to look futuristic to be functional! And what better way to explore a solar system than in a homemade wooden spaceship? It may be made up of bits and pieces, but *The Spaceship* has a wonderful tool: a computer that records all the discoveries made during the adventure.	Bioware and Bungie teamed up for a 2017 crossover update, offering *Destiny* players the chance to pick up a spaceship inspired by *Mass Effect*'s art direction. More specifically, the famous *Normandy*. Bungie took on the task of cleaning up the lines of an already Concorde-inspired design.	A gleaming yacht reminiscent of the heyday of the Republic, the *Mantis* bears little resemblance to the *Millennium Falcon* and its cousins. But it's still a charming home for the crew, with a '70s-style kitchen and living room. This ship adds a touch of style to the fight against the Empire.

First multi-platform game

Spacewar!

Coded in the early 1960s by Steve Russell (helped by volunteer hackers), *Spacewar!* was a showcase for the new PDP-1 (below) at the MIT computer lab in Cambridge, Massachusetts, USA. The two-player space combat game was a hit with local students, and as they graduated and moved on to other universities, they took the *Spacewar!* code with them, adapting it to whatever machine they could find. Soon, it was running on 14 other models of computer. In Oct 1972, *SpaceWar!* was the basis of the Intergalactic *Spacewar!* Olympics – the **first videogame tournament** and **first esports event**.

XP

Date: 1961–62
Developer: Steve Russell
First platform: PDP-1

> "Everybody who was interested in computers in the 1960s knew about it."

 Steve Russell, interviewed in 2011

The start of another US space programme

When Steve Russell was trying to think of better ways than generating patterns to demonstrate the PDP-1's power, he had just finished Edward E Smith's *Lensman* sci-fi novels. "The obvious thing to do was spaceships," he told *Rolling Stone* in 1972. "He had some very glowing descriptions of spaceship encounters."

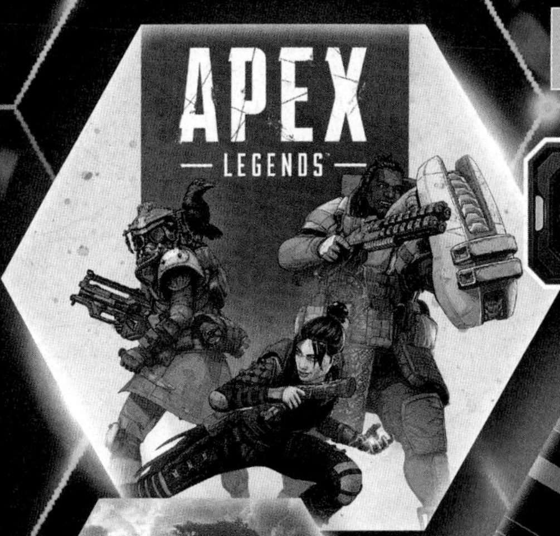

APEX LEGENDS

XP

Launch:
4 Feb 2020
Subscribers:
25 million
Games: 1,827

LIFE IS STRANGE 2

6

Tom Clancy's Rainbow Six Siege (Ubisoft, 2015)

Conqueror's Blade (Booming Tech, 2019)

R N G

25,000,000

Number of subscribers, as of Feb 2024. That is a sharp rise from the 10 million the California-based corporation announced in Apr 2021.

Monster Hunter Rise (Capcom, 2021)

Largest game-streaming service

41

GeForce NOW

As internet connections get faster, and the hardware needed to run games gets bigger and more demanding, some people are turning to cloud streaming services. These allow you to remotely play a game running on a datacentre server and stream it to your laptop, TV or phone. The services had a rough start, but Nvidia's GeForce NOW rode it out. As of 24 Feb 2024, 1,827 games were licensed to play via partnerships with Epic, Xbox, Steam and others. For those with no gaming PC but a good internet connection, it offers the chance to play titles such as those scattered around this page.

Counter-Strike 2 (Valve, 2023)

Best-selling PC exclusive

Garry's Mod

The 2006 open-world physics game *Garry's Mod* started life as the bedroom project of solo developer Garry Newman (right), running as a modified version of Valve's *Half Life 2*. It has gone on to become one of the most enduringly popular games on PC, selling more than 20 million copies.

"GMod" was created using the 3D game engine *Source,* developed by Valve. It poses no challenges and has no story, instead offering players a blank canvas that they can use to make games, animate movies... or even hack together cannons that fire watermelons! As Garry explains: "It's a sandbox. We give you the tools and leave you to play."

XP

Date: 2006
Developer: Facepunch Studios
Publisher: Valve

A line in the sandbox

In 2012, Garry said one of his "big regrets" was not renaming his mod phenomenon *Sandbox*. That explains why, when he started work on a follow-up title, he named it *S&box* (get it?). The game is powered by a highly modified version of Source 2, and Facepunch is at pains to point out "it's not going to be *Garry's Mod 2*".

s&box

Fastest-selling PC exclusive

While *Garry's Mod* has been a slow and steady performer, *Shadowlands* – the eighth expansion for the MMORPG *World of Warcraft* (Blizzard, see p.24) – sold more than 3.7 million units in its first 24 hours in Nov 2020. This beat the previous record of 3.5 million set by *Diablo III* (2012), another Blizzard title.

KOI, the esports team co-founded by Ibai in 2021

XP

Name: Ibai Llanos Garatea
Born: Bilbao, Spain
DoB: 26 Mar 1995

Ibai (left) streaming from the *League of Legends* Mid-Season Invitational in May 2023

R N G
75,742

Ibai's average concurrent Twitch audience, ranking him fourth overall as of Mar 2024. At No.1 is Michou (aka Miguel Mattiol, FRA), with an average of 108,862 viewers.

Highest peak viewership on Twitch

39

Ibai !

Counting up the days

When he's not organizing boxing events or managing his esports team KOI (above), Ibai spends most of his Twitch time just chatting – a whopping 2,256 hours (or 96 entire days) of chinwagging, as of 24 Apr 2024. His 15.5 million followers have also logged in to watch him spend 1,291 hr (53 days) playing *League of Legends*, 428 hr (17 days) on *Minecraft* and 240 hr (10 days) tackling *Among Us*.

On 1 Jul 2023, streamer Ibai (ESP) amassed 3.4 million concurrent viewers on Twitch while broadcasting his boxing event, *La Velada del Año 3* (*The Evening of the Year 3*), from the Metropolitano Stadium in Madrid, Spain. Various real-world bouts were fought that day, but it was the final one, between streamer Coscu and comedian Germán Garmendia, that attracted the biggest audience. The previous record of 3.35 million viewers was also set by Ibai, at *La Velada del Año 2* in 2022.

XP

Name:
Paweł Siciński
Teams: 46
Seasons: 520

FOOTBALL MANAGER 2018™

SEGA

38 Longest single game of *Football Manager*

Paweł Siciński

As verified in Jul 2023, Paweł (POL, above right) finished a mammoth *FM* session that lasted an in-game equivalent of 528 years 137 days. In 310 years as boss of an Icelandic club, he won 301 national titles. "My biggest achievement," he says. Set that against the average job duration in England's Premier League: in Oct 2022, it was two years four days!

🔓 INORITE!

When a Chilean *FM* fan noticed in a game that current Sheffield United striker Ben Brereton was half-Chilean, he fought for Ben to be part of the real national team. Since his debut, Ben (far right) has scored seven goals (one against world champions Argentina). To honour his heritage, he now calls himself Ben Brereton Díaz.

Match abandoned

Darren Bland (UK, below) spent 154 seasons as boss of Fiorentina (ITA) in *FM 2010*. Only an accidental drinks spill on his laptop stopped him from continuing. That's probably gaming's equivalent to a waterlogged pitch! Still, at the time, it was enough to set the record before Paweł came along.

Money makes the ball go round

Reflecting the increased interest of the Middle East in the sport, Al-Ittihad (KSA) is the **richest club in *Football Manager 2024***, measured by its balance of $454 m (£359.7 m). The top three is completed by Saudi teams Al-Hilal and Al-Nassr, followed by Manchester City, Tottenham Hotspur and Manchester United.

Largest playable area in a handcrafted open-world game

Silk

The RPG *Silk* is played out over a map that covers 3 million sq mi (7.7 million km²). It follows the ancient Silk Road route as it was in the third century CE and – incredibly – is not dynamically generated but hard-coded into the game. *Minecraft* (Mojang Studios, 2011) has 1.5 billion sq mi (3.8 billion km²) but is generated procedurally. There's a lot to see and do, but whether you're looking to explore, conquer or set up a trading empire, colourful characters known as Advisors are on hand to help.

XP

Date: 2019
Developer: ihobo
Publisher: Huey Games

R N G

37

Number of times bigger *Silk*'s world is compared with the 80,823 sq mi (209,331 km²) of previous holder *The Elder Scrolls II: Daggerfall* (Bethesda, 1996).

The long and winding road

The game's map follows a historic trade route from Roman Damascus (in modern-day Syria) to Three Kingdoms China. The final destination is Chengdu, a trek of 6,284 km (3,905 mi), not taking into account any diversions – roughly equivalent to walking to the centre of the Earth!

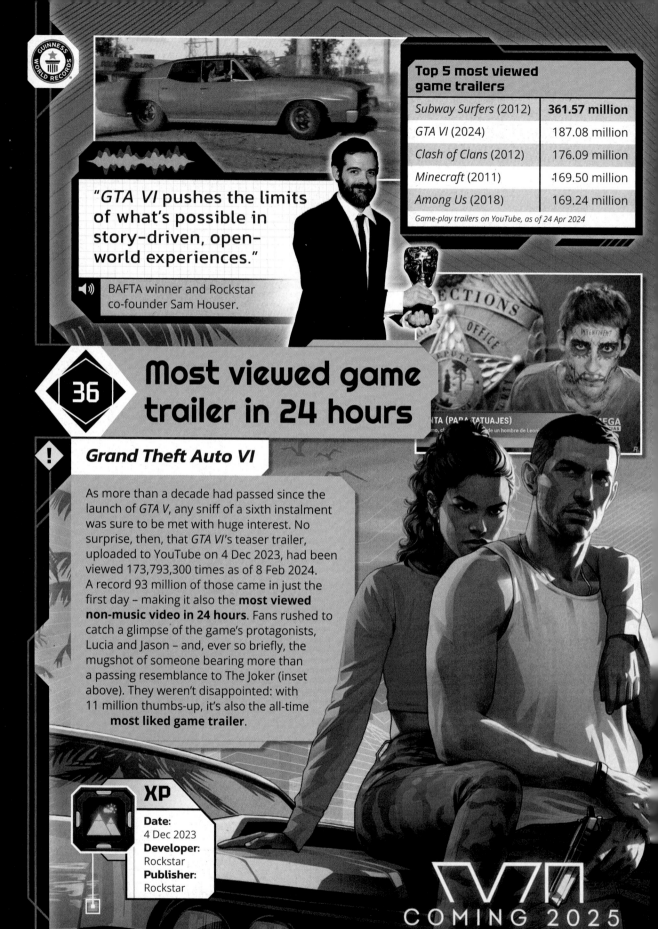

Top 5 most viewed game trailers

Top 5 most viewed game trailers	
Subway Surfers (2012)	**361.57 million**
GTA VI (2024)	187.08 million
Clash of Clans (2012)	176.09 million
Minecraft (2011)	169.50 million
Among Us (2018)	169.24 million

Game-play trailers on YouTube, as of 24 Apr 2024

"GTA VI pushes the limits of what's possible in story–driven, open–world experiences."

BAFTA winner and Rockstar co-founder Sam Houser.

36 Most viewed game trailer in 24 hours

Grand Theft Auto VI

As more than a decade had passed since the launch of *GTA V*, any sniff of a sixth instalment was sure to be met with huge interest. No surprise, then, that *GTA VI*'s teaser trailer, uploaded to YouTube on 4 Dec 2023, had been viewed 173,793,300 times as of 8 Feb 2024. A record 93 million of those came in just the first day – making it also the **most viewed non-music video in 24 hours**. Fans rushed to catch a glimpse of the game's protagonists, Lucia and Jason – and, ever so briefly, the mugshot of someone bearing more than a passing resemblance to The Joker (inset above). They weren't disappointed: with 11 million thumbs-up, it's also the all-time **most liked game trailer**.

XP

Date:
4 Dec 2023
Developer:
Rockstar
Publisher:
Rockstar

VI
COMING 2025

First interactive game documentary

Atari 50 **!**

Back to the Future

As if *Atari 50*'s 103 original games aren't enough, there are also six new titles from Digital Eclipse that take inspiration from the company's back catalogue. They are *Haunted Houses*, *VCTR-SCTR* and *Yars' Revenge Enhanced* plus, pictured below left to right, *Swordquest: Airworld*, *Quadratank* and *Neo Breakout*.

In 2022, game developer Digital Eclipse released a documentary celebrating the golden anniversary of the US electronic entertainment pioneer Atari. Unlike your regular, passive Netflix or YouTube experience, though, *Atari 50: The Anniversary Celebration* allows console and PC users the chance to play along with more than 100 games from the company's history, including *Asteroids*, *Pong* and *Missile Command*.

R N G
9

Number of launch titles in 1977 for the Atari 2600. The games included *Air-Sea Battle*, *Indy 500*, *Basic Math*, *Video Olympics*, *Black Jack* and *Combat*.

XP

Date: 2022
Developer: Digital Eclipse
Publisher: Atari

XP

Name: Yang Binglin
DoB: 10 Dec 1935
Nickname: Gamer Grandpa

Oldest streamer

34

Yang Binglin

Even after a career that involved the demands of scientific research and engineering for oil and gas, Yang Binglin (CHN, b. 10 Dec 1935) wasn't ready for a quiet retirement. Introduced to games by his family, he was soon blasting zombies in *Resident Evil* and has gone on to complete more than 300 games. At 88 years 131 days as of 19 Apr 2024, he regularly live-streams and posts videos as a content creator for the site Bilibili, sharing notes and strategies. His 270,000+ subscribers watch him in action playing games such as *Battlefield V* (DICE, 2018) and *Gran Turismo Sport* (Polyphony Digital, 2017, above).

Binglin enjoys the challenges posed in the FPS *Battlefield V*

CERTIFICATE

The oldest videogames Bilibili content creator (male) is Yang Binglin (China, b. 10 December 1935), who is 88 years and 15 days old, as verified in Luzhou, Sichuan, China, on 25 December 2023

OFFICIALLY AMAZING

RECORD HOLDER

"I want to contribute more in the role of a game blogger, guiding young people."

Yang Binglin

Oldest gaming YouTuber

The current matriarch of gaming YouTubers is Hamako Mori (JPN, b. 18 Feb 1930, left), who streams as "Gamer Grandma". As of 19 Apr 2024, Hamako was still streaming aged 94 years 61 days. She claimed the title in 2019 from Shirley Curry (USA, right), who, as of the same date, was 88 years 17 days old.

Most concurrent players for a debut on Steam

33

Terraria

HELLDIVERS II

Hogwarts Legacy

Palworld

!

It's often the case that a game's player base builds steadily off the back of good reviews and word-of-mouth buzz. Given the pre-release hype around *Palworld* (see p.66), it enjoyed a more direct route to the top. On 27 Jan 2024, its colourful, building-and-blowing-up gameplay attracted a high of 2,101,867 players, just eight days after release. In that short time, it also raced past Larian Studios' *Baldur's Gate 3* and FromSoftware's *Elden Ring*. The only game ahead of it as of 25 Apr 2024 was *PUBG: Battlegrounds* (PUBG Studios, 2017), which had a peak of a gargantuan 3,257,248 players in Jan 2018.

Most played open-world games on Steam

Game	Plays
Palworld (2024)	2,101,867
Cyberpunk 2077 (2020)	1,054,388
Elden Ring (2022)	953,426
New World (2021)	913,634
Hogwarts Legacy (2023)	879,308
Valheim (2021)	502,387
Terraria (2011)	489,886
Fallout 4 (2015)	472,962
HELLDIVERS II (2024)	458,709
Sons of the Forest (2024)	414,257

steamdb.info, all-time peaks as of 25 Apr 2024

Most concurrent players on Steam in 24 hours

At the time of going to press, *Counter-Strike 2* (Valve, 2023) sat proudly at the top of the Steam chart of most played games over the last 24 hours, more than twice as popular as *PUBG: Battlegrounds* at No.2. Indeed, despite being over a decade old, the *Counter-Strike* franchise continues to be a constant feature on Steam, rarely far from the top spot.

XP

Date: 2024
Developer: Pocket Pair
Publisher: Pocket Pair

Most popular social simulation

A happy Sim family in 2023's *Growing Together* expansion pack

The Sims 4

Help lonely Sims build careers, families and homes... or orchestrate a series of bizarre and fatal household accidents? Life is full of choices, and thanks to the *Sims* franchise, which started in 2000, we can live as many lives as we desire from the comfort of our (actual) homes. As of Apr 2023, more than 70 million of us had indulged the urge to play god thanks to the fourth game in this record-breaking social-sim series.

XP

Date: 2014
Developer: Maxis
Publisher: EA

INORITE!

The ninth game pack for *The Sims 4* takes you on a journey far, far away to the Outer Rim and the desert planet of Batuu. There, you must choose which faction to follow: team up with Rey as a Resistance fighter or join Kylo Ren and the First Order. *Star Wars* characters old and new pop up in this 2020 release – the **first Sims pack based on a movie franchise**.

The sim games are all Wright

The creator of *The Sims*, Will Wright (USA), is the brains behind some of the biggest life-sim games of all time, including the hugely successful city-builder *SimCity* (1989). The idea for *The Sims* came to him after his California house burned down during wildfires in 1991. Wright began to think about building a home from scratch – and so *The Sims* was born.

Most critically acclaimed Harry Potter game

LEGO® Harry Potter: Years 1–4 (Traveller's Tales, 2010) has a Metacritic score of 79 as of 12 Feb 2024, making it the best received of all the titles featuring the orphan wizard. The game allows you to play the main events of the first four films/books in lovable LEGO form.

Most critically acclaimed Harry Potter games

Game	Metascore
LEGO Harry Potter: Years 1–4	79
Harry Potter: Magic Awakened	78
LEGO Harry Potter: Years 5–7	77
Harry Potter and the Chamber of Secrets	71
Harry Potter and the Prisoner of Azkaban	70

Metacritic, as of 12 Feb 2024

Most viewed single-player game on Twitch

31

Hogwarts Legacy

On 9 Feb 2023, during its early-access period on Twitch, the much-anticipated Wizarding World action RPG attracted 1,280,000 concurrent viewers. The game – set at Hogwarts School of Witchcraft and Wizardry 100 years before the events of the Harry Potter novels – was a triumph for Warner Bros., selling more than 24 million units as of Jan 2024 and raking in well over $1 bn (£788 m). With a Metacritic score of 84, it is also the **most critically acclaimed Wizarding World game**.

XP
Date: 2023
Developer: Avalanche Software
Publisher: Warner Bros. Games

Largest Xbox Studio launch

30

Forza Horizon 5

The fifth edition of Playground Games' open-world *Horizon* series got off to a flying start, welcoming 4.5 million players in its first 24 hours (and 10 million by the end of the week). Since then, the player total on the in-game leaderboard has kept ticking upwards – it stood at 37 million as of 12 Feb 2024. Despite the game being three years old, players continue to carve up the dirt roads and highways of its lush Mexican setting. More than 500 customizable cars and a constantly updating roster of challenges keep racers coming back for more.

Take the wheel for a spin in Barbie's Chevy

On 26 Jun 2023, ahead of the release of the *Barbie* movie, *Forza* players were gifted a copy of Barbie's famous pink Corvette and Ken's open-top Hummer H2. These weren't just custom paint jobs, however: both limited-edition cars were all-electric and, just like the real things, at slightly the wrong scale – meaning players' heads stuck out above the windshields!

Barbie The Movie

XP

Date: 2021
Developer: Playground Games
Publisher: Xbox Game Studios

INORITE!

The first expansion pack for *FH5* revisited a history of working with die-cast model-maker Hot Wheels, which started with *FH3*. Ten HW cars were added to action that takes place on an orange racetrack high in the clouds above Mexico. Such collaborations are a two-way street; Mattel released a series of HW die-cast cars from the *FH5* line-up.

Fastest-selling PlayStation exclusive

29

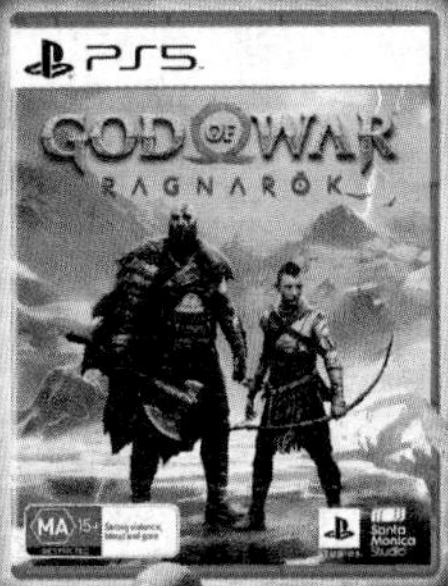

God of War Ragnarök

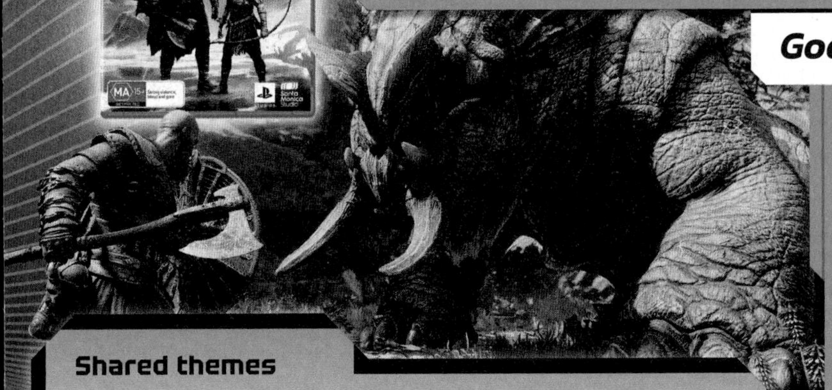

Even after 17 years and eight previous adventures, the mighty Kratos is still hacking and slashing at the record books with his lethal Leviathan Axe. Following its launch on 9 Nov 2022, *God of War Ragnarök* sold 5.1 million copies for the PS4 and PS5 in just five days. By 22 Jan 2023, that sales figure had more than doubled to 11 million. At the close of 2023, it had hit 15 million. In comparison, *Spider-Man 2* (2023), which enjoyed stronger first-day sales (see p.32), has shifted "only" 10 million units to date.

Shared themes

The DLC *God of War: Valhalla* (2023, below) transports Kratos into the sacred "hall of the slain". Exploring this part of Norse mythology was also the theme for another expansion pack, *Assassin's Creed Valhalla: Dawn of Ragnarök* (Ubisoft Montreal), published the year before.

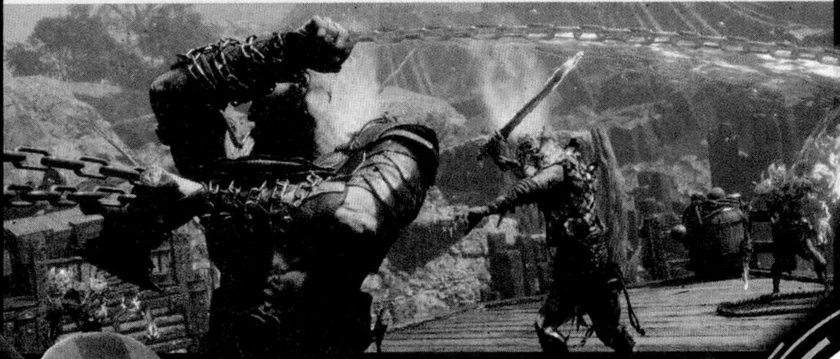

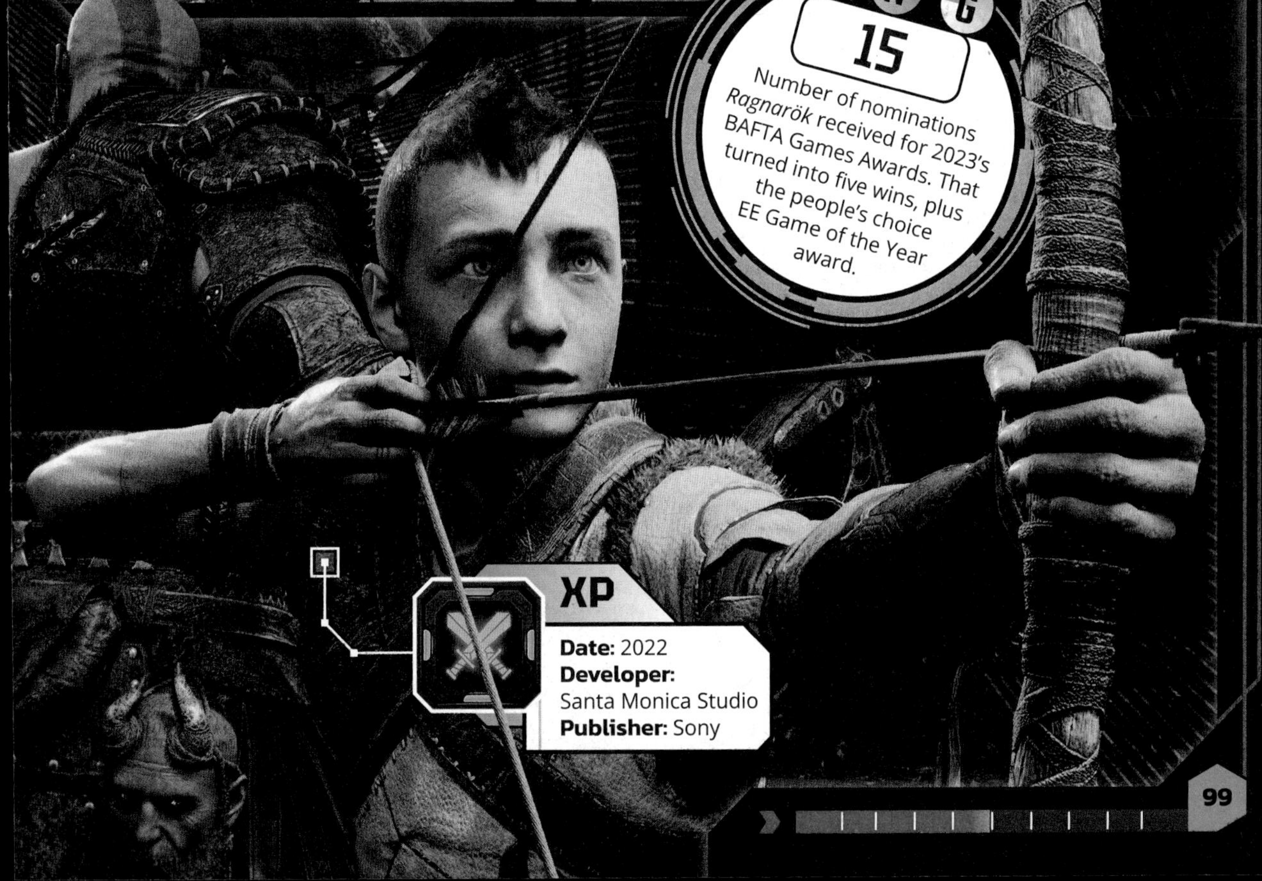

RNG

15

Number of nominations *Ragnarök* received for 2023's BAFTA Games Awards. That turned into five wins, plus the people's choice EE Game of the Year award.

XP

Date: 2022
Developer: Santa Monica Studio
Publisher: Sony

Top 10 most streamed videogame soundtracks

Ever since designer Tomohiro Nishikado wrote the looping background music for 1978's *Space Invaders*, soundtracks have been a key component of the gaming experience. Here's the top 10 most popular soundtracks, using Spotify data for the number of track plays within a soundtrack to create album totals.

10
ORIGINAL SOUNDTRACK
THE MUSIC OF RED DEAD II TION II
139,868,091

Red Dead Redemption II
(Rockstar, 2018)

Powerful, melancholic tracks from superstars such as D'Angelo and Willie Nelson make for a soundtrack that perfectly accompanies the game's depiction of the United States during the Wild West's decline.

9
FERDK
To Metal
bute to NieR.Automata
148,512,656

NieR: Automata
(PlatinumGames, 2017)

Keiichi Okabe's exhilarating soundtrack, recorded with the help of other members of his band Monaca, offers as eclectic a mix of songs as *NieR* does gameplay mechanics. "City Ruins (Rays of Light)" is the standout.

8
CALL OF DUTY
BLACK OPS
ZOMBIES
SOUNDTRACK
Composed By Treyarch Sound
202,216,472
ACTIVISION

Call of Duty: Black Ops – Zombies (Ideaworks, 2011)

It's not often that a game mode gets its very own soundtrack – one that includes heavy metal tracks that play during *Zombies* itself, as well as many of the musical Easter eggs found in the various maps.

7
ORIGINAL SCORE BY GUSTAVO SANTAOLALLA
THE LAST OF US
277,784,315

The Last of Us
(Naughty Dog, 2013)

Gustavo Santaolalla's delicate, dark soundtrack reinforces the sense of loss that permeates Joel and Ellie's cross-country adventure. The sweeping title track was also used in the intro to HBO's TV adaptation.

6
grand theft auto FIVE
395,431,087

Grand Theft Auto V
(Rockstar, 2013)

Rockstar created an in-game radio that lets you tune in to 16 stations packed with more than 441 tracks of licensed music. The score complements *GTA V*'s urban antics with a mix of rap, R&B, electro, pop and more.

5
DOOM
449,186,377

Doom
(id Software, 2016)

The *Doom* reboot's music is worthy of the groundbreaking original; a heart-pounding, hard rock soundtrack that pushes the player into increasingly violent acts of demon slaying. It also contains lots of cool Easter eggs!

 Spotify

Once Upon A Time
Toby Fox

4 481,247,306

3 672,206,070

2 1,424,286,360

The Witcher 3: Wild Hunt
(CD Projekt Red, 2015)

This is as rich and atmospheric as the grand adventure of the game itself. Composer Marcin Przybyłowicz enlisted the help of the Brandenburg State Orchestra in Frankfurt, Germany, and the Polish folk music group Percival to create an epic sound largely inspired by the traditional Slavic culture of central and eastern Europe.

The Elder Scrolls V: Skyrim
(Bethesda Game Studios, 2011)

Skyrim is all about dragons, so it's fitting that its theme song, "Dragonborn", contains lyrics written in Dovahzul, the game's fictional dragon language. Jeremy Soule's epic soundtrack transports the listener back to Whiterun, Solitude and, of course, the wilderness of Tamriel's untamed northern province.

Minecraft
(Mojang Studios, 2011)

Minecraft's soundtrack comprises two albums, *Volume Alpha* and *Beta*, both by German musician Daniel Rosenfeld (aka C418). Each track in this enduring collection of ambient electronica is hugely popular; the standout is the low-key "Sweden", which has had an incredible 153 million spins and perfectly matches the gameplay.

 1 1,487,185,270

Undertale (Toby Fox, 2015)

Toby Fox's smash-hit 2D role-playing adventure has an equally popular retro-infused soundtrack, which he wrote himself. Most of the 101 tracks have millions of plays, but the catchy, chiptune-esque "MEGALOVANIA" is top of the pops with an eye-watering 164 million streams alone as of 16 Mar 2024 – enough to make it the **most popular videogame song on Spotify**. "MEGALOVANIA", which plays during a boss fight against Sans the Skeleton, has been memed and remixed countless times across social media, and even appeared in other games.

Bizarrely, in 2022 a band played "MEGALOVANIA" during a live circus performance for Pope Francis at the Vatican! While we don't know if the pontiff is a fan of *Undertale*, he certainly looked like he enjoyed himself – he thanked the performers and said that "beauty guides us to God".

Largest first-person shooter battle

PlanetSide 2

Responding to a call to arms on 5 Nov 2022 by developer Rogue Planet Games, 1,530 players grabbed their guns, blasters and cannons before heading to the war-torn world of Auraxis. The enormous virtual showdown was the result of a challenge to break the previous record of 1,158, set back in 2015 by players of the same game. In a tweet following the new mark, publisher Daybreak promised to award participants a special in-game title, adding: "Thank you for the madness."

XP

Date: 2022
Developer: Rogue Planet Games
Publisher: Daybreak Game Company

That is one busy birthday party!

PlanetSide 2 was launched in Nov 2012, so the record attempt was Daybreak's 10th birthday present to its free-to-play game. This massively multiplayer online first-person shooter (MMOFPS) has earned a cult following with players who prefer the mayhem of its large battles to the tense, twitch-reaction skirmishes of the *Call of Duty* series.

Vanguard tank rolling into action for the New Conglomerate

❗ Pwn! ☐ ☒

Don't whiz through the character creator! There are three Empires to choose from, each with access to unique weapons, tanks and aircraft. The Terran Republic has the fastest vehicles, the New Conglomerate relies on heavy tanks and the Vanu Sovereignty loves lasers. Choose wisely!

Most Game of the Year awards

27

Elden Ring !

In the wide world of gaming, 2022 belonged to *Elden Ring*. There were 599 Game of the Year awards up for grabs and From-Software's action RPG won 435 (72.6%) of them. Nothing guarantees success, but the involvement of Hidetaka Miyazaki (*Dark Souls*) as director and George R R Martin (*Game of Thrones*) for world-building has had a major impact. If you have time to spare, the names of print titles, websites and podcasts that voted for *Elden Ring* form the background to this image of The Tarnished One.

XP

Date: 2022
Developer: FromSoftware
Publisher: Bandai Namco Entertainment

ELDEN RING

Godrick the Grafted, an optional Demigod Boss

Longest-running videogame series

XP

Debut: 1971
Developers: MECC
Publisher: Various

The Oregon Trail

TOT captured the trek by both day and night

The 2,000-mi (3,218-km) trek west to find a new life in mid-19th-century America was tough, taking an average of 160 days. So it's fitting that the educational game charting the Oregon Trail has been equally hardy. As of 19 Feb 2024, it had been rolling on for 52 years 78 days. Over that time, it's seen many changes. Originally, it was a text-only tool to teach children about pioneer life, but over the years, it has developed into a graphically rich series of choose-your-own adventures, such as 2022's *The Oregon Trail: Boom Town* (Tilting Point).

Telling the whole story

Back in 1971, the game's intent to recreate the Oregon Trail faithfully didn't apply to its Native American characters. After consulting experts, the makers of the 2021 version tackled prejudice and stereotypes about customs, speech and dress, and made characters more a part of the gameplay.

INORITE!

The Oregon Trail is the source of a number of classic memes, chief among them being the game-over message "You have died of dysentery". Players run the risk of contracting this intestinal infection by failing to keep good standards of hygiene, not checking water sources or eating contaminated food. In real life, it's estimated that one in 10 pioneers didn't finish the trail.

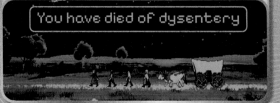

You have died of dysentery

Largest covered wagon

Hand-built from oak and steel by David Bentley (USA), this real-life wagon is 40 ft long and 25 ft tall (12.2 x 7.6 m). The super-sized prairie schooner – located on Route 66 in Lincoln, Illinois, USA – has only one traveller: former president Abraham Lincoln, who has been rendered in 12-ft-tall (3.6-m) fibreglass form.

XP

Date: 2003
Developer: CCP Games
Publisher: CCP Games

GUINNESS WORLD RECORDS

EVE
ONLINE

Largest multiplayer PvP battle

25

EVE Online – Fury at FWST-8

From *Star Trek* to *Mass Effect*, every sci-fi franchise loves an epic space battle, but none has been bigger than this showdown in CCP Games' sprawling space sim. On 6 Oct 2020, two massive player alliances – PAPI and the Imperium – clashed over control of a sector called FWST-8, drawing 8,825 players into a 12-hour battle. At its peak, there were 6,557 pilots on the field – the **most concurrent participants in a PvP battle**. The Imperium prevailed, but the battle exacted a heavy cost on both sides, with the loss of 1,308 battleships, 836 cruisers and 414 destroyers.

Largest virtual theft in an MMO

The economy of New Eden revolves around Interstellar Kredits (ISK), a currency denoted by the symbol Ƶ. And like real-world money, ISK is at risk from looting. The most audacious heist to date occurred, without a single shot fired, in Apr 2023, when two players forced the takeover of a corporation of 299 members. As a result, Event Horizon Expeditionaries was stripped of assets worth 2.2 trillion ISK – a real-world equivalent of £17,904 ($22,497).

24 Most critically acclaimed superhero game

Batman: Arkham City

XP
Date: 2011
Developer: Rocksteady Studios
Publisher: Warner Bros.

The second game in Rocksteady's *Batman: Arkham* series was a runaway success: it shifted 12.5 million copies in its first year on sale, won a batcave-full of awards, and earned a mighty Metascore of 94 based on 87 critic reviews, as of 21 Feb 2024. The plaudits are plentiful – *The Guardian* said it was "the best Batman game of all time". This action-adventure classic allows you to roam around the open world of Arkham City, either as Batman or Catwoman (Robin and Nightwing were available as DLC), fighting a who's who of Bat-villains.

Arkham City is now available on the Switch as part of 2023's *Arkham Trilogy*

RNG
23
Number of perfect 100 scores for *Arkham City* on Metacritic. Only five critics rated it below 90. *Game Informer* labelled it "the best licensed videogame ever made".

Hamill's performance is no joke

Mark Hamill, best known for playing Luke Skywalker in the Star Wars movies, has played Batman's nemesis, The Joker, several times since 1992, both in animated TV series and video-games. He reprised his portrayal in *Arkham City* – and won a Best Performer BAFTA for his efforts.

Top 5 most critically acclaimed superhero games

Game	Metascore
Batman: Arkham City	94
Batman: Arkham Asylum	92
Marvel's Spider-Man 2 (right)	90
Injustice 2: Legendary Edition (left)	88
Marvel's Spider-Man	87
Metacritic, as of 17 Apr 2024	

RNG

4,483,253

Average number of hours of WoW content watched weekly on Twitch, as of Mar 2024, attesting to its ongoing popularity.

XP

Date: 2004
Developer: Blizzard
Publisher: Blizzard

Most critically acclaimed MMORPG

23

World of Warcraft !

The Azeroth-set epic sits atop the Metacritic MMORPG chart with a score of 93 from 57 critic reviews, one point ahead of *Final Fantasy XIV: Endwalker* (Square Enix, 2021), as of 17 Apr 2024. Blizzard have revealed that development of the game cost them a mighty $63 million (£50 m) and took the best part of five years. *WoW* was released 10 years after the first game in the Warcraft series (*Orcs & Humans*, 1994) and remains the **best-selling MMO** – see p.24 for more.

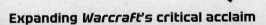

91 **91** **90** **88** **87**

Expanding *Warcraft*'s critical acclaim

Metacritic's top-10 MMORPG list includes five *WoW* expansion packs, which means that more than half of the most acclaimed MMORPGs of all time are part of the *Warcraft* universe. The top 10 also includes three *Final Fantasy XIV* expansions – *Endwalker* (92); *Shadowbringers* (90) and, in joint 10th place, *Stormblood* (87) – plus *Guild Wars 2* (90) and *Dark Age of Camelot* (88).

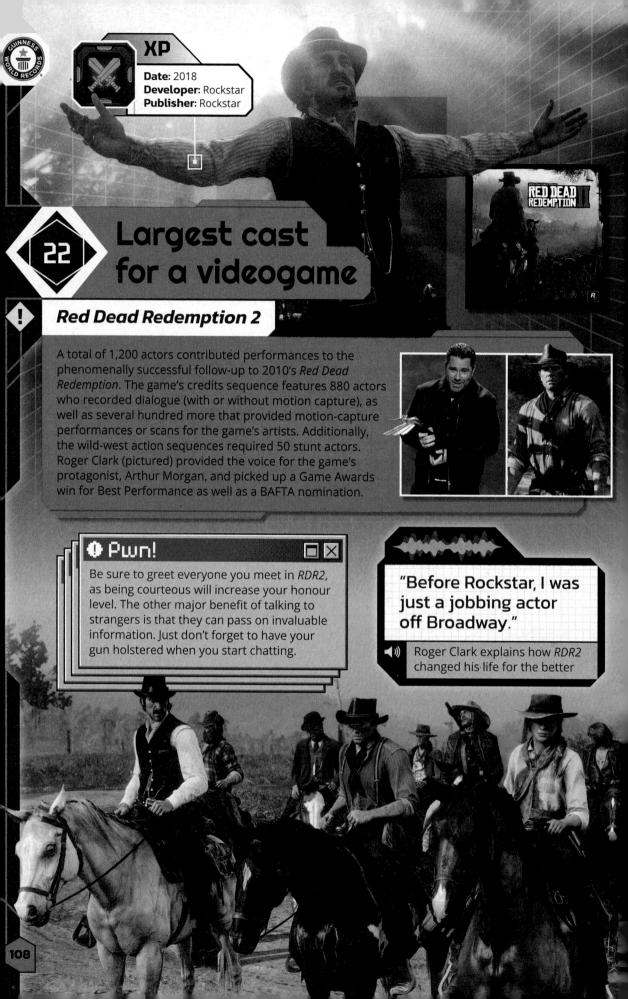

XP

Date: 2018
Developer: Rockstar
Publisher: Rockstar

22 Largest cast for a videogame

! Red Dead Redemption 2

A total of 1,200 actors contributed performances to the phenomenally successful follow-up to 2010's *Red Dead Redemption*. The game's credits sequence features 880 actors who recorded dialogue (with or without motion capture), as well as several hundred more that provided motion-capture performances or scans for the game's artists. Additionally, the wild-west action sequences required 50 stunt actors. Roger Clark (pictured) provided the voice for the game's protagonist, Arthur Morgan, and picked up a Game Awards win for Best Performance as well as a BAFTA nomination.

! Pwn! □ ✕

Be sure to greet everyone you meet in *RDR2*, as being courteous will increase your honour level. The other major benefit of talking to strangers is that they can pass on invaluable information. Just don't forget to have your gun holstered when you start chatting.

> "Before Rockstar, I was just a jobbing actor off Broadway."

◀)) Roger Clark explains how *RDR2* changed his life for the better

The legends behind the liquid

Victor "Nazgul" Goossens (right) founded Team Liquid as a *StarCraft: Brood War* clan in 2000. When *StarCraft II: Wings of Liberty* came out in 2010, Liquid signed up their first pro gamers. In 2015, they merged with Team Curse, bringing Steve "LiQuiD112" Arhancet (left) on board. Steve and Victor are the current CEOs.

Team Liquid

The Netherlands-based esports giants had brought home a total of $48,783,762.69 (£39,018,716) as of 19 Apr 2024, according to esportsearnings.com. That princely sum leaves them more than $10 million (£7.9 m) ahead of OG in second place. Liquid have made their money from 2,754 tournaments, with their highest-earning game being *Dota 2*, from which they've netted $28.6 m (£22.8 m). At the opposite end of the spectrum, they've banked just $840 (£662) from *FIFA*. The current team's highest earner is Samuel "Boxi" Svahn (SWE), who has made $1,228,691 (£982,744) from playing *Dota 2*.

XP

Debut: 2000
Base: Netherlands
Main sponsor: Honda

There were 16 rosters within Team Liquid, as of Mar 2024

Alien base in California

Pictured here is Team Liquid's Alienware Training Facility in Los Angeles, California, USA (there's another one in Utrecht, Netherlands). Alienware, who manufacture gaming computers, are one of the team's main sponsors. According to Liquid, the facility is designed to "advance the cognitive performance of high performers".

Most downloaded mobile exclusive

Subway Surfers

In Mar 2018, this graffiti-spraying delinquent dash became the **first Android game to reach 1 billion downloads**. In May 2019, seven years after its launch, it hit the 2.5 billion mark and showed no signs of slowing down. Indeed, it continued to gain momentum, and has since reached more than 4 billion downloads worldwide. *Subway Surfers* was already a smash hit before viral videos on TikTok made it a 2020s speedrunning favourite. It's now the **most speedrun game** on speedrun.com, having notched up 44,663 runs as of 18 Apr 2024. On the website's chart, it sits behind only *Seterra* (1997), the **most speedrun quiz** with 62,828 runs.

XP

Date: 2012
Developer: SYBO
Publisher: Kiloo & SYBO

Most watched game trailer on YouTube

With more than 361.5 million views on YouTube as of Mar 2024, the "Official Google Play Trailer" for *Subway Surfers* tops the list of most viewed videogame adverts, ahead of the likes of *Clash of Clans* and *Minecraft*, and sitting far ahead of the second-place promo for *Grand Theft Auto VI*, with 187.08 million views (see p.92).

Animated surfing!

In 2018, SYBO Games launched *Subway Surfers: The Animated Series* on YouTube. To coincide with the launch, SYBO hosted a street party at Venice Beach Skate Park in California, USA, with live skate and game challenges. The series content has generated over two millennia of collective watch-time on YouTube!

Fastest time to collect 10,000 coins

LiYueee (CHN) collected 10,000 *Subway Surfer* coins in a speedy 18 min 32.33 sec on 27 Sep 2023, according to speedrun.com. LiYueee's time is a full 27 seconds faster than second-placed L0rdN4tsu_ (BRA). Think you've got what it takes to outpace LiYueee? Find out how to register an official record attempt on pp.8–9.

🔓 INORITE!

Ten years after the original, SYBO released an Apple Arcade exclusive title, *Subway Surfers Tag* – a top down, arena-based game that pits players against the series' antagonist "Guard" and his drones. It won Best Apple Arcade Game 2022 at the Pocket Gamer Awards, and along with *Marvel Snap* (Second Dinner, 2022), shared the award for Game of the Year 2023 at the Mobile Games Awards.

R N G
20 million

Number of daily active users of *Subway Surfers* as of Jan 2024. The game has an average of 150 million monthly active users.

Largest game convention

Some 320,000 people attended Gamescom 2023

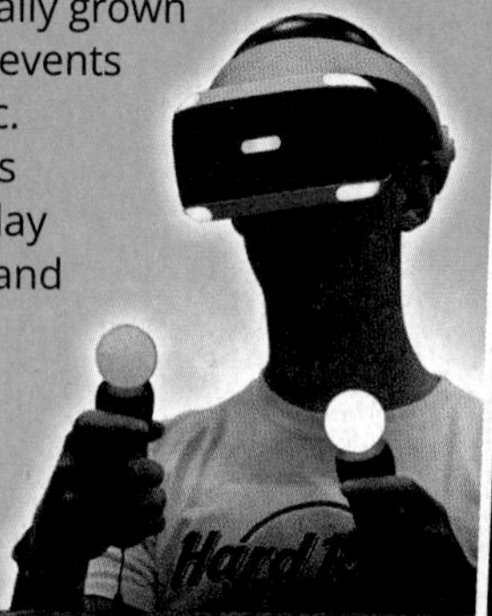

Gamescom 2019

Gamescom, an annual industry trade fair and convention held in Cologne, Germany, has been running since 2009. The 2019 edition of the event took place between 20 and 24 Aug and welcomed 373,000 visitors, including 31,300 industry professionals representing 1,153 developers and publishers. Gamescom started out as an industry-only trade event, but has gradually grown to incorporate more events for the general public. These include esports competitions, a cosplay village, various talks and presentations, and an indie area where gamers can meet developers and try out new titles.

It comprises one trade–only day and four days of public events, including esports

There's also a cosplay contest with four categories: Best Costume, Best Dress, Best Built and Fan Favourite

R N G
180,000,000
Number of online views of Gamescom 2023 content. Some 20 million people alone worldwide watched the opening night.

XP

Where: Cologne
When: Aug 2019
Participants: 373,000

The 10 biggest conventions in 2023	
Event	**Attendees**
ChinaJoy (Shanghai, China)	338,000
Brasil Game Show (São Paulo, left)	328,000
Gamescom (Cologne, Germany)	320,000
Taipei Game Show (Taiwan, China)	320,000
Tokyo Game Show (Japan)	243,000
G-Star (Busan, South Korea)	197,000
SPIEL (Essen, Germany)	193,000
Paris Games Week (France)	180,000
San Diego Comic-Con (USA)	150,000
PAX West (Seattle, USA)	120,000

Various sources, as of 27 Feb 2024

Colossal conventions

Gaming gatherings are big business. Not a month goes by without a major event being held for both industry professionals and members of the public alike. As the table here shows, huge annual conventions now take place across the globe. As well as the general gatherings, there are more niche ones, such as BlizzCon (right) in California, which showcases and celebrates developer Blizzard's games, and *Eve Online*'s *Eve* Fanfest (far right) in Iceland.

🔓 INORITE!

Minecraft's annual convention, Minecraft Live, now takes place entirely online. But the first gathering of fans was a spontaneous event held in Bellevue, Washington, USA, in 2010. Around 30 people showed up – including the game's creator, Markus Persson. A year later, more than 5,000 people attended the first official convention in Las Vegas, USA.

18

Most concurrent views for an esports event

WORLDS 23

League of Legends World Championship 2023

On 19 Nov 2023, an online audience of 6,402,760 people logged in to witness the much-hyped showdown between esports giants Weibo Gaming (CHN) and T1 (KOR) at the final of the *League of Legends* World Championship. "Worlds" has long been one of the biggest events in the esports calendar, but this match – which came at the conclusion of a dramatic 40-day tournament – beat the previous record of 5,415,990 by almost a million viewers. In the end, on home ground in Seoul, T1 comprehensively defeated Weibo 3–0.

The 16,744–seat Gocheok Sky Dome, venue for the 2023 tournament final

🔓 INORITE!

T1 have the **most wins of the *League of Legends* World Championship**, but the changing line-ups of teams means that only Faker (see facing page, top right) has been present for all four victories. For the rest of the quintet – Choi Woo-je (aka Zeus), Moon Hyeon-joon (Oner), Lee Min-hyeong (Gumayusi) and Ryu Min-seok (Keria) – it was a career first.

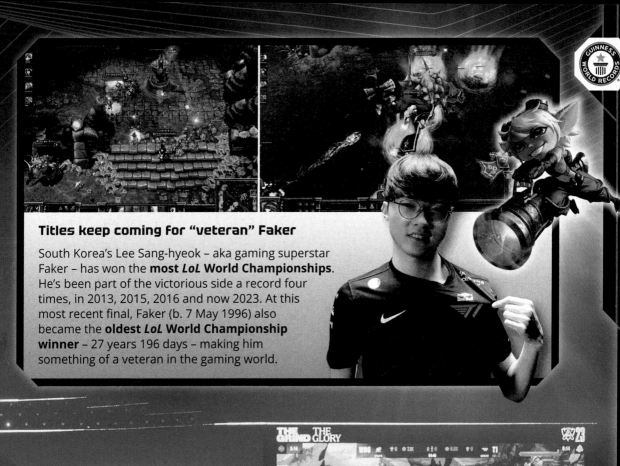

Titles keep coming for "veteran" Faker

South Korea's Lee Sang-hyeok – aka gaming superstar Faker – has won the **most *LoL* World Championships**. He's been part of the victorious side a record four times, in 2013, 2015, 2016 and now 2023. At this most recent final, Faker (b. 7 May 1996) also became the **oldest *LoL* World Championship winner** – 27 years 196 days – making him something of a veteran in the gaming world.

R N G

13.19

The patch (update) number of *League of Legends* introduced at Worlds 2023. It included the new skin of La Ilusión Nidalee (left).

XP

Event: 10 Oct –19 Nov 2023
Teams: 22
Winners: T1 (KOR)

ACCESSIBILITY IN GAMING

More than 400 million gamers have disabilities that can make playing games frustrating or even painful. In many cases, these problems could be solved by simple accessibility fixes, so a community of disabled gamers and advocacy groups have mobilized in recent years to raise the profile of the disabled gaming community and push for the adoption of these enabling features.

Games

UNCHARTED 4: A THIEF'S END

Naughty Dog's 2016 blockbuster *Uncharted 4* raised the bar for adaptive options in big-budget games. It featured a dedicated accessibility menu with options for players who struggle with twin-stick controls and button-mashing. In 2021, the developer announced 9.5 million players had used the menu.

FORZA HORIZON 5

VR puzzler *Moss* (Polyarc, 2018) was the **first commercial game with sign language**, but the feature made its triple-A debut in *Forza Horizon 5* (2021), which provided American Sign Language translations for cutscenes and in-game voiceovers.

Hardware

NINTENDO CONTROLLER

This hands-free controller came out for the NES in 1985. It weighed 2.5 lb (1.1 kg) and was worn around the neck. Puffing/sipping into a tube triggered the A/B buttons. It was only available via Nintendo's customer service line.

XBOX ADAPTIVE CONTROLLER

The large programmable buttons of its central hub caught the eye in 2018, but the huge plus for many was the controller's 21 ports, most offering customization. Microsoft consulted AbleGamers (see right) during its development.

SONY'S ACCESS CONTROLLER

With remappable buttons and sensitivity for a control stick that also has an adjustable extension arm, this 2023 controller for the PS5 addressed challenges faced by players with limited motor control, including holding a controller for long periods.

PARA GHOST

PARA.GHOST

The five members of this Swedish Counter-Strike team all have Duchenne muscular dystrophy. Martin Stengård founded the group in 2021 to help his son Sigge (second from left) deal with social isolation. See p.28 for another para esports team, Permastunned Gaming.

MOBILE LEGENDS BANG BANG

First esports appearance at a para-sports event

In Jun 2023, the popular MOBA *Mobile Legends: Bang Bang* was included as a demonstration event at the ASEAN Para Games, appearing alongside established para sports such as wheelchair basketball and goalball. The Philippine team won gold.

the ablegamers charity

ABLEGAMERS

Mark Barlet founded this charity in 2004 to support a friend with multiple sclerosis. AbleGamers has now trained more than 600 developers, including those from a number of major studios, in how to create games that are accessible as well as enjoyable. Pictured left, using his tongue to push the buttons on his controller, is *Street Fighter* champion and AbleGamers affiliate BrolyLegs, aka Michael Begum, who sadly passed away in Mar 2024.

Best-selling first-person shooter series

! Call of Duty

In the front line of first-person shooter gaming, a war has been raging for the last two decades. As the smoke clears, the name that emerges as king of the hill is *Call of Duty*. As of Jun 2022, total sales of the franchise had topped 425 million. Including the series debut in Oct 2003, there are more than 20 main-series *CoD* games, set in a wide range of locations and time periods (see pp.120–21). For many players, however, the single-player campaigns take a distant second place behind the series' overwhelmingly popular online multiplayer.

R N G

3

Number of game franchises that have sold more copies than *CoD* (425 million): *Pokémon* (481 million), *Super Mario* (494 million) and *Tetris* (520 million).

XP

Debut: 2003
Developer: Infinity Ward
Publisher: Activision

Most popular *Call of Duty* speedrun

Call of Duty's Zombies mode – which started as an off-the-books side project during the development of *World at War* – pits the series' grizzled veterans against endless waves of the living dead. The fan favourite is the most popular part of *CoD* with speedrunners. The Zombies mode in 2015's *Black Ops III* had a record 5,161 runs on speedrun.com as of 18 Apr 2024.

Operator Ateret "Doc" Dahan from *Modern Warfare III*'s multiplayer mode

Balance in the gaming world

A survey in 2013 by the Entertainment Software Association found that 45% of gamers were female. The **first *Call of Duty* game to feature female soldiers** arrived the same year. *Ghosts* offered the option of female troops who had been added to the game's multiplayer mode.

Most critically acclaimed *Call of Duty* games

Game	Metascore
Call of Duty: Modern Warfare 2 (2009)	94 (100 reviews)
Call of Duty 4: Modern Warfare (2007)	94 (70 reviews)
Call of Duty (2003)	91
Call of Duty 2 (2005)	89
Call of Duty: Modern Warfare 3 (2011)	88

Metacritic, as of 18 Apr 2024

Fastest Any% completion of Modern Warfare III

Sledgehammer Games' 2023 entry into the series offers two modes for an Any% completion. At the level of **Recruit**, Mourie (AUT) finished his mission in 1 hr 3 min 40.41 sec on 10 Mar 2024, shaving 5 sec off the previous record. Taking the **Veteran** route, PC gamer Russian_Zone (USA) completed the course on 10 Nov 2023 in a blistering 1 hr 29 min 9.95 sec.

Call of Duty through the ages

CoD games span a significant period of time, from World War II via the Vietnam War to a bleak future in which all of Earth's resources have been exhausted. Here we chart the series' chronological order of gameplay through the 20th and 21st centuries.

Call of Duty 2
1941–45

Vanguard
1945

Call of Duty 3
1944

Black Ops
1961–68

Black Ops Cold War
1981

Modern Warfare
2011

1942–45
Call of Duty World at War

1940–1945
WWII

1975–79
Black Ops: Declassified

1986–89
Black Ops II (Alex Mason Missions)

2019
Modern Warfare

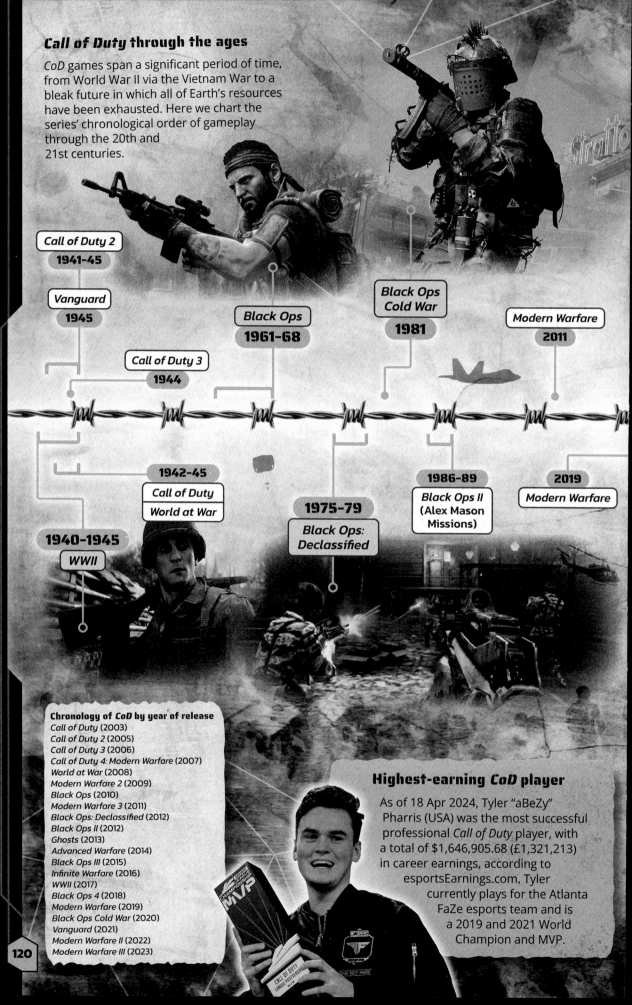

Chronology of *CoD* by year of release
Call of Duty (2003)
Call of Duty 2 (2005)
Call of Duty 3 (2006)
Call of Duty 4: Modern Warfare (2007)
World at War (2008)
Modern Warfare 2 (2009)
Black Ops (2010)
Modern Warfare 3 (2011)
Black Ops: Declassified (2012)
Black Ops II (2012)
Ghosts (2013)
Advanced Warfare (2014)
Black Ops III (2015)
Infinite Warfare (2016)
WWII (2017)
Black Ops 4 (2018)
Modern Warfare (2019)
Black Ops Cold War (2020)
Vanguard (2021)
Modern Warfare II (2022)
Modern Warfare III (2023)

Highest-earning *CoD* player

As of 18 Apr 2024, Tyler "aBeZy" Pharris (USA) was the most successful professional *Call of Duty* player, with a total of $1,646,905.68 (£1,321,213) in career earnings, according to esportsEarnings.com. Tyler currently plays for the Atlanta FaZe esports team and is a 2019 and 2021 World Champion and MVP.

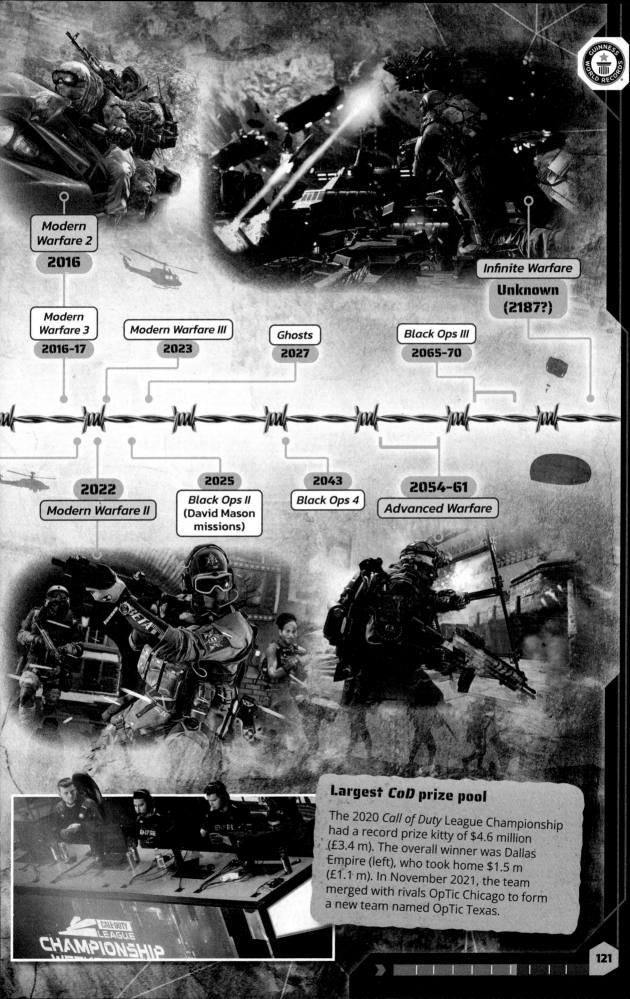

Modern Warfare 2
2016

Infinite Warfare
Unknown (2187?)

Modern Warfare 3
2016-17

Modern Warfare III
2023

Ghosts
2027

Black Ops III
2065-70

2022
Modern Warfare II

2025
Black Ops II (David Mason missions)

2043
Black Ops 4

2054-61
Advanced Warfare

Largest *CoD* prize pool

The 2020 *Call of Duty* League Championship had a record prize kitty of $4.6 million (£3.4 m). The overall winner was Dallas Empire (left), who took home $1.5 m (£1.1 m). In November 2021, the team merged with rivals OpTic Chicago to form a new team named OpTic Texas.

16 Longest videogame marathon

Carrie Swidecki

Carrie Swidecki (USA) is the undisputed dancing queen of gaming. The teacher from California played Ubisoft's *Just Dance 2015* on 11–17 Jul 2015 for a total of 138 hr 34 sec. That's the longest continuous play on *any* game – check out other marathon records on pp.124–125. Carrie's brilliant boogie also gives her records for the **longest marathon playing a dance game** and **rhythm game**, and she separately achieved the **most high scores on a dance game series in 24 hours** when she earned the maximum five-star rating for 276 different songs in 11 *Just Dance* titles. Carrie encourages the use of games to help get children fit and tackle obesity, and has raised a total of $100,000 (£78,000) for charity during her various record attempts.

PS4
JUST DANCE 2015
42 NEW HITS

XP

Holder: Carrie Swidecki
Time: 138 hr 34 sec
Location: Bakersfield, California, USA

Happy OK   Jazzy PERFECT   Crazy OK

Carrie lost 75 lb (34 kg) while playing dancing games

Perry good, Katy!

With 15 songs in the franchise, Katy Perry (USA, right) holds the record for the **most *Just Dance* appearances by one artist**. Six hits from her 2012 album *Teenage Dream: The Complete Confection* appear in the series – the **most songs from a single album in *Just Dance***.

Simone and Aly just love dancing

A few months after scooping four golds at the 2016 Rio Olympics, legendary gymnast and GWR record holder Simone Biles (USA, far left) took part in the launch of *Just Dance 2017*. Biles and fellow gold medallist Aly Raisman (far right) got members of Kips Bay Boys & Girls Club in New York City, USA, busting some moves to, among others, "Single Ladies (Put a Ring On It)" by Beyoncé and Sia's "Cheap Thrills". It was a gold medal effort all round!

🔓 INORITE!

The dance party isn't ending any time soon. In 2023, 14 years after the debut title, Ubisoft released *Just Dance 2024 Edition*, the 15th game in the series. Billie Eilish, BTS and Olivia Rodrigo are among the artists whose songs feature in the game. Subscription service Just Dance+, which launched in 2022, continues to offer gamers access to 300 songs and in-game events.

A UBISOFT ORIGINAL

JUST DANCE 2024 EDITION

King of the Kids' Choice Awards

Just Dance 2019 won the Favorite Video Game gong at the 32nd Nickelodeon Kids' Choice Awards, beating some stiff opposition, including *Super Mario Party* (NDcube) and *Super Smash Bros. Ultimate* (Bandai Namco/Sora). It was the eighth win in this category for a *Just Dance* title following prizes every year since 2011.

LONGEST VIDEOGAME MARATHONS

Following on from the overall winner, we split these amazing feats of endurance into a huge range of gaming genres. Whatever the challenge, these record breakers have two things in common: skill and determination!

Ken, *Super Smash Bros. Ultimate*

RACING GAME
Gran Turismo 7

During his epic 2023 journey (29 Jun to 3 Jul), Csépe Szabolcs (HUN) – aka "GrassHopper" – set himself the challenge of driving all 474+ stock cars in the game. By the end, he had covered more than 9,100 km (5,654 mi).

90 hr

FIGHTING GAME
Super Smash Bros. Ultimate

TCNick3 (CHL) went into his record bid thinking that, if he set his mind to achieve something, he could make it happen. He did just that in New Jersey, USA, from 23 to 26 Jun 2022.

69 hr 4 min 20 sec

MMORPG
World of Warcraft

Chef Barnabás Vujity-Zsolnay (HUN) served up a *WoW* marathon on 26–28 Sep 2022. He beat the previous record by nearly 14 hours. It was all live-streamed, with proceeds from the broadcast being donated to charity.

59 hr 20 min 12 sec

ROLE-PLAYING GAME
Assassin's Creed Valhalla

Starting on a Friday morning and finishing late on a Sunday afternoon, Wout Lenaerts, aka CasualGorilla (BEL), emerged with this record on 16 Oct 2022.

54 hr 32 min 10 sec

STRATEGY GAME
StarCraft

Francisco Javier Muros Ponce (left) and Carlos García Muñiz (both ESP) outlasted the previous record by six hours in Dec 2020. "The only way in each life goal is to do our best until being exhausted," said Francisco.

50 hr 21 min 5 sec

SPORTS GAME
Football Manager

Kevin Chapman (UK) not only set a record in Sep 2023, he was also part of a test to see if applying deodorant helped to reduce sweating in a marathon record attempt. "I still smell great," he tweeted.

50 hr 8 min 13 sec

VIRTUAL REALITY GAME
Minecraft VR Mode

The intention for Robin Schmidt and Based AF (both NLD) was to play a variety of games on 18–20 Oct 2023. As is often the case, they got consumed by *Minecraft VR* and the other games stayed unplayed!

50 hr

SOCCER GAME
FIFA 22

David Whitefoot (UK) briefly held the overall **sports game** record (above) for playing *FIFA 22* for an epic 50 hours between 4 and 6 Mar 2022. Although he was beaten by Kevin Chapman, he still holds the *FIFA* record.

50 hr

Minecraft

FIFA 22

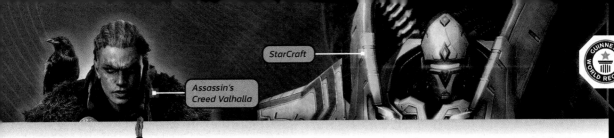

SURVIVAL-HORROR GAME
State of Decay 2

In a post-apocalyptic landscape, Samuel Steele (UK) repelled a never-ending wave of various zombiefied abominations for the equivalent of two days from 2 to 4 Aug 2019.

48 hr

BATTLE-ROYALE GAME
Call of Duty: Warzone

Grant Taylor (UK) planned to declare a ceasefire after 36 hours of his record bid, which ran from 19 to 20 Sep 2020. A late burst of energy saw him keep fighting for another two hours.

38 hr 17 min

MINECRAFT

The game's player base grew by 25% at the start of the pandemic. While his country was in a COVID-19 curfew, from 5 to 7 Jun 2021 Alexandre Jouniaux (FRA) used his time to take on this marathon (non-VR) record as a personal challenge.

38 hr 1 sec

POKÉMON GAME
Pokémon Shield

Cody Harbidge (CAN) picked his birthday – 17 Jun 2021 – to start his challenge. His record-breaking efforts raised CAN$2,000 ($1,640; £1,165) for Alberta Children's Hospital Foundation.

36 hr 12 sec

PUZZLE GAME
Tetris Effect

Versatile multiple record breaker Csépe Szabolcs (see the *Gran Turismo 7* box opposite) says he overcame sleepiness during this attempt in Dec 2021 by setting *Tetris Effect* to a higher difficulty, presenting him with faster speeds.

32 hr 32 min 32 sec

NARUTO GAME
Narutimetto Akuseru 2

In Mar 2021, Csépe Szabolcs displayed more of his all-round gamer excellence. This time it was with the fifth instalment of the *Ultimate Ninja* series. "I am a patient type," he said afterwards.

PLAYER: [PXL] GrassHopper

28 hr 11 min 32 sec

DRUMMING ON ROCK BAND
Rock Band 4

Douglas Spears (USA) trained for more than a year in preparation for his attempt across 16–17 Feb 2020. His forearms were not the only thing to benefit: Spears was also raising money for charity.

27 hr 45 min 20 sec

LEAGUE OF LEGENDS

Jorell Rolle (USA) first entered Riot Games' battle arena in late 2014, but waited until Dec 2021 to stream his record attempt on twitch.tv/jrealli. "I wanted to provide an entertaining experience for my viewers," he told GWR.

24 hr 27 min 49 sec

Longest-running soccer series

Kylian Mbappé, cover star of *FIFA 2023*, probably the last in the franchise

FIFA/EA Sports FC

XP

Debut: 1993
Developer: EA Vancouver
Publisher: EA Sports

An era that kicked off on 15 Dec 1993 with *FIFA International Soccer* seemingly came to an end with the release of *FIFA 2023* on 30 Sep 2022 – that's 28 years 289 days. In that time, there has been at least one *FIFA* game released every year, sometimes several, bringing the total number of titles in the series to 41. Soccer is often referred to as the "global game", and the franchise's success reflects this with editions of *FIFA* released in more than 50 countries. It's also the **best-selling sports franchise**, with more than 325 million sales. But the final whistle has been blown; EA and FIFA have dissolved their partnership, and the franchise has been reborn as *EA Sports FC* – developed by the same team but without FIFA's endorsement.

Most critically acclaimed *FIFA* game

The winner of the Metacritic league for *FIFA* games turns out to be a three-way split between *10*, *12* and *13* (right), all with a rating of 90. The **most critically acclaimed football game** is *World Soccer Winning Eleven 7 International* (KCET/Konami, 2003), with a metascore of 93. It was called *Pro Evolution Soccer 3* in most territories outside the US.

#EQUAL GAME

Poetry in motion

FIFA 18 was the first game of the franchise to record motion-capture performances with stars such as Cristiano Ronaldo. On the training ground, the then Real Madrid icon wore a bodysuit that allowed his movements, from his electrifying sprints to those defender-bamboozling tricks, to be more accurately reproduced in game.

R N G

26,400,000

Sales of *FIFA 18*, reported by EA in early Feb 2019, making it the **best-selling soccer game** as well as the **best-selling FIFA game**.

First women on a *FIFA* cover

For *FIFA* 16, Alex Morgan (USA), Steph Catley (AUS, right) and Christine Sinclair (CAN) topped the polls in votes for the first female players to appear on the cover of a *FIFA* game. Each of them featured alongside Argentina forward Lionel Messi on their respective regional covers. It's also the **first FIFA game with women's football in playable mode.**

Longest marathon playing *FIFA*

David Whitefoot (UK, below) played *FIFA 22* for 50 hours on 4–6 Mar 2022. Originally, he was aiming for 48 hours to raise funds for a hospital, then altered his target to beat the then record of 48 hr 49 min. His feat was praised by the RAF Video Gaming & Esports Association. See pp.122–25 for other marathon records.

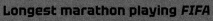

Crossing over

As well as featuring icons of the game in *FIFA 23*, there are those of more modest on-field achievements. Ted Lasso – played by Jason Sudeikis – is the star of the Apple TV+ comedy drama and now part of the *FIFA* family. He's joined by his AFC Richmond squad. But would you pick the former American football coach to take charge of your team?

HISTORY OF THE GENRE

Given soccer's enormous popularity across the globe, it's no surprise that the sport has been a regular fixture in gaming for more than 40 years. Here, we chart the evolution of the beautiful [video]game.

1980

NASL SOCCER

Various *Pong*-like paddle games were marketed as "soccer" titles as early as 1973, but arguably the **first soccer videogame** was released in 1980 by Mattel for their Intellivision console. This game-changing title allowed players to control their team from a side perspective (aka the "stadium camera"), which would later become the standard for almost all soccer games. The NASL was the pro soccer league in the USA and Canada from 1968 until 1984.

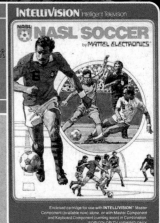

1994

VIRTUA STRIKER

By the mid-1990s, the soccer genre was flying. Sega's *Virtua Striker* was the **first soccer game to use 3D graphics**. It spawned a decade of titles – the series got up to *Virtua Striker 4* in 2004, and ports were later produced for the Xbox 360 and PS3.

1993

FIFA INTERNATIONAL SOCCER

The sport's global governing body got in on the act in 1993. EA Sports' first *FIFA* title opted for an isometric viewpoint, where the game is seen from an angle. There were 48 national teams, all made up of fictional players. The game was a huge success.

1995

ACTUA SOCCER

Developers Gremlin were based in Sheffield, UK, and used players from Sheffield Wednesday FC for motion capture. *Actua* was the **first football game with a full 3D graphics engine**. It was promoted with a dig at its rival – "there's nothing virtual about *Actua*".

2001

PRO EVOLUTION SOCCER

Konami's *Pro Evo* series (aka *PES*) – which evolved from their 1995 *International Superstar Soccer* (aka *Winning Eleven*) franchise – formed a legendary rivalry with *FIFA*. The first *PES* game launched in 2001, while the most recent, *eFootball 2024*, was released in Sep 2023. In 2003, Pierluigi Collina (ITA) became the **first referee to appear on a videogame cover**.

PELÉ'S SOCCER

The biggest star in the NASL was Brazilian legend Pelé, so it follows that he got his own game, Atari's imaginatively titled *Pelé's Soccer*. The superstar striker, who won the **most FIFA World Cups** (3), was also the **first soccer player to headline a game**.

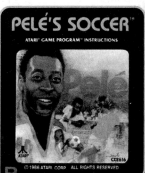

1985

TEHKAN WORLD CUP

This top-down arcade hit, known simply as *World Cup* in Japan, utilized a trackball controller and bird's-eye view of the pitch. The game was released in the run-up to the 1986 World Cup in Mexico. It was released on the PS2 and Xbox in the mid-noughties.

1992

SENSIBLE SOCCER

With an eye-catching title (often shortened to *Sensi*) and Dutch legend Ruud Gullit on the cover, this was a smash hit. Developers Sensible Software packed it with national, club and custom teams, and several sequels followed, including *Sensible World of Soccer* (2007's Xbox version below right).

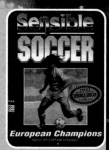

1989

KICK OFF

Italian-British developer Dino Dini released this bird's-eye-view classic in 1989, and things really, well, kicked off for him – he went on to develop nine more soccer games. Pictured below left is the original, and on the right is Windows title *Kick Off 98*.

2023

EA SPORTS FC 24

EA Sports' first soccer title following the end of their long partnership with FIFA was hotly anticipated. EA said 11.3 million gamers played *EA Sports FC 24* in its first week after launch. While Norway's Erling Haaland is the cover star for the standard edition, the cover for the Ultimate Edition (right) features a diverse mix of current and retired footballers.

How many players can you name?

USA star Trinity Rodman

Answers on p.191

Longest-running fighter series

XP
Debut: 1987
Developer: Capcom
Publisher: Capcom

Street Fighter

When the first *Street Fighter* hit the arcades in 1987, few could have predicted the groundbreaking phenomenon that would follow. Designer and director Takashi Nishiyama is the brains behind the brawler. He says the idea came to him during a long, boring meeting with the sales staff at Capcom! It may not have been the first close-contact, side-on fighter – that credit goes to Sega's *Heavyweight Champ* (1976) – but the *SF* series, and in particular *SFII* (see right), quickly defined the conventions of the genre. Nearly 40 years later, there have been six main titles and dozens of spin-offs, crossovers, ports and compilations. The most recent game in the series is 2023's *Street Fighter 6*, which features a *Teenage Mutant Ninja Turtles* crossover (right).

Largest *Street Fighter* prize won

The Capcom Cup 2024 made an instant millionaire of Chinese Taipei player UMA, aka Wang Yuan-hao. The event – Capcom's first *Street Fighter 6* championship – came to a nail-biting close on 25 Feb 2024 with UMA's Juri defeating Chris Wong's Luke 3–0 in the Grand Final. Wong had to settle for the second-place prize of $300,000 (£236,705).

INORITE!

Since 2015, Red Bull Kumite has brought together the world's best fighting gamers. The ninth edition Main Event, staged in Brooklyn, New York, USA, on 17 Mar 2024, saw 16 players duke it out in a *Street Fighter 6* "best of nine" eliminator. Emerging victorious was MenaRD (USA), whose Blanka comprehensively eradicated NuckleDu's Guile in the final showdown.

Red Bull Kumite 2023 in Pretoria, South Africa

Changing the game

The original *Street Fighter* may have blazed the trail, but it was the sequel that changed the fighting genre for good. *Street Fighter II*, originally released on arcades in 1991, introduced a roster of eight playable characters, each with their own moveset and special abilities. By 2017, it had amassed an inflation-adjusted total revenue of $10.61 bn (£7.8 bn).

Best-selling *Street Fighter* games

Title	Units sold
Street Fighter V (2016)	7.4 million
Street Fighter II (1991)	6.3 million
Street Fighter II Turbo (1994)	4.1 million
Street Fighter IV (2008)	3.5 million
Street Fighter 30th Anniversary Collection (2018)	3.0 million
Street Fighter 6 (2023)	2.9 million
Ultra Street Fighter IV (2014)	2.0 million
Super Street Fighter II: The New Challengers (1993)	2.0 million

Capcom, as of 1 Jan 2024

Decapre, *USF IV*

Sagat, *SF V*

Chun-Li, *SF II Turbo*

GAME THE RECORD

World records can be broken at any age – just look at the gamers on p.94. For those of you under 16, we have had six records specially made. Scan the QR code for our *Game the Record* episodes full of action and advice, pick up some tips below – and maybe you'll be a record breaker!

Highest score in a "Bob-omb Blast" match in *Mario Kart 8 Deluxe* in one minute

In this battle mode, matches can turn very explosive very quickly. Run down the item boxes so you can arm yourself. Bombing those boxes might also catch a rearming enemy. Do you prefer throwing your bombs forward or dropping them behind? Whichever, it usually pays to have an aggressive approach.

Most sunflowers picked in one minute in *Minecraft*'s "Sunflower Field" with a controller

Picking sunflowers has never been this nerve-racking! Starting out by leaping out of a tree, you'll need to be speedy and accurate to gather up as many of the tall blooms as you can. And watch out for cows and creepers that try to slow you down. Take Steve's advice – don't forget that you only have 60 seconds. Happy harvesting!

Fastest time to complete the first 10 levels of the *Find the Button* map in *Fortnite*

Don't think that this is a break from BR mode – haring around a special map to find a series of fiendishly secreted buttons is a challenge on its own! Educated guesses and sparks of inspiration are just as crucial as speed when levels become tougher. Always keep the unexpected in mind...

Fastest time to win a 1v3 match on *Nickelodeon All-Star Brawl*

Don't be fooled when choosing your character in the crossover fighting game. Even SpongeBob's usually lazy friend Patrick has the moves and powers to beat a trio of Teenage Mutant Ninja Turtles or a triple threat of Reptars. Fight for your right to stay on the platform – if you fall off, it's game over!

Fastest time to complete the GWR Speed Track course on *Hot Wheels Unleashed*

Our special GWR track is waiting for fast and furious action as budding speed kings show what they can do. You can choose any car, even models that have been upgraded. How about racing around in the Batmobile? Be careful with your boosts, especially on tight corners. Spin-offs can cost you time!

Fastest hat-trick with the goalie on *EA Sports FC 24*

Deep down, many goalkeepers probably dream of being a striker. Make those wishes come true by scoring three goals as your team's keeper. You have to run through the opposition from one end of the pitch to the other, so save energy for your shots. Then all you have to do is score two more – just don't lose the ball!

**Ready to apply?
Scan here!**

YOUNGEST GAME DEVELOPER

In 2023, Simar Khurana (CAN, b. 17 May 2016) started taking coding lessons. After a moment of self-discovery – "I used to eat a lot of junk food!" – she used her coding skills to make the game *Healthy Food Challenge*. When her achievement was verified, Simar was a day short of her seventh birthday!

Most pre-orders for a PC game

! *Cyberpunk 2077*

This Keanu Reeves-led dystopian action RPG launched on 10 Dec 2020, after eight years in development. According to developers CD Projekt Red, it had more than 8 million pre-order sales, with 59% of those for PC – that's 4.72 million copies. Unfortunately, the game's console release, on the PS4 and Xbox One, was fraught with problems. Glitches, bugs and crashes on launch day led to Sony briefly pulling the game from digital sale, and both they and Microsoft offered customers refunds. But CD Projekt Red took swift action, issuing an apology and releasing patches to fix the problems. The game is now widely considered a triumph, with total sales of more than 25 million by the end of 2023.

The mercenary known as V: the game's player-controlled character

Tech company Razer released a Viper Ultimate Cyberpunk 2077 Edition mouse

XP

Date: 2020
Developer: CD Projekt Red
Publisher: CD Projekt

From *Fortnite* guy to *Cyberpunk* engram

Actor Keanu Reeves provides the voice and likeness of rockstar-terrorist Johnny Silverhand, who, by the year 2077, exists only as a digitized consciousness known as an "engram". Though not a gamer, Reeves is no stranger to videogames – he first appeared in pixellated form in the NES adaptation of his hit movie *Bill & Ted's Excellent Adventure* (USA, 1989). To some, however, he's best known as "*Fortnite* guy", due to the resemblance that a popular skin called "The Reaper" bears to his film character, John Wick. After he'd figured out why people were calling him "*Fortnite* guy" in the street, Reeves reached out to Epic games, who have since included an official John Wick skin in *Fortnite* (right)!

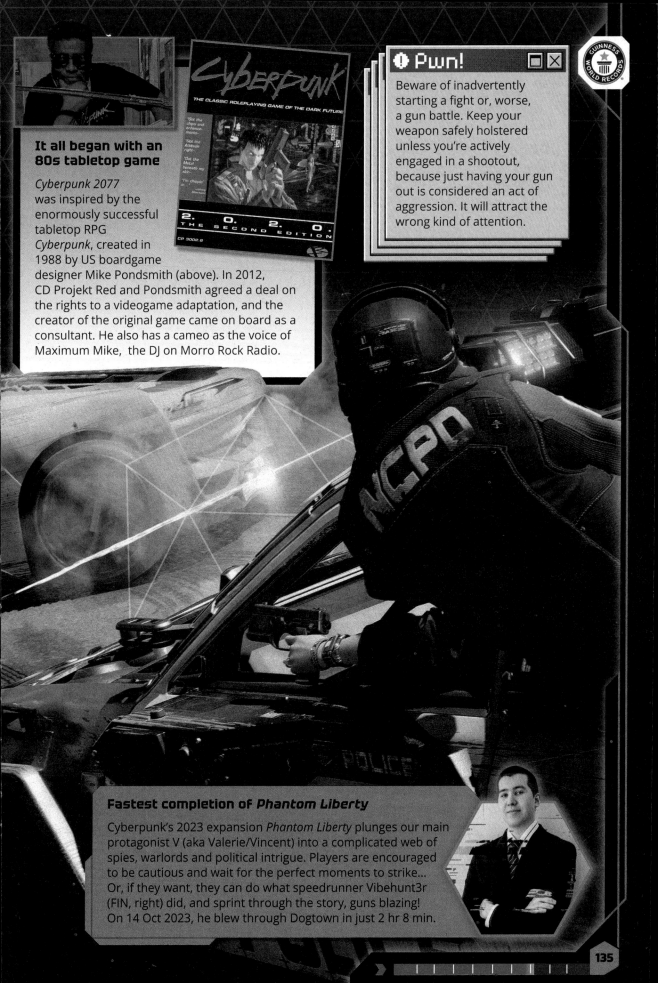

It all began with an 80s tabletop game

Cyberpunk 2077 was inspired by the enormously successful tabletop RPG *Cyberpunk*, created in 1988 by US boardgame designer Mike Pondsmith (above). In 2012, CD Projekt Red and Pondsmith agreed a deal on the rights to a videogame adaptation, and the creator of the original game came on board as a consultant. He also has a cameo as the voice of Maximum Mike, the DJ on Morro Rock Radio.

⚠ Pwn! ☐ ☒

Beware of inadvertently starting a fight or, worse, a gun battle. Keep your weapon safely holstered unless you're actively engaged in a shootout, because just having your gun out is considered an act of aggression. It will attract the wrong kind of attention.

Fastest completion of *Phantom Liberty*

Cyberpunk's 2023 expansion *Phantom Liberty* plunges our main protagonist V (aka Valerie/Vincent) into a complicated web of spies, warlords and political intrigue. Players are encouraged to be cautious and wait for the perfect moments to strike... Or, if they want, they can do what speedrunner Vibehunt3r (FIN, right) did, and sprint through the story, guns blazing! On 14 Oct 2023, he blew through Dogtown in just 2 hr 8 min.

Largest gathering of people dressed as game characters

Polaris Convention 2023

A gaming con in Germany on 15 Oct 2023 played host to a posse of 492 on-screen favourites, ranging from Mario and the Junker Queen to Aloy and Geralt of Rivia. This colourful collective of cosplayers amassed at the finale of the annual Polaris Convention in Hamburg, where a GWR representative was on hand to do the official count. It's a good job that no one backed out, because the previous effort, set in Finland in 2013, numbered 491, meaning that the Polaris attempt beat the record by the narrowest of margins: just one person! How many of the gaming heroes and villains can you name in the picture below?

GWR adjudicator Şeyda Subaşı–Gemici hands over the official certificate

XP

Where: Hamburg
When: 15 Oct 2023
Participants: 492

> "I love the large cosplay area. I think it's cool to admire all the elaborate costumes in the halls."
>
> YouTuber Jasmin Sibel, aka Gnu

Largest cosplay gatherings

People just like dressing up as their favourite characters...

Harry Potter	997	Perth, Australia	22 Nov 2017
Superman	867	Cumbria, UK	27 Jul 2013
Batman	542	Alberta, Canada	18 Sep 2014
Doctor Who	492	Mexico City, Mexico	19 Mar 2016
Mario	230	Chifeng City, China	18 Aug 2010

Largest gathering of people dressed as Steve...

"Steve" was just a nickname for the default player skin in *Minecraft*, suggested by game creator Markus Persson. But that didn't stop 337 fans taking on his likeness in Peterborough, UK, at MineVention on 12 Sep 2015. As per GWR guidelines, everyone wore a pixelated brick head, trademark blue jeans and blue untucked shirt.

... and Lara Croft!

To celebrate the launch of the movie *Tomb Raider* (USA, 2018), an entire roomful of 316 fans dressed in the green top and black shorts of the film's titular heroine Lara Croft. The event was organized by Warner Bros. Pictures in Beijing, China, as part of their PR for the reboot of the franchise, which starred Alicia Vikander in the role previously played by Angelina Jolie.

Hollow Knight's horned hero stands out among the crowd!

Best-selling console

!

PlayStation 2

XP
Year: 2000
Sales: 160,000,000
Generation: 6th

The Sony PS2 towered over its sixth-generation rivals, dominating the gaming landscape to a degree not seen since the NES in the 1980s (see p.44). It launched in Japan in Mar 2000 (and worldwide in the autumn), hitting shelves 18 months ahead of its Microsoft and Nintendo rivals (see opposite) and just as Sega's soon-to-be-discontinued Dreamcast was faltering. As well as a sleek design and impressive graphics, it lured gamers in with features such as backwards compatibility with the original PS and a built-in DVD player (at a time when these were the next big thing). The result? Sales of an unprecedented 160 million units.

PS2 gamers could save their game progress on 8-MB memory cards

Our pick of popular PlayStations

PlayStation 4
117 million (Nov 2013)

PlayStation
102.4 million (Dec 1994)

PlayStation 3
87.4 million (Nov 2006)

PlayStation Portable
76.4 million (Dec 2004)

PlayStation 5
54.8 million (Nov 2020)

PlayStation Vita
15–16 million (Dec 2011)

PlayStation 2

First game to offer cross-platform play

Playing an online game against someone using a different console is now common. Not so in 2001. Sega's Dreamcast and the PS2 were competing consoles that joined forces for the fighting sequel *Capcom vs. SNK 2: Mark of the Millennium 2001* (Capcom, 2001). The technology gap between the consoles was bridged using an internet-enabled "multi-matching" service.

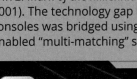

🔓 INORITE!

The best-selling console was precious to millions of fans, but Dan Holmes (UK) took his devotion to a new level in 2002 by legally changing his name to Mr. PlayStation 2. Sony was impressed at the news: "This shows enormous loyalty."

Console warfare

As the 1990s became the 2000s, it looked like the battle for dominance in the new world of sixth-generation consoles would be a four-way fight. But Nintendo's GameCube (21 million sales, six years in production), Sega's underperforming Dreamcast (9 million, three years) and Microsoft's Xbox (24 million, five years) soon fell by the wayside. That left the PlayStation 2 as the undisputed champ, spurred on by a series of mega-selling games covering a variety of genres (below).

Best-selling PS2 games

(10) **Final Fantasy XII (2006)** 6 million

Kingdom Hearts (2002) 5.9 million

(8=)

(8=) **Tekken 5 (2005)** 6 million

(7)

(6)

Final Fantasy X (2001) 8.5 million

(5) **Grand Theft Auto III (2001)** 8.3 million

Gran Turismo 3: A-spec (2001) 14.89 million

(4)

(3)

Grand Theft Auto: Vice City (2002) 10.5 million

(2)

(1)

Metal Gear Solid 2: Sons of Liberty (2001) 7.03 million

Grand Theft Auto: San Andreas (2004) 17.33 million

Gran Turismo 4 (2004) 11.76 million

10

Best-selling videogame heroine

!

Lara Croft

XP

DoB: 14 Feb 1968
Debut: 1996
Main games: 12

As of Dec 2022, the *Tomb Raider* series had sold more than 95 million units. Soon after her 1996 debut, the game's legendary archaeologist, Lara Croft, quickly became a gaming icon on a par with Mario, Sonic, Link and PAC-MAN. By 1999, she had crossed over into a recognizable figure beyond gaming, becoming the **first female game protagonist to record an album**. Aptly enough, its title was *Female Icon*. Lara has now appeared in 30 games, including limited-release UK-only titles. It could all have been so different: she was originally going to be a Latina heroine called Laura Cruz, but developers Core Design changed their minds and got the name "Croft" from a British phone directory!

1996   2003   2007   2012   2018

Stamp of approval

In 2020, Britain's Royal Mail released a set of 12 postage stamps marking the history of the UK gaming industry. Four of them (below) were of *Tomb Raider* games; 15 years earlier, Lara had become the **first female videogame protagonist on a stamp** when she was honoured on a set in France (right).

ADVENTURES OF LARA CROFT – 1998

TOMB RAIDER – 1996

TOMB RAIDER – 2013

TOMB RAIDER CHRONICLES – 2000

At the movies

Cinematic Croft is just as well known as the gaming version. Angelina Jolie (USA, below left) played her in 2001's *Lara Croft: Tomb Raider* (USA) and the sequel *The Cradle of Life* (USA, 2003). Alicia Vikander (SWE, below right) took on the role in 2018 reboot *Tomb Raider* (USA).

Unreal makes it so real

In Dec 2022, developer Crystal Dynamics and publisher Amazon Games announced they were working on a new *Tomb Raider* game using Unreal Engine 5. When the impressive engine was revealed in 2020, it was showcased with *Lumen in the Land of Nanite* (above), a real-time demo running live on a PS5. The game's artwork, packed with billions of polygons, looked a lot like a *Tomb Raider* game, leaving Croft fans excited about how detailed the next instalment will look.

🔓 INORITE!

Lara Croft's simple, striking costume – tank top, shorts, boots and holster – has made her a popular choice for cosplayers and occasional fancy-dressers alike. There's even a website dedicated to the art of dressing up as Lara: there are more than 7,400 pics on laracroftcosplay.com, as well as clothing, hair and make-up tutorials.

How many iconic female characters can you name?

Answers on p.191

Most ported videogame

The relentless building block video puzzle.

TETRIS

Tetris

Since the four-part blocks ("Tetriminos") began falling in 1984, more than 200 official *Tetris* variants have been developed for 70+ unique systems. Boot up anything even vaguely computer-like, and you'll probably find a compatible version. Aside from the research computers it was made for, and the Game Boy release that made it a global hit, how about the obscure Philips CD-i? Or the TRS-80? Despite all the variations, *Tetris*'s "easy to learn, hard to master" gameplay (see p.83 for a killer *Tetris* record!) is the same, and has resulted in an estimated 520 million sales in all its designs, making it, unofficially, the **best-selling game** (see pp.176–81).

XP

Debut: 1984
Creator:
Alexey Pajitnov
Variants: 200+
Sales: 520 million
(all versions)

Tetris (1989) NES

Tetris (1989)
Game Boy

Dr. Mario (1990) Game Boy

Tetris Beat (2021) Apple Arcade

Tetris Effect (2018) PS4

Tetris Party Deluxe (2010) Wii

Taking shape

Despite no real characters and no story, *Tetris* is surprisingly popular with cosplayers. If you and your friends have some blocky costumes to hand, consider having a go at setting the official GWR record for the **largest gathering of people dressed as *Tetris* blocks**. If you want to make a claim, find out how to go about it on pp.8–9.

An Apple Original Film
TARON EGERTON
TETRIS™

Youngest *Tetris* world champion

The fast-paced world of competitive *Tetris* (see p.82–83) is a young person's game. In the final of the 2020 Classic Tetris World Championship, 15-year-old Andrew "P1xelAndy" Artiaga was defeated by his younger brother Michael (aka "Dog"), who was 13 years 16 days old. Not to be outdone, on 4 Jan 2024, P1xelAndy became only the third player to reach the killscreen (see p.83) and went on to achieve the **highest score in *NES Tetris*** – 8.9 million points!

Battling for the eastern block

The 1980s race to patent the addictive puzzle game was at the heart of the well-reviewed 2023 film. Rather than trying to do the impossible – dramatizing falling blocks – the film follows the high-stakes international intrigue involved in publishing the game outside the Soviet Union.

P1xelAndy

Dog

Most followers on Twitch

Ninja

Ninja started out as a pro gamer with a love of *Halo*

Since joining Twitch on 17 Nov 2016, Ninja, aka Richard Tyler Blevins (USA), has risen to become the streaming platform's biggest star. As of 3 Apr 2024, his 19 million followers put him well clear of his closest rivals, auronplay (16.2 million) and ibai (15.5 million; see p.89). The rise of Ninja as the king of gaming streamers happened almost hand in hand with the massive growth of *Fortnite* in the late 2010s. A *Fortnite* Twitch stream with superstar rapper Drake on 14 Mar 2018 was also a major factor in raising Ninja's profile. At the time, it had the **most concurrent viewers for a Twitch stream by an individual** (a peak of 667,000), showing the drawing power of "personality" streams.

XP

Name: Ninja
DoB: 5 Jun 1991
Favourite game: *Fortnite*

First Pro-Am *Fortnite* contest

The pairing of Ninja and DJ/producer Marshmello (USA) prevailed against 49 other duos in Los Angeles in Jun 2018. This was despite Marshmello playing in his famous helmet! The charity tournament – which paired professional players with celebrities – sent *Fortnite* to the top of the Twitch viewership charts on 12 Jun, with 700,000 concurrent viewers.

Ninja's Top 5 most streamed games

FORTNITE

PUBG

Z1: BATTLE ROYALE

VALORANT

LEAGUE OF LEGENDS

Gaming at the movies

Free Guy (USA, 2021) follows a seemingly nondescript bank teller called Guy (played by Ryan Reynolds) who finds out that he is actually a non-player character in an MMORPG. The film occasionally cuts away to streamers, including Ninja, DanTDM, Pokimane and LazarBeam, who react to the action unfolding in Guy's fictional game.

THE WORLD NEEDED A HERO
THEY GOT A GUY
FREE GUY
JULY 3

🔓 INORITE!

A sign in 2019 of how Ninja was making the jump from gaming megastar to mainstream celebrity happened when no one could see his face! Dressed as Ice Cream, he performed a couple of songs as part of season two of *The Masked Singer* competition on TV in the USA. "100% the scariest thing I have ever done," posted Ninja after he had been unmasked on the first show.

Top 5 Twitch accounts

Account	Followers
Ninja	19,021,412
auronplay	16,225,658
ibai	15,545,710
Rubius	14,913,186
xQc	11,979,700

Source: Social Blade, as of 3 Apr 2024

Largest user-generated content platform

7

Roblox

This online game-creation platform just keeps on growing, reaching a remarkable 71.5 million daily active users at the end of 2023 – that's almost a quarter more than the year before. *Roblox* also boasted more than 200 million monthly active users in the last three months of 2023. With over 4.4 million active games (aka "experiences") spanning multiple genres, it's easy to see why its mostly young user base keeps on coming back for more. According to Roblox themselves, over half of American under-16s – and three quarters of 9–12-year-olds – are on the platform.

Most popular *Roblox* game

According to stats monitored by Roblox, the RPG *Brookhaven RP*, created by Wolfpaq (left), had attracted more than 46.6 billion visits as of 25 Apr 2024. It boasts 485,526 players notching up an average playtime of 15 min 32 sec. *Brookhaven RP* is described as a place where you can "own and live in amazing houses, drive cool vehicles and explore the city". The majority of in-game items, houses and vehicles are free, though some do require Gamepasses.

Most visited *Roblox* games

Game	Visits
Brookhaven RP	46.6 billion
Adopt Me!	36.0 billion
Blox Fruits	32.8 billion
Tower of Hell	22.9 billion
MeepCity	15.9 billion

roblox.com, as of 25 Apr 2024

XP

Debut: 2006
Developer: Roblox Corp.
Publisher: Roblox Corp.

Brookhaven RP's Fire Station and, far right, the Police Station

R N G

5.8 billion

Number of registered accounts on *Roblox*. There are more than 2.4 million developers on the platform and 19.4 million "group" communities.

Highest-rated official *Roblox* concert

According to RoMonitorStats.com, the Saweetie Super Bowl Concert in Feb 2023 had an approvals rating of 95.86% – a full four points ahead of K-pop sensations NCT 127 in second place. The American rapper performed hits including "Tap In" and "Icy Grl" on Warner Music's *Rhythm City* RP game, now known as *Harmony Hills*.

Most visited branded game in *Roblox*

The little blue hedgehog's MMO platformer *Sonic Speed Simulator* tops the list of official branded experiences on *Roblox*, with 933.65 million visits as of 25 Apr 2024. Developed for Sega by Gamefam Studios (USA), this smash hit was released in Apr 2022 and has 230 million more visits than second-placed *Miraculous RP: Ladybug & Cat Noir*.

Roblox collabs

Companies are keen to promote their brands on *Roblox*. In 2024, Squishmallows, the cuddly toys that went viral on TikTok in 2020, collaborated with fashion retailer H&M in real life and in game (top); the *Galactic Speedway Creator Challenge* (centre) was sponsored by the movie *Star Wars: The Rise of Skywalker* (USA, 2019); and a *Stranger Things 3* promotion in 2019 offered users two free marketplace items and four promo code items.

GREATEST GAMER'S EDITION

PHOTO SHOOTS

One of the best ways to visualize gaming record holders is to drop them straight into their favourite games! Here, *GE* Picture Editor Lucy Talavera picks her favourite recreations from over the past 15 years, capturing devotion, invention and, above all, a sense of fun.

Back in 2010, Ryan Hart (UK) channelled his inner Ryu to visualize the **most tournaments won on games in the Street Fighter series** – 30. His worthy adversary was Marie-Laure Norindr (FRA), aka Kayane: the **first woman to win a pro Street Fighter event**.

Back in Oct 2016, Daniel Middleton (UK), aka DanTDM, was the king of *Minecraft* content creators. The *Minecraft* channel, loved for its focus on videos on his YouTube channel, had been watched more storytelling and characters, earning him the **most views for a single-game YT channel**. He's still going strong, with than 9 billion times, earning him the **most views for a** a total of almost 20 billion views, though he now plays other games in addition to *Minecraft*.

To illustrate the *Red Dead Redemption* record for the **fastest donkey ride from Dixon Crossing to Gaptooth Ridge**, we dressed up gamer Dan White (UK) as a cowboy and stuck him on the back of an ass. How better to show him braying his way across the game's map in 11 min 7 sec?!

To picture the **most goals scored in a game of Rocket League by a team of two** (then 56), we magically transported schoolboys Shashipreetham Rao Ravella (IND, left) and Jamal Gianni Ragno (UK, right) into the middle of a madcap vehicular soccer match. Goooooaal!

In 2018, Alex Tan (USA) donned a hard hat, overalls and fake moustache to help us illustrate the **most difficult level created in Super Mario Maker**. *Pit of Panga: U-Break* had been completed just 367 times from 4,805,934 tries, which means it foxed 99.99% who played it! (See p.171 for the **longest time to complete a Super Mario Maker level**.)

...female gamer for the 2016 book resulted in a memorable photoshoot for Kat "Mystik" Gunn (USA) in the dramatic landscape of Vasquez Rocks, California. As a Halo esports pro, what outfit could she wear except The Master Chief's Mjolnir armour? The record has since changed hands and is now with Sasha "Scarlett" Hostyn (see p.27).

Never doubt the devotion of a gamer who broke one of his *Super Mario Kart* records just after midnight on Christmas Day 2013! Sami Cetin (UK) had to steer clear of real-life banana skins on this track at Revolution Karting in London's Mile End. To complete the photoshoot, GWR adjudicators Gaz and Liz dressed up as Donkey Kong and Peach!

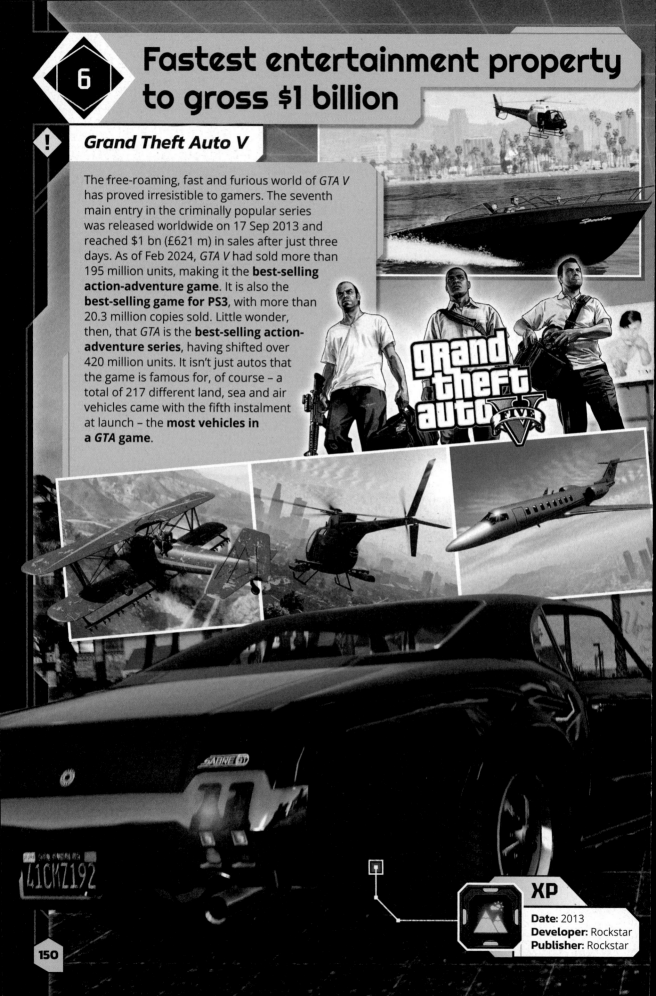

Fastest entertainment property to gross $1 billion

! **Grand Theft Auto V**

The free-roaming, fast and furious world of *GTA V* has proved irresistible to gamers. The seventh main entry in the criminally popular series was released worldwide on 17 Sep 2013 and reached $1 bn (£621 m) in sales after just three days. As of Feb 2024, *GTA V* had sold more than 195 million units, making it the **best-selling action-adventure game**. It is also the **best-selling game for PS3**, with more than 20.3 million copies sold. Little wonder, then, that *GTA* is the **best-selling action-adventure series**, having shifted over 420 million units. It isn't just autos that the game is famous for, of course – a total of 217 different land, sea and air vehicles came with the fifth instalment at launch – the **most vehicles in a *GTA* game**.

XP

Date: 2013
Developer: Rockstar
Publisher: Rockstar

Fastest games and movies to make $1 billion

Property	Format	Time taken
GTA V (2013)	Videogame	3 days
Avengers: Endgame (2019)	Movie	5 days
Call of Duty: Modern Warfare II (2022)	Videogame	10 days
Avengers: Infinity War (2018)	Movie	11 days
Star Wars: The Force Awakens (2015)	Movie	12 days
Spider-Man: No Way Home (2021)	Movie	12 days

Source: The-Numbers.com, as of 25 Apr 2024

Top-down top game

The first *GTA*, released in 1997, looks very different to later games in the series. It has a top-down perspective, and its open world is a lot less, well, open. But the game was just as controversial as its successors – upon release, it was banned by the Ministry of Justice in Brazil.

Speeding citation

Want to beat the record for **fastest 100% completion of *GTA V*?** As of Mar 2024, you'll need to do better than UnNameD (POL), who finished all 69 missions (without taxis) in 9 hr 53 min 10 sec on 19 Sep 2023. You can choose any ending – but no skipping failed missions.

⬡ Pwn! ▢ ✕

Thanks to the Mar 2024 update to *GTA Online*, you can now finally board and drive the game's iconic freight train! To gain control, you'll need to play the Cluckin' Bell Farm Raid missions, which challenges you to steal the locomotive from the drug cartel's compound.

A gaming era started with two *Pocket Monsters* games

Wild PIDGEY appeared!

GAME BOY. Nintendo

ポケットモンスター 赤

GAME BOY. Nintendo

ポケットモンスター 緑

XP

Debut: 27 Feb 1996
Country: Japan
Platform: Game Boy

R N G

82

Most Pokémon identified in one minute – in New York on 17 Sep 2022 by Jen Molly Walker (USA). Could you beat that record? See pp.8–9.

5 Best-selling RPG series

! *Pokémon*

On 27 Feb 1996, two games – called *Pocket Monsters Red* and *Green* – made their debut on the Game Boy in Japan. They were positively reviewed, but there wasn't much hype surrounding their release on the ageing handheld. The games proved to be a surprise hit, however, aided by word-of-mouth popularity and an innovative game mechanic that allowed players to trade Pokémon using a link cable. By the end of 1997, *Red* and *Green* had sold 4.7 million copies in Japan alone and an international release – *Red* and *Blue* – was in the works. *Pokémon* has since become an entertainment-industry juggernaut, selling more than 480 million units across 41 releases and inspiring numerous spin-offs.

Zap, zap, zap! Pikachu's here...

Despite being 15 years younger, Pikachu rivals Mario in videogame appearances, popping up in everything from sleep trackers (see opposite) to fighting games such as *Super Smash Bros*. Since debuting in 1996, Pikachu has appeared in 79 games, making the electric mouse the **most ubiquitous RPG character**.

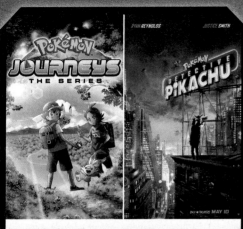

A media phenomenon

With 24 feature-length animations and one live-action release (2019's *Detective Pikachu*, USA), *Pokémon* holds the record for the **most movie spin-offs from a game series** and is the **highest-grossing film franchise from a game series**, having generated over $1.5 bn (£1.18 bn). What's more, running on TV since 1997, *Pokémon: The Series* has racked up more than 1,200 episodes – the **longest-running anime series based on a game**.

First player to reach level 50 in *Pokémon GO*

When the level cap for *GO* was raised from 40 in late 2020, there was a stampede of gamers fully focused on being the first to 50. On 26 Jan 2021, Daniel "FleeceKing" Amos (AUS) reached the maximum. Completing 999 excellent throws and catching five Legendary Pokémon were just two of the tasks that had to be completed before getting to the summit. FleeceKing covered an amazing 20,614 km (12,809 mi) and caught close to 800,000 Pokémon on the way.

🔓 INORITE!

Pokémon Sleep was released in Jul 2023. Less than two months later, the gamified sleep tracker had been downloaded 10 million times. As well as a good night's sleep being rewarded with rarer Pokémon, the voice of Pikachu lets you know when it is time to sleep or wake up.

Fastest Any% completion of *Scarlet* and *Violet*

Joshua "halqery" Cullins (USA) completed *Scarlet* and *Violet* on the Switch in 5 hr 19 min 25 sec on 30 Nov 2023, according to speedrun. com. As of 25 Apr 2024, the brisk Texan holds lots of other *Pokémon* records, including the **fastest completion of *Scarlet* and *Violet* Treasure Hunt** (3 hr 48 min 50 sec), ***Pokémon Legends: Arceus* Any%** (3 hr 37 min 29 sec) and ***Legends: Arceus* Catch 'em All** (13 hr 59 min 33 sec).

❗ Pwn!

In *Pokémon Scarlet* and *Violet*, you're well advised to keep a steady supply of Poké Dolls with you. If you end up fighting wild Pokémon, these dolls allow you to immediately escape the battle. And make sure your trainer eats regular meals and snacks – they'll give plenty of vital boosts.

Poké-merch

Pokémon is jointly owned by three companies: Nintendo, Game Freak and Creatures. The latter oversees the mountain of licensed merchandise inspired by the *Pokémon* games. The first major tie-in was the trading cards (above) that launched in 1996 – nearly 53 billion had been produced as of May 2023. Over the years, everything from clothes, shoes, plush toys and even cars (like this one-off Mini Cooper concept vehicle) have been emblazoned with Pokémon-themed artwork.

Gotta win 'em all!

The *Pokémon* World Championships has brought together card game and videogame Trainers from all over the globe annually since 2004. The 2023 edition took place in Yokohama, Japan, from 11 to 13 Aug. Shohei Kimura was the videogame Masters Division Champion, while ItsAXN bagged the top prize in *Pokémon GO*. Shao Tong was the trading card game Junior Division Champion, while Brazil's Gabriel Fernandez took the Senior Division title.

ItsAXN

Shao Tong

Gabriel Fernandez

Shohei Kimura

Luminosity Gaming were the *Pokémon Unite* champions in 2023

Largest Pokemon balloon costume

Tom Kent (UK) is a wizard with modelling balloons! He used 350 yellow, black and red balloons to create this blow-up Pikachu, which stood 262 cm (8 ft 7 in) tall. In 2021, Tom secured the overall record for the **largest balloon costume** with his inflatable Hulk (right), which stood a mighty 353 cm (11 ft 7 in) tall.

4 Most critically acclaimed videogame

! The Legend of Zelda: Ocarina of Time

Released for the Nintendo 64 console in 1998, this action-adventure classic – the first in the *Zelda* series to use 3D graphics – is the only game to achieve a score of 99 on the reviews aggregator site Metacritic. The fifth title in the hugely popular franchise remains at No.1 on the chart, ahead of *Grand Theft Auto IV* and *SoulCalibur*, which share second place on 98. GameSpot's critic rightly predicted that *Ocarina* was a "masterpiece that people will still be talking about 10 years down the road". A glossy remake released on the 3DS in 2011 was also praised, achieving a respectable Metascore of 94.

XP

Date: 1998
Developer: Nintendo EAD
Publisher: Nintendo

R N G

150,740,000

Games sold in *The Legend of Zelda* franchise worldwide as of Apr 2023. More than 30 million of those are for 2017's *Breath of the Wild* alone.

Largest collection of *Zelda* memorabilia

At the last official count, Anne Martha Harnes (NOR) owned a mighty 1,816 *Zelda*-themed items. She started her collection in 2008, and it includes toys, life-size statues, costumes and – her favourite piece – a Zoraxe fish-bone guitar!

Fastest 100% completion of *The Legend of Zelda: Tears of the Kingdom*

The 20th mainline title in the *Zelda* series (see pp.160–61) was completed in its entirety – i.e., all main quests, side adventures, shrine quests and memories – by Tippi (UK), who played for 1 day 5 hr 45 min 16 sec on 15 Oct 2023. By comparison, topping Speedrun's *Ocarina* **100%** chart, as of Feb 2024, is glitchymon (CAN), who, on 7 Jan 2024, took just 3 hr 45 min 41 sec to complete every challenge.

⚠ Pwn! ▢ ✕

Here's a *Tears of the Kingdom* tip. The Recall power lets you freeze time and send objects backwards. So when you're battling an enemy who's using a bow, use Recall to stop time while their arrow is still airborne. Select the arrow, and it will glide back and damage your foe.

Rarest N64 *Zelda* game

Of all the nearly 400 games for the N64, one 2000 release – limited to 1,000 copies – has been of particular interest for collectors. With a copy of the game, a soundtrack CD, a watch, a T-shirt and pin badges, the "Limited Edition Adventure Set" of *The Legend of Zelda: Majora's Mask* also came with a numbered certificate of authenticity. A copy on eBay as of 16 Apr 2024 was listed at €50,000 ($53,159; £42,725)!

Fifteen years after the original, *Majora's Mask* was remade for the 3DS

R N G
325,000+
Number of US consumers who put down deposits for their copies of *Ocarina of Time* before release – at the time, the **most advance orders for a game.**

Who rules Hyrule?

When *The Super Mario Bros. Movie* (USA, 2023) became the **highest-grossing film adaptation of a videogame** (see pp.68–69), questions were inevitably asked about a *Zelda* live-action release. At the time of going to press, very little has been confirmed, which means speculation is rife. Above, from left, the likes of Tom Holland and Thomas Brodie-Sangster have been Link-ed to the project, with Hunter Schafer and Zendaya in the running for the role of Zelda.

Fastest time to defeat Ganon

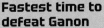

Ganon, aka Ganondorf Dragmire, looms ominously over these pages as well as over the *Zelda* franchise. The jump to 3D in *Ocarina of Time* (1998) made Ganon even more fearsome than before, but Amateseru (FRA) went from Link's bed in the Kokiri Forest to defeating Ganon's castle-sized final form in 10 min 33.45 sec on 24 Mar 2024.

CGC UNIVERSAL GRADE
8.0
SEALED

The Legend of
ZELDA
Includes invaluable maps and strategic playing tips.
ENTERTAINMENT SYSTEM

🔓 *INORITE!*

The **most expensive Zelda game sold at auction** was a mint example of *The Legend of Zelda* (1986). It went for $870,000 (£631,374) in 2021! The game was in the news again in Feb 2024, when another copy sold for $288,000 (£227,577). The seller, a 22-year-old from California, USA, had expected to get no more than $20,000 (£15,800) for this family heirloom.

Most critically acclaimed character

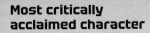

Links appears nine times in the Top 100 all-time best-reviewed games on Metacritic. This list includes two versions of *Ocarina of Time* (the original and the 3DS remake), but doesn't include the original *Legend of Zelda*, with a score of "just" 84. Nintendo stablemate Mario is second with six (including 2008's *Super Smash Bros. Brawl*); and *Metal Gear*'s Solid Snake takes third place for Konami with four appearances.

THE TIMELINES OF THE LEGEND OF ZELDA

To fully immerse yourself in the Zelda universe, you might want to play the games in story order. But it's not quite as simple as it sounds. This timeline maps the epic series' famously confusing chronology, which splits following the events of *Ocarina of Time*.

The Wind Waker (2002)

Link stays an adult, Ganon is resurrected and the world floods.

A Link to the Past (1991)

Oracle of Seasons / Oracle of Ages (2001)

Link is defeated by Ganon and the world falls into ruin.

Link's Awakening (1993)

Skyward Sword (2011)

Four Swords (2002)

The Minish Cap (2004)

Ocarina of Time (1998)

Link goes back to childhood then travels through a portal to the world of Termina.

Majora's Mask (2000)

Twilight Princess (2006)

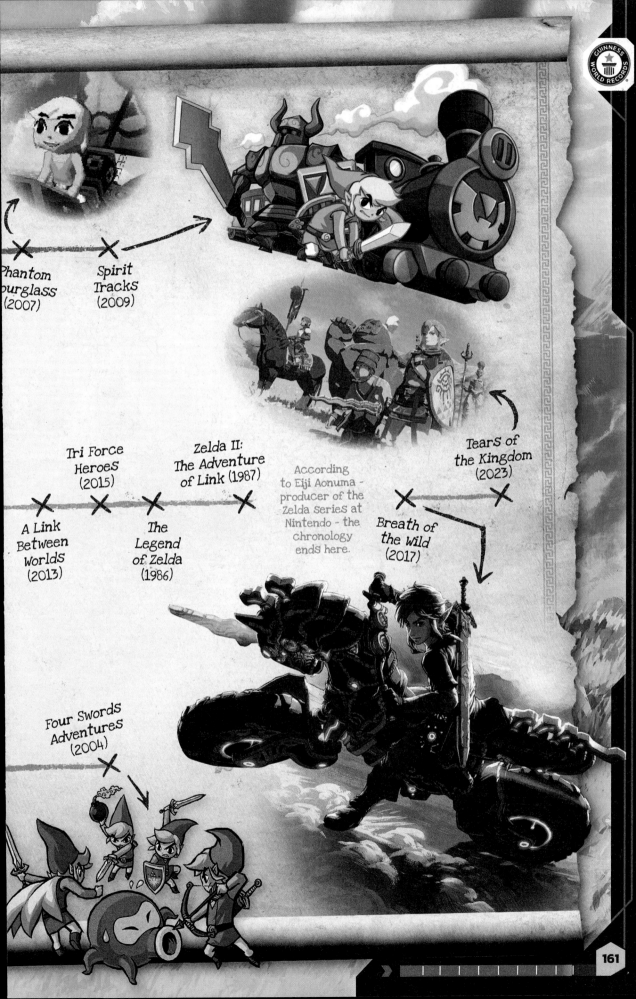

Phantom
Hourglass
(2007)

Spirit
Tracks
(2009)

Tri Force
Heroes
(2015)

Zelda II:
The Adventure
of Link (1987)

According
to Eiji Aonuma -
producer of the
Zelda series at
Nintendo - the
chronology
ends here.

Tears of
the Kingdom
(2023)

A Link
Between
Worlds
(2013)

The
Legend
of Zelda
(1986)

Breath of
the Wild
(2017)

Four Swords
Adventures
(2004)

METAVERSE GAMING

Ever since the first computers were networked together, people have talked about the idea of a shared virtual world, or metaverse, where anything could be made possible...

The first steps towards this were made in the late 1970s, when students started coding multiplayer *Dungeons & Dragons*–style games for their university networks and science-fiction writers started to speculate on the possibilities the future might hold. (The term itself comes from the 1992 cyberpunk sci-fi classic *Snow Crash*, by Neal Stephenson.) At this point, we're not quite ready for an all-encompassing *Ready Player One* VR, but we are on the cusp of a virtual world becoming a home not just for play, but for everyday life.

EVE Online (2003)

EVE Online is an ultra hardcore space MMO that offers perhaps the most immersive virtual world ever created. This shared, persistent universe lets players live out their sci-fi fantasies, role-playing as miners, pirates, traders, and more. If you're looking for a metaverse with a razor-sharp edge, *EVE Online* is the one.

Ultima Online (1997)

The first big, commercially successful MMO, this was also Origin Systems' first persistent online game. It established many of the mechanics seen in modern MMORPGs such as *WoW*, which make the world of the game feel like a real place where time passes and events take place even in a player's absence.

Roblox (2006)

User-generated content platforms such as *Roblox* realize another aspect of the metaverse concept. Here, users are not simply inhabiting a pre-built world, but have the power to mould and shape their virtual environment and what happens in it.

Habitat (1986)

Known for point-and-click games, LucasArts also created the first graphics-based large-scale virtual community. *Habitat* is arguably the first metaverse, and a forerunner of the massively multiplayer online role-playing game.

Second Life (2003)

Launched 20 years ago, *Second Life* is the closest thing to the vision of the metaverse presented in the novel *Snow Crash* (see below). Developer Linden Lab insists it's not a game. Rather, the focus is on avatars interacting with avatars in a virtual world, with no manufactured conflict and no set objective.

1935	1955	1986	1992	1997	2003	2006	2011

The history of virtual reality (VR) arguably started with Stanley G. Weinbaum's short story *Pygmalion's Spectacles*, in which a character wears goggles offering "sight and sound... taste, smell and touch".

In 1955, US film-maker Morton Heilig conceived of a "cinema of the future" offering 3D images, physical movement, aromas and weather effects. He built his prototype sit-in "Sensorama" in 1962, simulating a motorcycle ride through New York.

The word "metaverse" was coined in the 1992 novel *Snow Crash* by US sci-fi author Neal Stephenson. It refers to a virtual world offering a way out of a bleak reality, but which is under threat by a mind-controlling virus.

Fortnite (2017)

Its globe-spanning popularity and the technical resources of its creator, Epic Games, have allowed *Fortnite* to become a platform for all sorts of virtual events. On 24 Apr 2020, for example, an amazing 12.3 million people attended the **largest concert in a videogame**, staged by US rapper Travis Scott. The in-game attendance for end-of-season events can be even higher, as millions of players log in to watch as spectacular set-pieces change the layout of the game's map. The Galactus event, which marked the end of Season 4, made *Fortnite* the **most concurrently played game**, with 15.3 million people (see pp.164–70).

No Man's Sky (2016)

While most games strive to create virtual worlds, *No Man's Sky* creates a virtual universe. Using procedural generation tech (see p.80), the developers at Hello Games offer a constellation that encompasses 18 quintillion planets. Although it had a rocky start, the game has gone on to become a cult classic, with a devoted community dedicated to exploring this boundless cosmos.

Minecraft (2011)

Mojang's open-world sandbox (see pp.176–82) has included an online mode since its early alpha stage in May 2009. *Minecraft* players can host their own persistent worlds, called servers, which allow large numbers of players to socialize and collaborate on massive projects such as those on pp.178–79.

Red Dead Redemption 2 (2018)

No game has come close to matching Rockstar's Western, with its living, breathing environments, memorable characters and ultra-realistic visuals. This is the cowboy fantasy made into a virtual reality.

The Sandbox (2012)

Not all metaverses are 3D. *The Sandbox* is a 2D experience that lets players craft their own universe as "Deity apprentice". Players mix various physics-based elements to create pixel block objects they can share with the entire community.

Cyberpunk 2077 (2020)

As the world depicted in classic cyberpunk sci-fi starts to look more and more like our own, the genre that invented the metaverse is experiencing a renaissance. This action RPG (see pp.134–35) gives players the opportunity to prowl the digital world as a tech-augmented "netrunner".

Rec Room (2016)

Forget virtual worlds – how about virtual *rooms*? This metaverse allows players to create rooms and games accessed from a recreation centre. Players use the Maker Pen tool to design the rooms and draw shapes in 3D. You can even code in "Circuits", Rec Room's own programming language.

| 2012 | 2014 | 2016 | 2017 | 2018 | 2020 | 2022 | 2024 |

Headsets by Oculus widened the options for immersive VR, including to gaming. Facebook (now Meta) recognized the potential and bought Oculus in Mar 2014.

Will the metaverse be a force for good or bad? That's the question at the heart of Matthew Ball's non-fiction primer. The "proto-metaverses" of *Roblox* and *Minecraft* are just a taste of what's to come, he argues, as the metaverse begins to revolutionize everything from healthcare and education to shopping and dating.

RayNeo AR glasses were launched at CES 2024 – another step closer to Weinbaum's *Pygmalion's Spectacles*?

MOST CONCURRENTLY PLAYED VIDEOGAME

3

!

Fortnite

There are countless stats to show how much of a phenomenon Epic Games's massive battle royale has become. One of them is from *Fortnite*'s Galactus event on 1 Dec 2020. In the Marvel-themed mission, superheroes engaged in battle with planet-eater Galactus, drawing a record peak of 15.3 million concurrent players to the Season 4 finale.

Fortnite really has been a game-changer. What started in 2017 as a multiplayer shooter pitting players against waves of computer-controlled enemies (*Save the World*) was transformed by a battle-royale mode inspired by *PUBG* (see p.30). The everyone-for-themselves fight for survival was a massive hit, and player counts have been growing ever since. A big part of its enduring popularity is the constantly evolving maps and new features. In the last few years, we've seen floods, black holes and meteor impacts. Who knows what's coming next?

In Season 10, a mysterious meteor hung ominously above the residents of Dusty Divot

Chapter 4's Raven Team Leader (left) and Renegade Lynx (right)

RNG

$3,618,205

Winnings accrued by Canadian esports team Lazarus from 30 *Fortnite* tournaments, making them the **highest-earning** *Fortnite* team.

Thunderbolt-flinger Zeus in Chapter 5: Season 2 – *Myths & Mortals*

XP

Date: 2017
Developer: Epic Games
Publisher: Epic Games

Chapter 4: Season OG took us back in time to the original island with some new skins

MOST PLAYED *FORTNITE* MAP IN 24 HOURS

Even for a game just six years old, the pull of the past can still be strong. On 3 Nov 2023, a return to the original *Fortnite* island from Season OG (Chapter 1, Season 5) drew 44.7 million players for a total of 102 million hours. It was the first of a series revisiting phases from the game's history but also bringing new items, such as the X-4 Stormwing (below).

ADDING SPEED AND SOUND TO THE *FORTNITE* SET LIST

In Dec 2023, Epic aimed to draw in players with diverse preferences via three new *Fortnite* releases. For fans of rhythm games, *Fortnite Festival* encouraged players to take to the main stage or have a jam session. Its first featured artist was The Weeknd. *Rocket Racing* – a mash-up of *Fortnite* with the physics-defying *Rocket League* – was for those who prefer burning rubber in fast cars. You can read about the third game on pp.168–69.

MOST EXPENSIVE *FORTNITE* SKIN

With the heavens swirling across a character's body, the Galaxy skin was a hot item in 2018. But you had to be pretty rich and pretty quick to get your hands on one. It was available only to buyers of a Samsung Galaxy Note 9 phone for $1,299.99 (£1,010), or a Tab S4 tablet at $999.99 (£777). To make it even more exclusive, the offer was only for a brief period from 10 Aug.

FIRST MARVEL CHARACTER IN *FORTNITE*

For a week in May 2018, Thanos – the year's baddest movie villain in *Avengers: Infinity War* (USA) – brought his brooding presence to the year's biggest game. In a special mode, "Infinity Gauntlet", players who found that item could transform into Marvel's Mad Titan, with powers to wipe out structures and players with merely a super-punch.

CELEBRATING THE FORTNITERS

From 16-year-old millionaires to 78-year-old streamers, here we celebrate the diverse record holders who continue to make *Fortnite* the phenomenon that it is.

HIGHEST-EARNING *FORTNITE* PLAYER

As of 11 Apr 2024, Kyle "Bugha" Giersdorf (USA, left) had earned $3,672,300 (£2,909,920) playing *Fortnite*. His most lucrative year was 2019, when at the age of 16 he won $3,080,191 (£2,348,045) – the majority of which came from the $3 m (£2.4 m) individual first prize at the *Fortnite* World Cup (see p.167). That remains the **largest payout for a single player in an esports tournament**.

The **highest-earning *Fortnite* player (female)** is Tina "TINARAES" Perez (USA, right), who has scooped $68,290 (£54,112) since 2018.

MOST WINS OF FORTNITE BATTLE ROYALE

Twitch streamer Ship (USA, below) has notched up 49,240 wins, according to fortnitetracker.com, as of 11 Apr 2024. That's 20,000 more than his nearest rival. Ship also holds the record for **most wins in *Fortnite* (squad)**, with 22,111 wins from 30,145 matches playing as part of a squad. He's the most deadly marksman, too, achieving the **most *Fortnite* Battle Royale eliminations** with 564,856 – a figure some 140,000 higher than his closest rival. Ship has achieved these stats by putting in more than 16,500 hours of game time.

MOST ELIMINATIONS IN *FORTNITE BATTLE ROYALE* USING A QUADSTICK MOUTH-OPERATED JOYSTICK

After an accident at the age of 19, Rocky Stoutenburgh (USA) was left with quadriplegia (paralysis below the neck). Playing as "RockyNoHands", and using a controller operated entirely with his mouth, he has fought his way to 15,573 Battle Royale eliminations. Rocky also boasts the **most Victory Royales using a quadstick** (1,100). He livestreams on Twitch and YouTube, and in 2020 he joined Luminosity Gaming, making him the **first quadriplegic to join a pro esports team**.

OLDEST *FORTNITE* STREAMER ON TWITCH (FEMALE)

Cath Bowie (UK), aged 75, plays *Fortnite* for up to six hours a day and streams it on her grumpygran1948 Twitch channel. As of 16 Apr 2024, she had 15,181 followers on the service, where her description text says she is "just as bad" as when she first started gaming five years ago! While playing, she has been known to sing old Scottish songs like "Ye Cannae Shove Yer Granny Aff a Bus"!

The **oldest male *Fortnite* Twitch streamer** is 78-year-old army veteran grand007pa (USA), who plays on a PC built by his grandson.

MOST PARTICIPANTS IN A VIDEOGAME EMOTE ROUTINE

Some 383 *Fortnite* fans gathered at Paris Games Week in Paris, France, on 28 Oct 2018. Participants turned out in Cuddle Team Leader hoodies and performed classic emotes including Fresh and Hype.

BEST OF THE REST...

As of 16 Apr 2024, the **most wins on *Fortnite* (solo)** was 14,592 by TTV R1xbox (THA); the **most global matches played** was 130,899 by Alien2K18; and the **most minutes played** was 996,149 by primesalad (USA) – equivalent to 691 solid days of gameplay!

CALLING FORTNITE FANS!

Have you collected a ton of *Fortnite* merch? If so, let us know about it! You might just set the record for the **largest collection of *Fortnite* memorabilia**.

Turn to p.8 for more.

LARGEST *FORTNITE* TOURNAMENT

The *Fortnite* World Cup (below), held at the Arthur Ashe Stadium in New York, USA, on 26–28 Jul 2019, reached a peak viewership of 2,334,826 on Twitch and YouTube – the most for a *Fortnite* competition. The event also boasted the **largest prize pool for an esports tournament (solo category)**, with a princely pot of $15,287,500 (£12.3 m). (For the **overall** record, see p.63). The World Cup was due to return in 2020, but the COVID-19 pandemic put paid to that. As of Apr 2024, Epic Games had no plans to resurrect it.

DJ Marshmello wows the crowds at the Arthur Ashe Stadium

It was a *Peely* good tournament!

167

LEGO FORTNITE®

FORTNITE GOES FOR BRICK

In Dec 2023, Epic released *LEGO® Fortnite*. Converting the player character into a LEGO Minifigure, you enter a brave new world which is either sandbox or survival mode – the decision is yours. You then get to work crafting tools, structures, a campfire and plenty more. Up to seven other people can jump into your world while you're in it, too.

Destruction can be just as fun as construction! In *LEGO Fortnite*, dynamite can be crafted

Chickens, cows and sheep enjoy being petted. Brutes? Not so much

❶ Pwn!

Build a wall that surrounds the village where your home base is located. If you don't, there's a good chance you'll be raided by enemies who spawn close and attack at night. Your best bet is going for a high wall that keeps the pesky Brutes out.

LARGEST LEGO-BRICK FORTNITE GUN CUSTOM SCALE MODEL

Built by LEGO designer and YouTuber Kyle L Neville (aka ZaziNombies) from Alberta, Canada, this scale replica of *Fortnite*'s powerful Minigun measures 140 cm (4 ft 6 in) long. It was built using more than 5,000 individual LEGO bricks and weighs over 8 kg (17 lb 10 oz). The giant assault weapon, first revealed on 22 Feb 2018, took Kyle around 60 hours – across seven days – to construct.

The in-game Minigun

Sydney, AUS

Tokyo, JPN

London, UK

New York, USA

LARGEST LEGO-BRICK *FORTNITE* SCULPTURE

This is a whole lot of llama! Teams of LEGO model builders from Enfield in Connecticut, USA, Kladno in Czechia and Jiaxing in Zhejiang, China, each spent 850 hours building 3.6-m-tall (11-ft 9-in) Fortnite llamas in Dec 2023. In the game, the iconic Supply Llama is famously packed full of loot, but these giant LEGO likenesses don't hold any treasure. However, they *are* each made up of 234,323 pieces, and would make a terrible mess if struck with a pickaxe!

The llamas have appeared in various cities around the globe

FORTNITE

LEGO LEGO

FORTNITE

Most ubiquitous videogame character

Number of official professions Mario has had, according to Nintendo. As well as being a plumber, Mario is also a doctor, racer, martial artist, basketball player, soccer player and pro baseball player!

Mario

Nintendo's iconic Italian plumber has appeared in more videogames than any other character over the course of his 43-year gaming career. As of 5 Mar 2024, Mario Mario (his full name) had popped up in 383 titles, including ports and remakes. While most of these appearances are within the *Mario* franchise, he's made cameos in all kinds of other games, too (see below). It all began with *Donkey Kong* (see p.172), which starred a 130-pixel sprite called Jumpman. The tiny red-and-blue character was later renamed after Mario Segale, a real-estate developer who rented a warehouse to Nintendo in Washington, USA. Mario's ubiquity is such there is even an international Mario Day, marked every year on 10 March (MAR10 Day – get it?!) Wahoo!

XP
Debut: 1981
Game: *Donkey Kong*
Total games: 383

Most game performances as the same character

"It's a-me, Mario!" The iconic catchphrase is the work of actor Charles Martinet (USA), who played the Italian plumber 114 times between 1995's *Mario's Game Gallery* and 2022's *Mario + Rabbids Sparks of Hope*. He has also portrayed Luigi, Wario and Waluigi. Martinet stepped down from the role in 2023.

Super Cameo World

Not content with headlining one of the biggest entertainment franchises, Mario has also popped up in a host of other games. He shot some hoops in 2005's *NBA Street V3* (above) and appeared in *Tetris DS* (2006, right). He has also made cameos in the *Zelda* and *Kirby* series, among many others.

Fastest-selling *Mario* game

Switch-exclusive platformer *Super Mario Bros. Wonder* sold 4.3 million units within the first two weeks of going on sale on 20 Oct 2023. Nintendo did point out that their data is limited to titles released for Wii and Nintendo DS onwards, but it's highly unlikely that any *Super Mario* game released on earlier hardware sold any quicker than *Wonder*. It also has a mighty Metacritic score of 92.

Fastest men's half marathon dressed as a videogame character

On 3 Sep 2023, Daniel Titcomb (UK) completed a half marathon in 1 hr 18 min 7 sec in London, UK, clad in a full Mario costume.

The **women's** record is 1 hr 35 min 56.2 sec, and was achieved by Jean Oh (USA) in Toronto, Canada, on 21 Oct 2018 while dressed as Mario's pal Yoshi.

Longest time to beat a level on *Super Mario Maker*

Super Mario Maker (2015) allows players to create and share their own Mario levels. When Braden "ChainChompBraden" Moor (CAN) designed *Trials of Death* in Jan 2016, he made it too hard for even him. Creators have to beat their own level before it can be shared, forcing Braden to endlessly replay his hellish creation. He didn't complete it until 30 Sep 2022, after 4,368 hours of attempts. Sadly, his triumph occurred after the game's servers were shut down, so the level was never relased to the public.

Top 10 best-selling *Mario* games

With total sales of over 700 million units, the plucky plumber heads up the **best-selling videogame franchise**. Here are the 10 biggest hitters, with some speedrun records from the past year.

1

Mario Kart 8 [inc. Deluxe] (2014/2017)
69.04 million

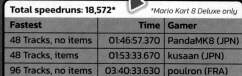

Total speedruns: 18,572*   *Mario Kart 8 Deluxe only

Fastest	Time	Gamer
48 Tracks, no items	01:46:57.370	PandaMK8 (JPN)
48 Tracks, items	01:53:33.670	kusaan (JPN)
96 Tracks, no items	03:40:33.630	poulron (FRA)
96 Tracks, items	03:52:27.080	poulron (FRA)

2

Super Mario Bros. (1985)
40.24 million

Total speedruns: 8,830

Fastest	Time	Gamer
Any% completion	04:54.631	Niftski (USA)

3

Mario Kart Wii (2008)
37.38 million

4

New Super Mario Bros. (2006)
30.80 million

5

New Super Mario Bros. Wii (2009)
30.32 million

6

Super Mario Odyssey (2017)
27.65 million

7

New Super Mario Bros. U Deluxe [inc. New Super Mario Bros. U + New Super Luigi U] (2012/2013/2019)
26.09 million

8

Mario Kart DS (2005)
23.6 million

9

Super Mario World (1990)
20.61 million

10

Super Mario Party (2018)
20.34 million

Super Mario 64 (1996)
Total speedruns: 43,197

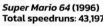

Fastest	Time	Gamer
120-star completion	01:36:21	Weegee (USA)
70-star completion	00:46:28	ikori_o (JPN)
0-star completion	00:06:16.600	Suigi (CAN, above)

Top 10 most critically acclaimed *Mario* games

The franchise's commercial success is matched by its critical acclaim. The rankings here are based on Metacritic scores as of 11 Apr 2024, with the top three games sharing the record for **most critically acclaimed platformer**.

1 **Super Mario Odyssey (2017)** 97

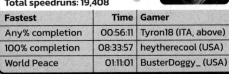

Total speedruns: 19,408		
Fastest	**Time**	**Gamer**
Any% completion	00:56:11	Tyron18 (ITA, above)
100% completion	08:33:57	heytherecool (USA)
World Peace	01:11:01	BusterDoggy_ (USA)

2 **Super Mario Galaxy 2 (2010)** 97

3 **Super Mario Galaxy (2007)** 97

4 **Super Mario Advance 4: Super Mario Bros. 3. (2003)** 94

5 **Super Mario 3D World (2013)** 93

6 **Mario Kart: Super Circuit (2001)** 93

7 **Paper Mario (2000)** 93

8 **Super Mario Bros. Wonder (2023)** 92

9 **Mario Kart 8 Deluxe (2017)** 92

Total speedruns: 1,687		
Fastest	**Time**	**Gamer**
Any% completion	01:22:59	Tsuake (JPN, above)
100% completion	04:57:55	Adr1anGD (USA)

10 **Super Mario Sunshine (2002)** 92

Total speedruns: 11,656		
Fastest	**Time**	**Gamer**
Any% completion	01:13:08	JJsrl (USA)
All Blue Coins	01:51:15	Nanashi745 (JPN)

All speedrun times in hours:minutes:seconds
Source: speedrun.com, as of 22 Apr 2024

Top 10 selection and order based on number of reviews

MARIO vs. DONKEY KONG™

First appearance of Mario

The careers of Mario and his nemesis-turned-friend, Donkey Kong, have been intertwined since their joint debut in 1981's *Donkey Kong*. Back then, it was DK that got top billing, with Mario appearing as "Jumpman". More than four decades later, *Mario vs. Donkey Kong* (2024) sees Donkey Kong slip back into his old ways after being told a toy he wants is out of stock everywhere. There are new worlds and enhanced graphics, but some things don't change with the moustachioed mascot: the game topped sales charts in both Japan and the UK.

Eyeing up Popeye

Shigeru Miyamoto's first choice for his game's hero was spinach-chomping cartoon icon Popeye, but he couldn't get permission. *Donkey Kong*'s success changed that, however, and Miyamoto got the go-ahead to make his Popeye game (a platformer simply called *Popeye*) in 1982.

Action from the 2024 remake of *Mario vs. Donkey Kong*

Best-selling game starring Luigi

In 2019, Mario's timid brother made his unwilling return to the ghost-busting business with *Luigi's Mansion 3* (Next Level Games). The game sees Luigi work his way through a haunted hotel called the ScareScraper, armed with a ghost-vacuum and assisted by his unsettling ectoplasm doppelganger, "Gooigi". As of 31 Mar 2023, it had shifted 13.98 million units worldwide. It also places *Luigi's Mansion 3* in the top 15 best-selling games for the Switch.

Cleaning up with the Poltergust 3000

Players face 17 phantom-filled floors in *LM3*

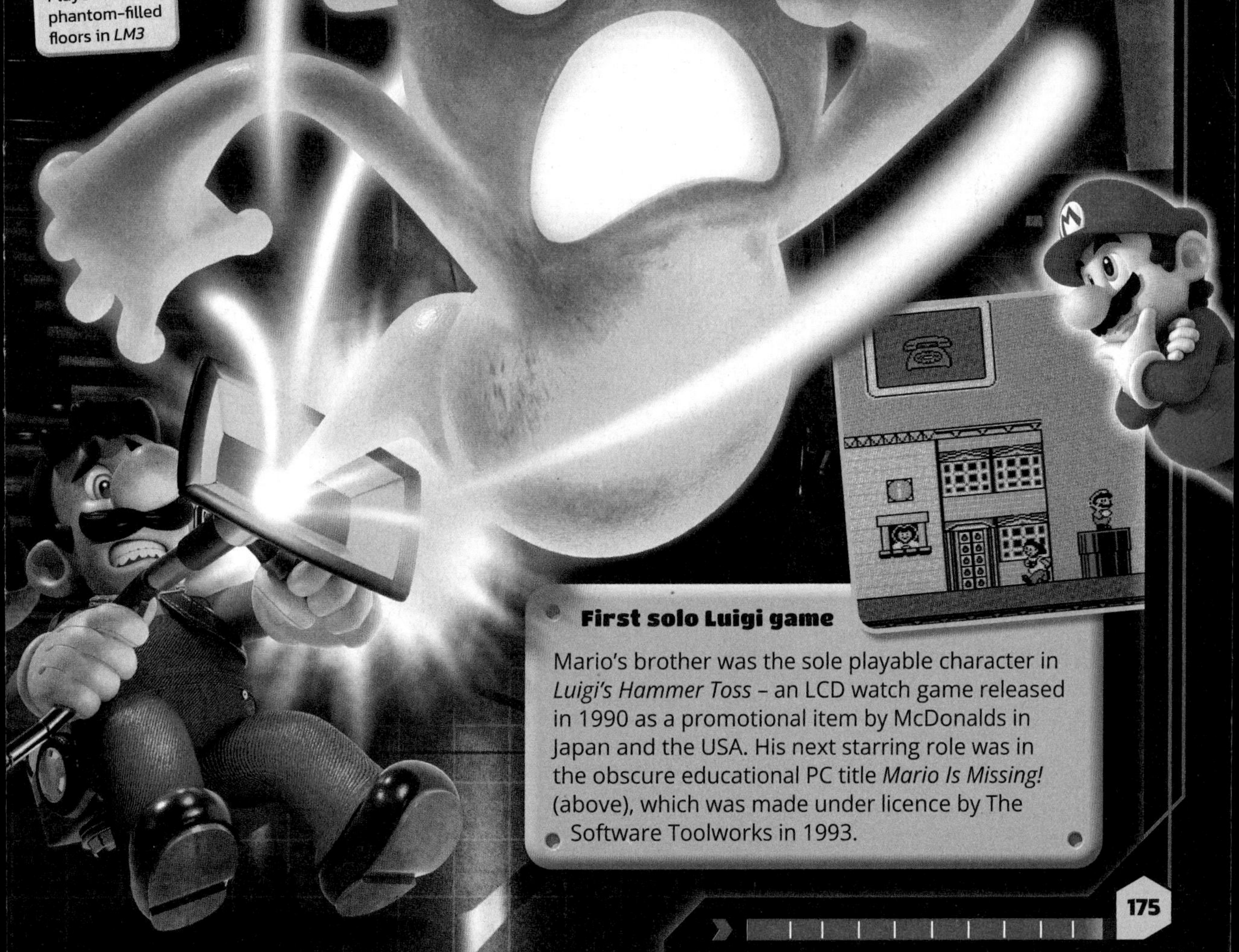

First solo Luigi game

Mario's brother was the sole playable character in *Luigi's Hammer Toss* – an LCD watch game released in 1990 as a promotional item by McDonalds in Japan and the USA. His next starring role was in the obscure educational PC title *Mario Is Missing!* (above), which was made under licence by The Software Toolworks in 1993.

BEST-SELLING VIDEOGAME

XP
Debut: 2011
Developer: Mojang
Publisher: Mojang

Minecraft

Sitting pretty at the top of our list of gaming records is the cultural phenomenon that is *Minecraft*. The game that launched online as a free-to-play demo in May 2009 has gone on to sell more than 300 million copies across numerous platforms. The block-building sandbox sensation has no pre-written story to complete and no mandatory goals to achieve. Despite three console generations passing since *Minecraft*'s launch, players keep coming back to their randomly generated worlds to build fantastical structures (see pp.178–79) and mighty fortresses, or just to walk through the changing landscape (see pp.176–77). In 2014, Microsoft bought Mojang for $2.5 billion (£2 bn) – proof that the block-builder had become a blockbuster!

SPINNING A MINECRAFT WEB

It's not all about the sandbox. A number of spin-off titles have spawned from the *Minecraft* mothership over the years. In 2015, *Minecraft: Story Mode* used the original game's setting to tell an interactive story and incorporate quick-time events. Choices you make in *Story Mode* affect both the episode you're playing and future ones. Five years later came *Dungeons* (right), an action-adventure hack-and-slash in which you conquer randomly generated dungeons. Finally, there is 2023's *Legends* (main picture), in which you're tasked with fortifying a settlement to survive an invasion of piglins from the Nether.

EDUCATIONAL *MINECRAFT*

Teachers have been using Minecraft in classrooms almost since its launch – indeed, the **first course built entirely in-game** was introduced to a Swedish school in 2013. In 2016, Microsoft launched a dedicated schools-focussed version, called *Minecraft Education*.

HIGHEST-EARNING *MINECRAFT* PLAYER ON YOUTUBE

Preston Arsement (USA) built his YouTube following with a series of viral *Minecraft* videos on his channel, "PrestonPlayz". As of 4 Mar 2024, he had 15.4 million subscribers and, according to Forbes, a net worth of $34.6 m (£28.3 m). Preston is pictured here with his wife, Brianna, who is also a YouTuber.

Fallout Mash-Up Pack

Super Mario Mash-Up Pack

Minions x Minecraft

CROSSING OVER TO 'CRAFT

Although *Minecraft* is best known for its fan creations, since 2012, it has featured official videogame, movie and TV crossovers in the form of downloadable "Skin Packs", a few examples of which you can see here. These are often handed out for free as part of promotional events – Mario and friends were added to mark the game's release on the Wii U, for example. Other recent gaming skins include blocky versions of *Street Fighter* (2022), *Sonic* (2021), *PAC-MAN* (2020).

The Simpsons Skin Pack

BEYOND THE HORIZON

When you load a new world in *Minecraft*, the landscape extends 30 million blocks in each direction before you reach the border. Or at least, it's supposed to. In older versions of *Minecraft* (before update 1.8 in Sep 2014), the numbers used to generate the Overworld would become too big to calculate after a certain distance. This created a wild, glitchy landscape that became known as the "Far Lands". The **first person to reach the Far Lands in Survival Mode** was KilloCrazyMan (USA), who completed the quest on 19 Jun 2020 during a blistering speedrun that took him nine months.

But not everyone seeking the Far Lands is in such a rush...

R N G

12,550,812

Blocks walked by *Minecraft* speedrunner KilloCrazyMan during his epic trek to the Far Lands (see left) – the equivalent of 12,550 km (7,800 mi)!

🔓 INORITE!

The most famous traveller to the Far Lands is probably Kurt J Mac (USA, pictured), who embarked upon a fund-raising pixelated pilgrimage back in Mar 2011 (see opposite). As of Apr 2024 – more than 13 years later – he's still walking, with about 58% of the journey ahead of him. Until he was overtaken by KilloCrazyMan (see above), Kurt held the GWR title for the **longest walk in *Minecraft***, covering 3,857,848 blocks as of Aug 2019.

Kurt accepting his official GWR certificate for the **longest walk in *Minecraft***

Kurt has had company on his marathon trek – faithful Wolfie

"It's about the journey not the destination," says Kurt

MOST MONEY RAISED IN A VIDEOGAME CHARITY WALK

Kurt J Mac (USA) from Tacoma in Washington, USA, is on an epic quest to reach the Far Lands, and has been documenting his trip on his YouTube channel "Far Lands or Bust!". As of Apr 2024, he'd walked 8,388,608 blocks (8,388 km; 5,212 mi), made nearly 1,089 videos and livestreams, and grown his audience to over 400,000 subscribers. Thanks to his loyal following, Kurt has raised $478,683.68 (£383,545) for charity during his walk, with beneficiaries including the Child's Play Charity, Direct Relief, PAWS and the Equal Justice Initiative.

BUILDERS KEEP ON BUILDING...

You've read all sorts about *Minecraft* in these pages – from record-breaking sales to gamers embarking on epic quests. Now we come to the building blocks of its success – it's literally just that! Well, that and those who never stop amazing us with their creations.

mine67 said he had to "relearn how to build"

LARGEST ANAMORPHIC ART IN *MINECRAFT*

Anamorphic art is a piece that looks "normal" only from one perspective, as with mine67's *Urban Buildings*. Look left and we see a street scene. Below is a shot from the side. That reveals it to be created in a series of layers, positioned perfectly so they line up to create the illusion. The Frenchman worked on the piece for at least 1,000 hours and took 15,000 screenshots after starting in 2022. "A lot of trial and error," he wrote.

R N G

850,246

Number of blocks used for the **longest tunnel made in *Minecraft* creative mode**, achieved by Samuel "beyond belief" Blight (UK) in London on 10 Jan 2024.

LONGEST *MINECRAFT* SENTENCE

On 14 Oct 2022, Benjamin Elcoate, aka Benjamin E (UK), used 128,358 blocks to create this quote by scientist Alexander Graham Bell. The 124-character sentence was made in 80-block-high letters. As each *Minecraft* block is one cubic metre, this means each letter would be six times the height of the Hollywood sign. The typographer inside Benjamin said he was "really proud of the Gs and the Ws" in his huge creation.

WHEN ONE DOOR CLOSES, ANOTHER OPENS; BUT WE OFTEN LOOK SO LONG AND SO REGRETFULLY UPON THE CLOSED DOOR THAT WE DO NOT SEE THE ONE WHICH HAS OPENED FOR US.

LARGEST LEGO® *MINECRAFT* DIORAMA

This 3D fantasy cityscape covered 17.13 m² (184 sq ft) at the Brick 2014 event in London. Visitors to the exhibition, especially children, didn't need asking twice to pitch into the project by building their own contribution on square boards. When these were assembled into one piece, it was 8.83 m (28 ft 11 in) long and 1.87 m (6 ft 1 in) wide at its broadest point.

MINECRAFT RECORDS YOU CAN ATTEMPT AT HOME

For these six *Minecraft* challenges, we've set you up below with some of the major do's and don'ts. Scan the QR code for the challenges, detailed official guidelines and instructions on how to register your application. Happy blocking!

Fastest time to flip a pig

This is a special record for our under-16 readers. Use a device with touch controls, such as a tablet or phone. To flip the pig, you need to use a "Dinnerbone" nametag, which has an unusual effect. When the pig is upside down, you're done. As with all these challenges – have fun!

Fastest time to build a castle

Gather your items quickly in our build challenges. Your castle has to have four walls, four turrets with battlements, an opening to the castle with a portcullis, a water-filled moat and a wooden bridge. The clock stops when you put a coloured banner at the top, making the castle yours!

Fastest time to build a house

Your home must cover at least a 4x4 block. Go as big as you like, but it'll take more time. Make sure you leave gaps for the door and a window. The house above isn't quite finished; it still needs a sloping roof. When you walk around your creation, the clock will stop.

Fastest time to build an iron golem

To create a golem, you'll need to place four iron blocks in a "T" shape and then put a carved pumpkin on top. You have to start with only 64 pieces of iron ore, though – everything else, including the shears you'll need to carve the pumpkin, have to be crafted from scratch.

Fastest time to make and eat 3 cakes

Grab your ingredients – milk, sugar, egg and wheat. The first cake must be made and scoffed (all six slices) before you can put the ingredients for the next one in the mixing bowl. No auto-crafting! We all hope that making and baking the cakes has given you a good appetite!

Largest LEGO brick *Minecraft* Steve

You can go solo on this record attempt, or you can team up with friends. First off, make sure your piece looks like Steve. Feel free to give him a sword or pickaxe or another prop from *Minecraft*. Send us photos and videos showing its dimensions. Then keep your fingers crossed!

ROUND-UP

Stop press! We're not quite finished yet. Here are some last-minute gaming additions to our Records Database, confirmed by our expert adjudicators just before *GWR Gamer's Edition 2025* went to press.

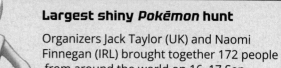

Largest shiny *Pokémon* hunt

Organizers Jack Taylor (UK) and Naomi Finnegan (IRL) brought together 172 people from around the world on 16–17 Sep 2022 for a livestreamed shiny Pokémon search. The pair also organized the **most shiny *Pokémon* variants collected in 24 hours by an online community** (588).

Dryang101

AsylixTheGreat

Longest winning streak as a duo in *Fall Guys*

On 27 Mar 2024, professional *Fall Guys* (Mediatonic, 2020) players AsylixTheGreat and Dryang101 (both USA) completed an impressive winning streak of 76 in a row. It took the duo three months' hard graft to defeat the previous world record of 68.

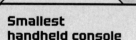

Smallest handheld console

Described by its makers Tiny Circuits (USA) as an "itty-bitty game system", the Thumby measures 29.5 x 18 x 8.5 mm (1.16 x 0.7 x 0.3 in) and has 2 MB of storage. It comes with preloaded games, and more are available to download. Try your hand (well, fingertip!) at rhythm game *Dance!*, driving game *Tiny Traffic* and puzzler *Maze Speedrun*.

ACTUAL SIZE

R N G

01:05:15

The **fastest glitchless completion of** *The Elder Scrolls V: Skyrim* (Bethesda, 2011), by Lithium_L (JPN) on 24 Apr 2024.

Highest score on NES *Tetris* (ROM hack)

On 15 Apr 2024, Alex "Alex T" Thach (USA) registered a high score of 16,700,760 on the NES classic. While this is significantly higher than the 8,952,432 achieved by P1xelAndy (see p.143), Alex T reached his record score using a ROM hack that bypasses the game's crash screen, allowing players to continue racking up more points. In line with the wider *Tetris* community, Guinness World Records considers this "no-crash" version a valid subcategory of the record.

Fastest 120-star completion of *Super Mario 64*

Weegee (USA) completed *Super Mario 64* (Nintendo, 1996) in 1 hr 36 min 21 sec on 16 Jan 2024, according to speedrun.com. He used the newly discovered "Carpetless" exploit to skip a section in the *Rainbow Ride* stage that requires Mario to ride a slow-moving magic carpet to the top of the level.

Largest collection of videogame kiosks

Travis Alfrey (right) of Austin, Texas, USA, has amassed 100 gaming kiosks. These marketing devices were placed in stores to draw attention to the latest consoles. "Kiosks have become a cultural phenomenon," says Travis, "and are as recognizable, important and iconic as the consoles themselves."

Highest score in *HELLDIVERS 2* mini-game *Stratagem Hero*

With a score of 13,059,604, Mellody Zanin (USA) became the first gamer to pass 10 million points in the *Stratagem Hero* mini-game within the third-person shooter *HELLDIVERS 2* (Arrowhead Game Studios, 2024). Mellody inputted memorized directions for almost six hours straight as her friends in voice chat cheered her on to victory during the gruelling marathon. Talk about dedication!

Bold entries in the index indicate an entry in our Top 100.

2K 42
7th Beat Games 15

A
AbleGamers 116, 117
Accessibility in Gaming 116–17
action-adventure games 66, 73, 75, 150–51, 174
Activision 28, 29, 35
Activision Blizzard 10, 56
Actua Soccer 128
Adopt Me! 52, 146
Adventure 37
Afghani, Kevin 10
Air–Sea Battle 93
Akupara Games 15
Alan Wake II 14, 15
Amanita Design 15
Among Us 52, 77, 78, 89, 92; *The Skeld* 39
Angry Birds 50, 53
Animal Crossing: New Horizons 61, 70, 79
Anthology of the Killer 15
Apex Legends 87
arcade cabinets 71, 74; LEGO® replica 37
arcade games 51, 60, 71
Arena of Valor 34
Arhancet, Steve 109
Arsement, Preston 177
Artiaga, Andrew 143
Artwick, Bruce 48
Asgard's Wrath 2 15
Asimov, Isaac 81
Assassin's Creed: Assassin's Creed II 76; *Assassin's Creed Valhalla* 124; *Assassin's Creed Valhalla: Dawn of Ragnarok* 99
Assetto Corsa 41
Asteroids 37, 93
Astro's Playroom 76
Atari 51, 93; *Atari 50* 93; Atari 2600 37, 93; LEGO® replica 37
Atlus 73
Atomic Heart 15
Avalanche Software 15, 97
Avengers: Age of Ultron 19; *Endgame* 151; *Infinity War* 151, 165
awards: BAFTA Games 14, 99; D.I.C.E. Awards 15; Emmys 57; The Game Awards 14; Game Developers Choice 15; Game of the Year 103; Golden Joysticks 14, 23; Independent Games Festival 15; Nickelodeon Kids' Choice 123; Steam Awards 15
Awards round-up 14–15

B
Baldur's Gate 3 10, 14, 15, 23, 95
balloon costumes 155
Balvin, J 110
Bandai Namco 28, 43, 74, 123
Barbie (movie) 98
Basic Math 93
Basketball! 42
Batman: Arkham Asylum 106; *Arkham City* 106; *The Telltale Series* 76

battle royale 29, 30, 53, 125, 164–65, 166
Battlefield V 94
Best-selling 1st-gen console 49
Best-selling 9th-gen console 45
Best-selling American sports game 42
Best-selling console 138–39
Best-selling farm-life sim 79
Best-selling fighting game series 43
Best-selling first-person shooter series 118–19
Best-selling game based on a movie 55
Best-selling game for Nintendo Switch 70
Best-selling game soundtrack 58
Best-selling game starring a solo female protagonist 40
Best-selling instrument game 35
Best-selling MMO 24
Best-selling Nintendo game 61
Best-selling Nintendo home console 54
Best-selling PC exclusive 88
Best-selling PS4 exclusive 32
Best-selling PS5 exclusive 21
Best-selling racing series 41
Best-selling RPG series 152–55
Best-selling videogame 176–77
Best-selling videogame heroine 140–41
Bethesda 10, 14, 56, 85, 91, 101
Biles, Simone 123
billion-dollar sales 35, 150–51
BioWare 50, 84, 85
Black, Jack 69
Blackjack 93
Bland, Darren 90
blindfolded speedrun 65
Blizzard 15, 24, 27, 64, 88, 107, 113
BlizzCon 113
Bloodborne 76
Bloodstained: Ritual of the Night 75
Blox Fruits 146
Bond movies 55
Bowie, Cath 167
Brasil Game Show 113
Breakout 51
Brereton Diaz, Ben 90
Brookhaven RP 146
BTS 123
Bungie 85
Burch, Ashly 40

C
Call of Duty 10, 28, 56, 102, 118–21; *Advanced Warfare* 120, 121; *Black Ops* 120; *Black Ops 4* 120, 121; *Black Ops II* 120, 121; *Black Ops III* 118, 120, 121; *Black Ops Cold War* 120; *Black Ops: Declassified* 120; *Black Ops – Zombies*

100, 118; *Call of Duty 2* 46, 119, 120; *Call of Duty 3* 120; *Call of Duty 4: Modern Warfare* 119, 120; *Ghosts* 119, 120, 121; *Infinite Warfare* 120, 121; *Mobile* 52; *Modern Warfare* 120; *Modern Warfare 2* 119, 120, 121; *Modern Warfare 3* 119, 120, 121; *Modern Warfare II* 120, 121, 151; *Modern Warfare III* 120, 121; *Vanguard* 120; *Warzone* 29, 125; *Warzone Mobile* 29; *World at War – Zombies* 118; *WWII* 120
Call of Duty League Championship 121
Candy Crush 53, 56
Capcom 14, 59, 73, 87
Capcom Cup 130
Capcom vs. SNK 2: Mark of the Millennium 2001 139
Catley, Steph 127
CCP Games 105
CD Projekt Red 14, 23, 30, 101, 134, 135
cel-shading 62
Centipede 37
Chapman, Kevin 124
charity fundraising: marathons 124, 125, 127; speedruns 65; tournaments 144; videogame walk 179
Chinajoy 113
Chrono Trigger 65
Chú Mó 15
Clark, Roger 108
Club Penguin 52
Cocoon 14, 15
collections, gaming 80; *see also* memorabilia
Collina, Pierluigi 128
Color TV-Game 49
Combat 93
ConcernedApe 79
Conqueror's Blade 87
consoles 44–46; best-sellers 45, 49, 54, 138–39; HD standard 46; LEGO® replicas 37, 39
conventions 19, 112–13, 136–37
Cordovilla, David 62
Core Design 31, 140
cosplay 19, 112, 136–37, 141, 143; marathons 171
Counter-Strike 53; *Counter-Strike 2* 30, 87, 95; *Global Offensive* 28
COVID-19 pandemic 11, 77, 79
Crash Bandicoot 56
Crazyracing Kartrider 52
cross-overs 72, 85, 130, 133, 177
Crossfire 53
Crystal Dynamics 141
Csépe, Szabolcs 124, 125
Cullins, Joshua 154
Cuphead 58
Curry, Shirley 94
Cyberpunk 2077 30, 95, 134–35, 163; *Phantom Liberty* 14, 135

D
D-pad 44
Dark Age of Camelot 107
Dave the Diver 14, 15
Degen, A. 15
Deltarune 65
DePetrillo, Thomas 19
Destiny 85
Detective Pikachu

(movie) 153
Diablo series 15, 88
Digimon 31
Digital Eclipse 93
Dini, Dino 129
disabilities, gamers with 116–17, 166; esports teams 28, 117; Quadstick 29
Dishonored 56
Donkey Kong 44, 71, 74, 170, 172, 174
Doom 56, 100
Dota 2 28, 30, 63, 109
Dragon Ball 43
Dragon Nest 52
Dreamcast 62, 138, 139
Dungeon Fighter Online 52
Dungeons & Dragons 10, 23

E
EA 11, 41, 46, 96, 126, 127, 128, 129
EA Sports FC 24 11, 129, 133
earnings: esports 27, 63, 64, 109, 120, 130, 149, 164, 166, 167; female gamers 27, 148, 166; YouTube streamer 177
Easter eggs 100
eFootball 2024 128
Eilish, Billie 123
Eiyuden Chronicle: Hundred Heroes 75
Elden Ring 95, 103
The Elder Scrolls 56; *Daggerfall* 91; *Skyrim* 101
Elite 84
Epic Games 52, 134, 163, 164, 167, 168
esports: earnings 27, 63, 64, 109, 120, 130, 149, 164, 166, 167; female players 27; LEC Championship 20; online audiences 114–15; para-esports 28, 117, 166
Evans, Barry 31
EVE Online 105, 113, 162; *Fury at FWST–8* 105; *War for New Eden* 105
EVE Fanfest 113
Eyedentity Games 52
Eyeguys 15

F
Fable 56
Facebook (now Meta) 163
Facepunch Studios 88
Fallout 38, 56; *Fallout 4* 95
Famicom 44
Fantasy Westward Journey 52
farming simulators 79
Fastest entertainment property to gross $1 billion 150–51
Fastest-growing non-mobile game 29
Fastest-selling Nintendo game 72
Fastest-selling PlayStation exclusive 99
female characters 40, 119, 140–41
FIFA 109; *FIFA 16* 127; *FIFA 18* 127; *FIFA 22* 124, 127; *FIFA 23* 126, 127; *International Soccer* 126, 128
fighting games 43, 124, 130–31
Final Fantasy (FF) 31; *FFVII Rebirth* 14; *FFVII Remake* 32; *FFVIII* 58; *FFX* 139; *FFXII* 139; *FFXIV: Endwalker* 107; *FFXIV: Shadowbringers* 107; *FFXIV: Stormblood* 107; *FFXV* 15; *FFXVI* 14

Firesprite 14
First console gamepad 44
First dog to hold a speedrun record 18
First HD videogame console 46
First interactive game documentary 93
First multi-platform game 86
First player to reach the killscreen in *Tetris* (NES) 83
Five Nights at Freddy's (movie) 68
Flight Simulator II 48
Football Manager 90, 124; *Football Manager 2010* 90; *Football Manager 2024* 90
Fortnite 52, 132, 134, 144, 163, 164–69; *Fortnite Battle Royale* 166; *Fortnite Festival* 165; *LEGO® Fortnite* 168–69; *Fortnite* sculpture 169
Forza series 41, 47; *Forza Horizon 3* 98; *Forza Horizon 5* 98, 116
Fox, Toby 65, 101
FPS games 30, 55, 102, 118–21
Francis, Pope 101
Free Guy (movie) 145
free-to-play games 102
FromSoftware 95, 103
Fruit Ninja 53
FS1 Flight Simulator 48

G
G-Star 113
Galaxian 84
Game & Watch 33, 44
The Game Awards 14
Game Boy 54, 67, 152
Game Boy Advance 54
Game Boy Color 67
Game Developers Choice Awards 15
Game Freak 154
Game Over podcast 62
Game the Record 132–33
Game of the Year awards 103
GameCube 139
Gamefam Studios 147
Games Done Quick 65
Gamescom 112, 113
Gaming at the Movies 68–69
Garatea, Ibai Llanos 89
Garry's Mod 88
Gears of War 56
GeForce Now 87
Geometric Interactive 14, 15
Ghost of Tsushima 32, 76
Gibson, Willis 3, 83, 143
Giersdorf, Kyle 166
GKART/QQ Speed 52
God of War 32, 76; *Ragnarök* 99; *Valhalla* 99
Golden Axe 80
Golden Joysticks 14, 23
GoldenEye (movie) 55
GoldenEye 007 55
González, Albert 62
Goossens, Victor 109
Gran Turismo (GT) 41, 47; *GT3: A-Spec* 139; *GT4* 139; *GT7* 124; *GT Sport* 94
Grand Theft Auto (GTA) 151; *GTA III* 139; *GTA IV* 156; *GTA V* 92, 100, 150–51; *GTA VI* 11, 92; *GTA Online* 151; *GTA: San Andreas* 139; *GTA: Vice City* 139
Greatest *Gamer's Edition* recreations 148–49

Greene, Brendan 30
Gremlin 128
Guerrilla 14, 40
Guild Wars 2 107
Guitar Hero III: Legends of Rock 35
Gunn, Kat 148
Gyromite 18

H
Haaland, Erling 129
Habitat 162
Half-Life 2 88
Halfbrick Studios 52, 53
Halo 56, 148; *Halo 2: Original Soundtrack and New Music, Volume One* (album) 58; *Halo 4* 58
Harbidge, Cody 125
Harmony Hills 147
Harnes, Anne Martha 157
Harry Potter videogames 15, 95, 97
Hart, Paul 15
Hart, Ryan 148
Haunted Houses 93
Healthy Food Challenge 133
Heavyweight Champ 130
HELLDIVERS 2 95
Hello Games 14, 81, 163
Hesse, Tyson 25
Hi-Fi Rush 14, 15
Highest peak viewership on Twitch 89
Highest-earning esports player 63
Highest-earning esports team 109
Highest-earning female esports player 27
Highest-grossing biographical movie based on a game 47
Hogwarts Legacy 15, 95, 97
Hollow Knight 137
Holmes, Dan 139
Homeworld 84
Honkai: Star Rail 14
Honor of Kings 34, 52
Honor of Kings International Championship 34
Horizon Zero Dawn series: *Call of the Mountain* 14; *Forbidden West* 38, 40; *Zero Dawn* 36, 40, 76
Hostyn, Sasha "Scarlett" 27
Hot Wheels Unleashed 133
How to be a record breaker 8–9

I
id Software 56, 100
Ideaworks 100
ihobo 91
Imangi Studios 53
Indy 500 93
Infamous: Second Son 76
Infinity Train 25
Infinity Ward 29, 46, 118
Infogrames 73
injuries, Wii-related 61
Injustice 2 106
Innersloth 52, 77, 89
Insomniac Games 11, 15, 21, 32, 76
Intel Extreme Masters 27
International Superstar Soccer 128

J
Jack in the Dark 73
Jagex 52
Jet Set Radio 62
Jetpack Joyride 52
Jolie, Angelina 31, 68, 137, 141

Jouniaux, Alexandre 125
Jovovich, Milla 59, 68
Just Dance 122–23

K
karting games 41, 70
KCET 126
Khurana, Simar 133
Kick Off 129
Kickstarter 75
Kiloo 53, 110
King 53
Kingdom Hearts 15, 139
Kirby: Planet Robobot 39
Konami 126, 128

L
Labyrinthine 15
Lara Croft 40, 137, 140–41
Lara Croft: Tomb Raider (movie) 31, 68, 141
Largest arcade cabinet 74
Largest cast for a videogame 108
Largest collection of *Tomb Raider* memorabilia 31
Largest esports team for people with disabilities 28
Largest first-person shooter battle 102
Largest Game Boy Color 67
Largest game convention 112–13
Largest game-streaming service 87
Largest gaming acquisition 56
Largest gaming collection 80
Largest gathering of people dressed as game characters 136–37
Largest human image of a Pokémon 60
Largest mobile game prize pool 34
Largest multiplayer PvP battle 105
Largest playable area in a hand-crafted open-world game 91
Largest playable Game & Watch device 33
Largest third-party Game Pass launch 66
Largest user-generated content platform 146–47
Largest Xbox Studio launch 98
Larian Studios 14, 23, 95
The Last of Us 57, 100; *The Last of Us Part I* 15; *The Last of Us Part II* 32
League of Legends 14, 22, 89, 125; LEC Championship 20; World Championship 114–15
Lee Sang-hyeok 115
The Legend of Zelda 38, 159, 161; *A Link Between Worlds* 161; *A Link to the Past* 160; *Breath of the Wild* 70, 72, 156, 161; *Four Swords* 160; *Four Swords Adventures* 161; *Link's Awakening* 160; *Majora's Mask* 158, 160; movie 11; *Ocarina of Time* 65, 156–59, 160; *Oracle of Seasons/Oracle of Ages* 160; *Phantom Hourglass* 161; series timeline 160–61; *Skyward Sword* 160; *Spirit Tracks* 161; *Tears of the Kingdom* 14, 15, 72, 157, 161; *The Minish

Cap 160; *The Wind Waker* 160; *Tri Force Heroes* 161; *Twilight Princess* 160
LEGO®: game map 38; gaming sets 36–37; *Minecraft* diorama 181; MOCs 38–39
LEGO® blockbusters 36–37
LEGO® Fortnite 168–69
LEGO® Harry Potter 97
LEGO® MOCs 38–39
LEGO® Star Wars: The Force Awakens 39, 50
Lenaerts, Wout 124
Lethal Company 15
Level Infinite 34
life sims 96
Light Tennis 49
Linden Labs 162
Longest game campaign/story 73
Longest single game of *Football Manager* 90
Longest videogame marathon 122–23
Longest-running arcade series 51
Longest-running esports game 64
Longest-running fighter series 130–31
Longest-running flight sim series 48
Longest-running gaming comic character 25
Longest-running gaming podcast 62
Longest-running gaming soccer series 126–27
Longest-running videogame series 104
Lost Ark 30
LucasArts 50, 162
Luigi's Hammer Toss 175
Luigi's Mansion 3 175
Lumen in the Land of Nanite 141

M
Mac, Kurt J 178, 179
Maddigan, Kristofer 58
Magnavox Odyssey 42
MapleStory 52
marathons 24, 35, 122–25, 127
Mardenborough, Jann 47
Mario 170–175: *Mario is Missing!* 175; *Mario vs. Donkey Kong* 174; *Mario's Game Gallery* 170; *Mario + Rabbids Sparks of Hope* 170; *Super Mario 3D World* 173; *Super Mario 64* 37, 172; *Super Mario Advance 4* 173; *Super Mario Bros.* 61, 172; *Super Mario Bros. 3* 71, 173; *Super Mario Bros. Movie* 24, 68, 69, 159; *Super Mario Bros. Wonder* 10, 11, 14, 171, 173; *Super Mario Galaxy* 173; *Super Mario Maker* 149, 171; *Super Mario Odyssey* 70, 172, 173; *Super Mario Party* 123, 172; *Super Mario Sunshine* 173; *Super Mario World* 172
Mario Kart: *Mario Kart 8* 61, 172; *Mario Kart 8 Deluxe* 70, 79, 132, 173; *Mario Kart DS* 61, 172; *Mario Kart Wii* 61, 172; *Super Circuit* 173; *Super Mario Kart* 149
Martin, George RR 103
Martinet, Charles 10, 170

Martinez, Christopher 83
Marvel's Spider-Man 21, 32, 76; *Marvel's Spider-Man 2* 11, 15, 21, 32, 106; *Marvel's Spider-Man 3* 21; *Miles Morales* 21; *Remastered* 21
Mattel 128
Maxis 96
Mediterranea Inferno 15
MeepCity 146
"Megalovania" 101
memorabilia 31, 157, 167
Messi, Lionel 127
Metal Gear Solid 139, 159
Metaverse gaming 162–63
Microsoft 10, 56, 139, 176; games 48; Xbox 10, 80, 129, 139; Xbox 360 46, 128; Xbox Adaptive Controller 116; Xbox Game Pass 66; Xbox One 42
Microsoft Flight Simulator 48
Middleton, Dan 148
Midnight Club 41
Midway 43
miHoYo 14
Minecraft 36, 52, 56, 66, 89, 91, 92, 101, 113, 125, 132, 137, 148, 163, 176–81; home challenges 181; *Dungeons* 176; *Education* 177; *Legends* 176; *VR Mode* 124; *Story Mode* 176
Minecraft Live 113
Mini World 52
Minions x Minecraft 175
Miniplay Inc. 52
Mintrocket 14
Missile Command 93
Miyamoto, Shigeru 11, 174
Miyazaki, Hidetaka 103
MMOFPS 102
MMORPGs 88, 107, 124, 162
MMOs 24, 107, 162
MOBAs 22, 30, 34, 63, 117
mobile gaming 29, 34
Mobile Legends: Bang Bang 117
Mojang 52, 89, 101, 176
Monster Hunter 73, 87
Monteiro, Antonio 80
Mori, Hamako 94
Mortal Kombat 14, 43
Moss 116
Most concurrent players for a debut on Steam 95
Most concurrent players on Steam 30
Most concurrent views for an esports event 114–15
Most concurrently played videogame 164–65
Most critically acclaimed MMORPG 107
Most critically acclaimed *Star Wars* game 50
Most critically acclaimed superhero game 106
Most critically acclaimed survival-horror game 59
Most critically acclaimed videogame 156–59
Most Emmy wins for a game adaptation 57
Most followers on Twitch 144–45
Most Game of the Year awards 103
Most Golden Joysticks won in a single year 23
Most money raised by a speedrunning event 65
Most planets in a game universe 81

Most platinumed PlayStation game 76
Most PlayStation trophies won 26
Most popular game (by monthly active users) 77
Most popular social simulation 96
Most popular virtual pet app 82
Most ported videogame 142–43
Most pre-orders for a PC game 134–35
Most speedrun videogame 110–11
Most ubiquitous videogame character 170–71
Most viewed game trailer in 24 hours 92
Most viewed game on Twitch 22
Most viewed single-player game on Twitch 97
Most viewers for a debut stream on Twitch 78
Most wins of the LEC 20
Most-funded game on Kickstarter 75
movies: biographical 47; body counts 59; box office 24, 47, 153; game-based 11, 24, 47, 57, 59, 68–69, 141, 153, 159; movie-to-game conversions 55; prolific videogame movie stars 59
MrBeast 82
Mundfish 15
Muñiz, Carlos Garcia 124
Muros, Francisco Javier 124
music: albums 58, 122, 140; concerts 58, 147, 163; from movies 69; scores 14; theme songs 58
My Talking Tom 82
Mysteries of the Sea/*Mysteries of the Deep* 33

N
N64 156, 158
Narutimetto Akuseru 2 125
NASL Soccer 128
Nathan, Alexander 28
Naughty Dog 15, 57, 100, 116
NBA 2K20 42
NBA Street V3 170
NDcube 123
Need for Speed 41, 46
Neople 52
NetEase Games 52
NetherRealm Studios 43
Neversoft 35
New Horizon Interactive 52
New World 95
Newman, Garry 88
Nexon 52
Next Level Games 175
Niantic 52
Nickelodeon All-Star Brawl 133
Nickelodeon Kids' Choice Awards 123
Nier: Automata 100
Ninja (Richard Tyler Blevins) 144–45
Nintendo 11, 139, 154, 171; 3DS 54, 156, 159; Color TV-Game 49; Famicom 44; Game & Watch 33, 44; Game Boy 54, 67, 152; Game Boy Advance 54; Game Boy Color 67; GameCube 139; games 11, 14, 18, 44, 61, 65, 71, 72,

74, 79; N64 156, 158; NES 37, 44, 138; Nintendo Controller 116; SNES 85; Switch 10, 11, 54, 55, 70, 79; Wii 54, 61; Wii U 54
Nintendo Campus Challenge 71
Nishikado, Tomohiro 51, 100
Nishiyama, Takashi 130
No Man's Sky 14, 81, 163
Norindr, Marie-Laure 148

O
Ocasio-Cortez, Alexandria 78
Octopus 33
Oculus 163
Okabe, Keiichi 100
Oldest streamer 94
Once Upon a Jester 15
open-world gaming 47, 66, 84, 91, 98
The Oregon Trail 104; *Boom Town* 104
Origin Systems 162
Outer Wilds 85
Outfit7 82
Outplay Entertainment 111
Overwatch 19, 56

P
PAC-MAN 60, 74
Palworld 30, 66, 95
Paper Mario 173
PARA.Ghost 117
Paris Games Week 113, 167
PAX West 113
PC gaming 48, 66, 88
Peanut Butter (dog) 18
Pelé's Soccer 129
Perez, Tina 166
Permastunned Gaming 28
Perry, Katy 122
Persona 5 73
Persson, Markus 113, 137
pets: *Adopt Me!* 52, 146; pet apps 82
Pharris, Tyler 120
Phonopolis 15
Pikachu 152, 153
Pillars of Eternity 75
Pin Bot 71
PlanetSide 2 84, 102
PlatinumGames 100
Playground Games 98
PlayStation 80, 99, 138; in-game trophies 26, 76; LEGO® replica 39
PlayStation 2 129, 138, 139
PlayStation 3 128, 138, 150
PlayStation 4 21, 42, 99, 138
PlayStation 5 11, 21, 32, 45, 99, 138
PlayStation Portable 138
PlayStation Portal 11
PlayStation Vita 138
PlayStation VR2 14
Pocket Pair 30, 66, 95
podcasts 62
Pokémon 38, 60, 118, 125, 152–55; *Blue* 61, 152; *Crystal* 61; *Diamond* 61; *Emerald* 61; *GO* 52, 69, 153; *Gold* 61; *Green* 61, 152; *Pearl* 61; *Platinum* 61; *Red* 61, 152; *Ruby* 61; *Sapphire* 61; *Scarlet* 72, 154; *Shield* 125; *Silver* 61; *Sleep* 153; *Violet* 72, 154; *Yellow* 61
Pokémon: Detective Pikachu (movie) 69
Pokémon: The Series (TV) 153
Pokémon World Championships 155
Polyarc 116
Polyphony Digital 47, 94

Pondsmith, Mike 135
Pong 93
Popeye 174
ported videogames 142–43
postage stamps 140
prize money 22, 27, 34, 63, 121, 130, 166, 167
Pro Evolution Soccer 126, 128
Przybylowicz, Marcin 101
Psychonauts 56
PUBG: Battlegrounds 30, 53, 95, 164; *Mobile* 53
puzzle games 125, 142–43

Q
Quadratrank 93
Quadstick 29, 166
Quake 56

R
racing games 41, 98, 124; *see also* kart racing games
Rage 56
Raisman, Aly 123
RAM: Random Access Mayhem 15
Rare 55
Rarest Nintendo game 71
Raven Software 29
RayNeo AR glasses 163
real-time strategy games 27
REC Room 163
Red Bull Kumite 131
Red Dead Redemption 148
Red Dead Redemption 2 15, 100, 108, 163
Redaelli, Lorenzo 15
Reeves, Keanu 134
Remedy Entertainment 14
Resident Evil 94; *Code: Veronica* 59; *Resident Evil 4* 14, 59
Resident Evil: Afterlife (movie) 59
Reynolds, Ryan 69
Rhythm Doctor 15
rhythm games 122, 125, 165
Riot Games 14, 20, 22, 89
Roberts, Rob 62
Roblox 52, 146–47, 162
Rock Band 35, 125
Rocket League 76, 149, 165
Rocket Racing 165
Rockstar 11, 15, 100, 108, 163
Rocksteady Studios 106
Rodrigo, Olivia 123
Rogue Planet Games 102
Rolle, Jorell 125
Ronaldo, Cristiano 127
Rosenfeld, Daniel 101
Rovio Entertainment 53
RPGs 10, 24, 30, 50, 58, 73, 84, 85, 91, 97, 124, 135, 146, 152–55, 163
Rules of Survival 52
Runescape 52
Russell, Steve 86

S
S&box 88
Sabotage Studios 14
Sad Owl Studios 14
San Diego Comic-Con 113
sandbox games 88, 162–63, 176; *see also* open-world gaming
Santa Monica Studio 99
Santaolalla, Gustavo 100
Santos, Rodrigo Martín 31
Sanzaru Games 15
Schmidt, Robin 124
Schwartz, Ben 69
sci-fi 50, 64, 84–85, 86, 162, 163
Sea of Stars 14

Second Life 162
Sega 11, 80, 128, 130, 138, 139, 147
Sensible Soccer 129
Shadowlands 88
Shenmue III 75
Shimomura, Yoko 15
Siciński, Paweł 90
Sifu 15
sign language 116
Silent Hill 31
Silk 91
SimCity 96
The Sims 96
simulations 48, 79, 96
skins 165, 175, 177
Sky Skipper 71
Skylanders 31
Sledgehammer Games 119
Sloclap 15
Smilegate 30, 53
SNES 70, 80, 85
Snow Crash (novel) 162
soccer 11, 124, 126–29; women's soccer 127
The Software Toolworks 175
Sonic the Hedgehog series: comic books 25; movie adaption 69; *Sonic Mania* 25; *Sonic Origin* 25; *Sonic Speed Simulator* 147; *Sonic Superstars* 11; *Sonic the Hedgehog* 31, 36; *Sonic the Hedgehog 2* 25
Sons of the Forest 95
Sony 11, 138; Access Controller 116; games 11, 21, 32, *see also* PlayStation
Sotala, Joona 64
SoulCalibur 156
Soule, Jeremy 101
soundtracks 51, 58, 100–101
Space Invaders 51, 100
Spacewar! 86
Spears, Douglas 125
speedruns 25, 79, 110–11, 118, 119, 135, 151, 154, 157, 159, 172, 173; blindfolded 65; charity fund-raising 65; dogs 18
Spider-Man 21; *No Way Home* 151; *Spider-Man 2* 32, 99; *Total Mayhem* 21
Spiel 113
SpongeBob SquarePants: Battle for Bikini Bottom – Rehydrated 26
Spotify 101
Spyro 56
Square Enix 14, 65, 107
Star Fox 85
Star Wars 50; *Jedi Fallen Order* 85; *Knights of the Old Republic* 50, 84; LEGO® 39; *The Force Awakens* 50, 151; *The Skywalker Saga* 39
StarCraft 27, 64, 124; *Brood War* 109; *Remastered* 27
StarCraft II 64; *Wings of Liberty* 27, 109
Stardew Valley 79
Starfield 10, 14, 15, 56, 85
State of Decay 2 125
Steam: concurrent players 30, 95; Steam Awards 15
Steele, Samuel 125
Stoutenburgh, Rocky 166
strategy games 64, 124
soundtracks 100–101
Street Fighter (SF) 31, 43, 117, 130–31, 148; *SF 6* 130, 131; *SF II* 109, 131; *SF II Turbo* 131; *SF IV* 131; *SF V* 131; *SF 30th Anniversary Collection* 131

Street Fighter (movie) 68
Strong National Museum of Play 74
Studio MDHR 58
Sublogic 48
Subway Surfers 53, 110–11
Summers, Jamie 62
Sundstein, Johan 63
Super Castlevania IV 80
Super Mario *see* Mario
Super Metroid 65
Super Smash Bros.; *Super Smash Bros. Brawl* 159; *Super Smash Bros. Ultimate* 43, 70, 72, 123, 124
survival-horror games 59, 125
Svahn, Samuel 109
Swidecki, Carrie 122
Switch 10, 11, 54, 55, 70, 79
Swordquest: AirWorld 93
SYBO Games 53, 110, 111

T
Taito 51
Tallest videogame cosplay costume 19
Tango Gameworks 14
Taylor, Grant 125
Team Fortress 2 92
Team Liquid 109
Teenage Mutant Ninja Turtles 130
Tekhan World Cup 129
Tekken 28, 43; *Tekken 5* 139
Temple Run 53
Tencent 34
Terraria 95
Tetris 61, 74, 83, 118, 142–43; *Tetris DS* 170; *Tetris Effect* 125
Tetris (movie) 143
Thecatamites 15
Tilley, Thomas 33
TiMi Studio Group 52
Tockstar 92
Tom & Friends 82
Tom Clancy's Rainbow Six Siege 87
Tomb Raider 31, 40, 140
Tomb Raider (movie) 137, 141
Tone, Tommy 15
Top 10 best-selling Mario games 172
Top 10 most critically acclaimed Mario games 173
Top 10 most streamed videogame soundtracks 100–101
Top 25 most played videogames 52–53
Torment: Tides of Numenera 75
Toss-Up 44
tournaments 63, 71, 86, 109, 144, 148, 167; *see also* esports
Tower of Hell 146
trailers 11, 92; app trailers 82
Transformers 19
Traveller's Tales 97
Triband 15
Tripod Studio 30
Twitch 22, 89, 97, 107; debut stream 78; viewership 89, 144–45

U
Ubisoft 87, 122, 123
Ubisoft Montreal 99
Uematsu, Nobuo 58
Uemura, Masayuki 44
Ultima Online 162

Uncharted 3: Drake's Deception 69
Uncharted 4: A Thief's End 116
Uncharted (movie) 69
Undertale 101
Unreal Engine 5 141
user-generated content platforms 146–47, 162

V
Valheim 95
Valko Game Studios 15
Valorant 14
Valve 28, 30, 87, 88, 95
Van Damme, Jean-Claude 68
VCTR-SCTR 93
Venba 15
Viana, Isaac 62
Video Olympics 93
Videogame spaceships 84–85
Viewfinder 14
Vikander, Alicia 68, 137, 141
Virtua Striker 128
virtual reality games 124, 162–63
Visai Games 15
voice actors 10, 40, 57, 69, 108, 135, 170
VSPO 34
Vujity-Zsolnay, Barnabás 24, 124

W
Wahlberg, Mark 69
Warcraft (movie) 69
Warcraft: Orcs & Humans 107
Warner Bros. Games 14
Welcome to Raccoon City 59
What the Car? 15
Whitefoot, David 124, 127
Whiteman, Matt 62
Wii 54, 61
Wii Sports 61
Wii U 54, 70
Williams, Lee 15
The Witcher 3: Wild Hunt 23, 101; *Wild Hunt: Blood and Wine* 23
Wizet 52
Wolfenstein 56
Wolfpaq 146
Wong, Faye 58
World Soccer Winning Eleven 7 International 126
World of Warcraft 24, 69, 88, 107, 124; *Dragonflight* 24; *Shadowlands* 24
Wright, Will 96

X
Xbox 10, 80, 129, 139
Xbox 360 46, 128
Xbox Adaptive Controller 116
Xbox One 42
Xbox Studio 98
Xylem Studios 15

Y
Yang Binglin 94
Yars' Revenge Reimagined 93
Year in gaming 10–13
YouTube 82, 148, 177
Ys Net 75

Z
Zeekerss 15
Zelda II: The Adventure of Link 161
ZeniMaxMedia 56
zombies 57, 118

FEATURED GAMES

Guinness World Records Gamer's Edition 2025 references a total of 432 unique videogames.

Actua Soccer
Gremlin Interactive, 1995
Adopt Me! Uplift Games, 2017
Adventure Atari, 1980
Air-Sea Battle Atari, 1977
Alan Wake II
Remedy Entertainment, 2023
Among Us Innersloth, 2018
Angry Birds Rovio
Entertainment, 2009
Animal Crossing: New Horizons
Nintendo, 2020
Anthology of the Killer
Thecatamites, 2024
Asgard's Wrath 2
Sanzaru Games, 2023
Assassins Creed II
Ubisoft Montreal, 2009
Assassins Creed Valhalla
Ubisoft Montreal, 2022
Assassins Creed Valhalla:
Dawn of Ragnarok
Ubisoft Montreal, 2022
Assetto Corsa
Kunos Simulazioni, 2014
Asteroids Atari, 1979
Astro's Playroom
Japan Studio, 2020
Atomic Heart Mundfish, 2023

Baldur's Gate 3
Larian Studios, 2023
Basic Math Atari, 1977
Basketball! Magnavox, 1973
Batman: Arkham Asylum
Rocksteady Studios, 2009
Batman: Arkham City
Rocksteady Studios, 2011
Batman: The Telltale Series
Telltale Games, 2016
Battlefield V DICE, 2018
Blackjack Atari, 1977
Bloodborne FromSoftware, 2015
Bloodstained: Ritual of the Night
ArtPlay, 2019
Breakout Atari, 1976
Brookhaven RP Wolfpaq, 2020

Call of Duty Infinity Ward, 2003
Call of Duty 2 Infinity Ward, 2005
Call of Duty 3 Treyarch, 2006
Call of Duty 4: Modern Warfare
Infinity Ward, 2007
Call of Duty: Advanced Warfare
Sledgehammer Games, 2014
Call of Duty: Black Ops
Treyarch, 2010
Call of Duty: Black Ops 4
Treyarch, 2018
Call of Duty: Black Ops II
Treyarch, 2012
Call of Duty: Black Ops III
Treyarch, 2015
Call of Duty: Black Ops Cold War
Treyarch/Raven Software, 2020
Call of Duty: Black Ops:
Declassified nStigate
Games, 2012
Call of Duty: Black Ops - Zombies
Ideaworks, 2011
Call of Duty: Ghosts
Infinity Ward, 2013
Call of Duty: Infinite Warfare
Infinity Ward, 2016
Call of Duty: Mobile
TiMi Studio Group, 2019

Call of Duty: Modern Warfare
Infinity Ward, 2019
Call of Duty: Modern Warfare 2
Infinity Ward, 2009
Call of Duty: Modern Warfare 3
Infinity Ward/Sledgehammer
Games, 2011
Call of Duty: Modern Warfare II
Infinity Ward, 2022
Call of Duty: Modern Warfare III
Sledgehammer Games, 2023
Call of Duty: Vanguard
Sledgehammer Games, 2021
Call of Duty: Warzone Raven
Software/Infinity Ward, 2020
Call of Duty: Warzone Mobile
Activision, 2024
Call of Duty: World at War
Treyarch, 2008
Call of Duty: WW II
Sledgehamer Games, 2017
Candy Crush Saga King, 2012
Capcom vs. SNK 2: Mark of the
Millennium 2001 Capcom, 2001
Centipede Atari, 1981
Chrono Trigger Square, 1995
Chú Mó Chú Mó Team, 2023
Club Penguin New Horizon
Interactive, 2005
Cocoon Geometric
Interactive, 2023
Combat Atari, 1977
Conqueror's Blade
Blooming Tech, 2019
Counter-Strike 2 Valve, 2023
Counter-Strike: Global Offensive
Valve, 2012
Crash Bandicoot
Naughty Dog, 1996
Crazyracing Kartrider
Nexon, 2004
Crossfire Smilegate
Entertainment, 2007
Cryptmaster Paul Hart/Lee
Williams/Akupara Games, 2024
Cuphead Studio MDHR, 2017
Cyberpunk 2077
CD Projekt Red, 2020
Cyberpunk 2077: Phantom
Liberty CD Projekt Red, 2023

Dark Age of Camelot
Mythic Entertainment, 2001
Dave the Diver Mintrocket, 2023
Deltarune Toby Fox, 2018
Diablo III Blizzard, 2012
Diablo IV Blizzard, 2023
Digimon Bandai, 1998–2022
Dishonored Arkane Studios, 2012
Donkey Kong Nintendo, 1981
DOOM id Software, 2016
Dota 2 Valve, 2013
Dr. Mario Nintendo, 1990
Dragon Ball various, 1986
Dragon Nest Eyedentity
Games, 2010
Driver Reflections
Interactive, 1999
Dungeon Fighter Online
Neople, 2005

EA Sports FC 24 EA Sports, 2023
eFootball 2024 Konami, 2023
Eiyuden Chronicle: Hundred
Heroes Rabbit and Bear
Studios, 2024
Elden Ring FromSoftware, 2022
The Elder Scrolls Bethesda, 1994
The Elder Scrolls V: Skyrim
Bethesda, 2011

The Elder Scrolls: Daggerfall
Bethesda, 1996
Elite David Braben/Ian Bell, 1984
EVE: War for New Eden
Titan Forge, 2024
EVE Online CCP Games, 2003

Fable Big Blue Box Studios, 2004
Fallout Interplay
Productions, 1997
Fallout 4 Bethesda, 2015
Fantasy Westward Journey
NetEase Games, 2001
FIFA 16 EA, 2015
FIFA 18 EA, 2017
FIFA 22 EA, 2021
FIFA 23 EA, 2022
FIFA International Soccer EA, 1993
Final Fantasy Square
Enix, 1987–2024
Final Fantasy VII Rebirth
Square Enix, 2024
Final Fantasy VII Remake
Square Enix, 2020
Final Fantasy VIII Square, 1999
Final Fantasy X Square, 2001
Final Fantasy XIV: Endwalker
Square Enix, 2021
Final Fantasy XIV:
Shadowbringers
Square Enix, 2019
Final Fantasy XIV: Stormblood
Square Enix, 2017
Final Fantasy XVI
Square Enix, 2023
Five Nights at Freddy's
Scott Cawthon, 2014
Flight Simulator II Sublogic, 1983
Football Manager
Sports Interactive, 2005
Football Manager 2010
Sports Interactive, 2009
Football Manager 2018
Sports Interactive, 2017
Football Manager 2024
Sports Interactive, 2023
Fortnite Epic Games, 2017
Fortnite Battle Royale
Epic Games, 2017
Fortnite Festival Harmonix, 2023
Forza Horizon 3
Playground Games, 2016
Forza Horizon 5
Playground Games, 2021
Fruit Ninja Halfbrick Studios, 2010
FS1 Flight Simulator
Sublogic, 1979

Galaxian Namco, 1979
Garry's Mod
Facepunch Studios, 2006
Gears of War Epic Games, 2006
Ghost of Tsushima Sucker Punch
Productions, 2020
GKART/QQ Speed
TiMi Studio Group, 2010
God of War
Santa Monica Studio, 2005
God of War Ragnarök
Santa Monica Studio, 2022
Golden Axe Sega, 1989
GoldenEye 007 Rare, 1997
Gran Turismo,
Polyphony Digital, 1997
Gran Turismo 4
Polyphony Digital, 2004
Gran Turismo 7
Polyphony Digital, 2022
Gran Turismo Sport
Polyphony, 2017

Grand Theft Auto DMA, 1997
Grand Theft Auto III DMA, 2001
Grand Theft Auto IV
Rockstar, 2008
Grand Theft Auto V Rockstar, 2013
Grand Theft Auto VI
Rockstar, 2023
Grand Theft Auto: San Andreas
Rockstar, 2004
Grand Theft Auto: Vice City 139
Guild Wars 2 ArenaNet, 2012
Guitar Hero III: Legends of Rock
Neversoft, 2007
Gyromite Nintendo, 1985

Habitat LucasArts, 1986
Half-Life 2 Valve, 2004
Halo Bungie, 2001
Halo 4 343 Industries, 2012
Harry Potter and the Chamber
of Secrets EA, 2002
Harry Potter: Magic Awakened
NetEase Games, 2021
Harry Potter and the Prisoner
of Azkaban KnowWonder, 2004
Haunted House Atari, 2022
Healthy Food Challenge
Simar Khurana, 2023
Heavyweight Champ Sega, 1976
HELLDIVERS II Arrowhead Game
Studios, 2024
Hi-Fi Rush
Tango Gameworks, 2023
Hogwarts Legacy
Avalanche Software, 2023
Hollow Knight Team Cherry, 2017
Homeworld
Relic Entertainment, 1999
Honkai: Star Rail miHoYo, 2023
Honor of Kings TiMi Studio
Group, 2015
Horizon Call of the Mountain
Guerrilla/Firesprite, 2023
Horizon Forbidden
West Guerrilla Games, 2022
Horizon Zero Dawn
Guerrilla Games, 2017
Hot Wheels Unleashed
Milestone, 2021

Indy 500 Atari, 1977
Infamous: Second Son
Sucker Punch Productions, 2014
Injustice 2 NetherRealm
Studios, 2017
Injustice 2: Legendary Edition
NetherRealm Studios, 2018
International Superstar Soccer
Konami, 1994

Jack in the Dark Infogames, 1993
Jet Set Radio Smilebit, 2000
Jetpack Joyride
Halfbrick Studios, 2011
Just Dance 2015 Ubisoft, 2014
Just Dance 2017 Ubisoft, 2016
Just Dance 2019 Ubisoft, 2018
Just Dance 2024 Edition
Ubisoft, 2021

Kick Off Dino Dini, 1989
Kingdom Hearts Square, 2002
Kirby: Planet Robobot
HAL Laboratory, 2016

Labyrinthine Valko Game
Studios, 2023
Lara Croft: Tomb Raider
Core Design, 1996
The Last of Us Naughty Dog, 2013
The Last of Us Part I
Naughty Dog, 2022
The Last of Us Part II
Naughty Dog, 2020

League of Legends Riot Games, 2009

The Legend of Zelda Nintendo, 1986

The Legend of Zelda: A Link Between Worlds Nintendo, 2013

The Legend of Zelda: A Link to the Past Nintendo, 1991

The Legend of Zelda: Breath of the Wild Nintendo, 2017

The Legend of Zelda: Four Swords Adventures Nintendo, 2004

The Legend of Zelda: Link's Awakening Nintendo, 1993

The Legend of Zelda: Majora's Mask Nintendo, 2000

The Legend of Zelda: Ocarina of Time Nintendo, 1998

The Legend of Zelda: Oracle of Seasons/Oracle of Ages Flagship, 2001

The Legend of Zelda: Phantom Hourglass Nintendo, 2007

The Legend of Zelda: Skyward Sword Nintendo, 2011

The Legend of Zelda: Spirit Tracks Nintendo, 2009

The Legend of Zelda: Tears of the Kingdom Nintendo, 2023

The Legend of Zelda: The Minish Cap Capcom/Flagship, 2004

The Legend of Zelda: The Wind Waker Nintendo, 2002

The Legend of Zelda: Tri Force Heroes Nintendo, 2015

The Legend of Zelda: Twilight Princess Nintendo, 2006

LEGO Fortnite Epic Games, 2023

LEGO Harry Potter: Years 1–4 Traveller's Tales, 2010

LEGO Harry Potter: Years 5–7 Traveller's Tales, 2011

LEGO Star Wars: The Force Awakens TT Fusion, 2016

Lethal Company Zeekerss, 2023

Lost Ark Smilegate/Tripod Studio, 2019

Luigi's Hammer Toss Nintendo, 1990

Luigi's Mansion 3 Next Level Games, 2019

MapleStory Wizet, 2003

Mario is Missing! Software Toolworks, 1993

Mario Kart: Super Circuit Intelligent Systems, 2001

Mario Kart 8 Nintendo, 2014

Mario Kart 8 Deluxe Nintendo, 2017

Mario Kart DS Nintendo, 2005

Mario Kart Wii Nintendo, 2008

Mario + Rabbids Sparks of Hope Ubisoft, 2022

Mario vs. Donkey Kong Nintendo, 2004

Mario's Game Gallery Presage Software, 1995

Marvel's Spider-Man Insomniac Games, 2018

Marvel's Spider-Man 2 Insomniac Games, 2023

Marvel's Spider-Man: Miles Morales Insomniac Games, 2020

Marvel's Spider-Man Remastered Insomniac Games, 2022

Mediterranea Inferno Eyeguys/Lorenzo Redaelli, 2023

MeepCity Alex Binello, 2016

Metal Gear Konami, 1987

Metal Gear Solid 2: Sons of Liberty Konami, 2001

Microsoft Flight Simulator Sublogic, 1982

Midnight Club Rockstar, 2000

Minecraft Mojang Studios, 2011

Minecraft Education Mojang Studios, 2016

Minecraft Legends Mojang Studios, 2023

Minecraft: Story Mode Telltale Games, 2015

Mini World Miniplay Inc, 2017

Miraculous RP: Ladybug & Cat Noir Toya/ZAG Games, 2021

Missile Command Atari, 1980

Mobile Legends: Bang Bang Moonton, 2016

Monster Hunter Freedom Unite Capcom, 2008

Monster Hunter Rise Capcom, 2021

Mortal Kombat Midway, 1992

Mortal Kombat 1 NetherRealm Studios, 2023

Moss Polyarc, 2018

My Talking Tom Outfit7, 2013

Narutimetto Akuseru 2 Bandai, 2007

NASL Soccer Mattel, 1980

NBA 2K20 Visual Concepts, 2019

NBA Street V3 IEA, 2005

Need for Speed: Most Wanted EA, 2005

Need for Speed/NFS Unbound EA, 2005

Neo Breakout Atari, 2022

New Super Mario Bros. Nintendo, 2006

New Super Mario Bros. U Deluxe Nintendo, 2019

New Super Mario Bros. Wii Nintendo, 2009

New World Amazon Games, 2021

Nickelodeon All-Star Brawl Ludosity/Fair Play Labs, 2021

Nier: Automata Platinum Games, 2017

No Man's Sky Hello Games, 2016

Octopus Thomas Tilley, 2017

Once Upon a Jester Bonte Avond, 2022

The Oregon Trail various, 1971

The Oregon Trail: Boom Town Tilting Point, 2023

Overwatch Blizzard, 2016

PAC-MAN Namco, 1980

Palworld Pocket Pair, 2024

Paper Mario Intelligent Systems, 2000

Pelé's Soccer Atari, 1981

Persona 5 P-Studio, 2016

Persona 5 Royal Atlus, 2019

Phonopolis Amanita Design, 2023

Pillars of Eternity Obsidian Entertainment, 2015

Pin Bot Nintendo, 1990

PlanetSide 2 Rogue Planet Games, 2022

Pokémon 38, 60, 118, 125, 152–155

Pokémon Blue Game Freak, 1996

Pokémon Crystal Game Freak, 2000

Pokémon Diamond Game Freak, 2006

Pokémon Emerald Game Freak, 2004

Pokémon GO Niantic, 2016

Pokémon Gold Game Freak, 1999

Pokémon Green Game Freak, 1996

Pokémon Pearl Game Freak, 2006

Pokémon Platinum Game Freak, 2008

Pokémon Red Game Freak, 1996

Pokémon Ruby Game Freak, 2002

Pokémon Sapphire Game Freak, 2002

Pokémon Scarlet Game Freak, 2022

Pokémon Shield Game Freak, 2019

Pokémon Silver Game Freak, 1999

Pokémon Violet Game Freak, 2022

Pong Atari, 1972

Popeye Nintendo, 1982

Pro Evolution Soccer Konami, 2001

Pro Soccer Evolution 3 Konami, 2003

Psychonauts Double Fine Productions, 2005

PUBG: Battlegrounds PUBG Studios, 2017

PUBG Mobile Lightspeed & Quantum Studios, 2018

Quadratank Atari, 2022

Quake id Software, 1996

Rage id Software, 2011

RAM: Random Access Mayhem Xylem Studios, 2023

Rec Room Rec Room, 2016

Red Dead Redemption Rockstar, 2010

Red Dead Redemption 2 Rockstar, 2018

Resident Evil Capcom, 1996

Resident Evil 4 Capcom, 2005

Resident Evil: Afterlife Capcom, 2010

Resident Evil – Code: Veronica Capcom, 2000

Rhythm Doctor 7th Beat Games, 2021

Roblox Roblox Corporation, 2006

Rock Band Harmonix, 2007

Rock Band 4 Harmonix, 2015

Rocket League Psyonix, 2015

Rocket Racing Psyonix, 2023

Rules of Survival NetEase Games, 2018

Runescape Jagex, 2001

The Sandbox Pixowl, 2012

Sea of Stars Sabotage Studios, 2023

Second Life Linden Lab, 2003

Sensible Soccer Sensible Software, 1992

Sensible World of Soccer Sensible Software, 2007

Shenmue III Deep Silver, 2019

Sifu Sloclap, 2022

Silent Hill Konami, 1999

Silk ihobo, 2019

SimCity Maxis, 1989

The Sims Maxis, 2000

The Sims 4 Maxis, 2014

Sky Skipper Nintendo, 1981

Skylanders various, 20011

Sonic the Hedgehog Sonic Team, 1991

Sonic the Hedgehog 2 Sega Technical Institute, 1992

Sonic Mania various, 2017

Sonic Origins Sonic Team, 2022

Sonic Speed Simulator Gamefam Studios, 2022

Sonic Superstars Arzest/Sonic Team, 2023

Sons of the Forest Endnight Games, 2024

SoulCalibur Bandai Namco, 1998

Space Invaders Taito, 1978

Spacewar! Steve Russell, 1962

Spider-Man 2 Insomniac Games, 2023

Spider-Man Total Mayhem Gameloft, 2010

SpongeBob SquarePants: Battle for Bikini Bottom – Rehydrated Purple Lamp Studios, 2020

Spyro Insomniac Games, 1998

Star Wars: Knights of the Old Republic LucasArts, 2003

Star Wars: The Force Awakens TT Fusion, 2016

Star Wars: The Skywalker Saga Traveller's Tales, 2022

StarCraft Blizzard, 1998

StarCraft II Blizzard, 2010

StarCraft II: Wings of Liberty Blizzard, 2010

StarCraft: Brood War Saffire/Blizzard, 1998

StarCraft: Remastered Blizzard, 2017

Stardew Valley ConcernedApe, 2016

Starfield Bethesda, 2023

State of Decay 2 Undead Labs, 2018

Street Fighter Capcom, 1987

Street Fighter 6 Capcom, 2023

Street Fighter 30th Anniversary Collection Digital Eclipse, 2018

Street Fighter II Capcom, 1992

Street Fighter II Turbo Capcom, 1993

Street Fighter IV Capcom and Dimps, 2009

Street Fighter V Capcom and Dimps, 2016

Subway Surfers Blast SYBO/Outplay Entertainment, 2023

Subway Surfers Kiloo/SYBO Games, 2012

Super Mario 3D World Nintendo, 2013

Super Mario 64 Nintendo, 1996

Super Mario Advance 4 Nintendo, 2003

Super Mario Bros. Nintendo, 1985

Super Mario Bros. 3 Nintendo, 1988

Super Mario Bros. Wonder, Nintendo, 2023

Super Mario Galaxy Nintendo, 2007

Super Mario Galaxy 2 Nintendo, 2010

Super Mario Kart Nintendo, 1992

Super Mario Maker Nintendo, 2015

Super Mario Odyssey Nintendo, 2017

Super Mario Party ND Cube, 2018

Super Mario Sunshine Nintendo, 2002

Super Mario World Nintendo, 1990

Super Metroid Nintendo, 1994

Super Smash Bros. HAL Laboratory, 1999

Super Smash Bros. Brawl Sora/Game Arts, 2008

Super Smash Bros. Ultimate Bandai Namco/Sora, 2018

Super Street Fighter II Capcom, 1994

Super Street Fighter II: The New Challengers Capcom, 1993

Super Castlevania IV Konami, 1991

Swordquest: AirWorld Atari, 2022

Team Fortress 2 Valve, 2007

Tehkan World Cup Tehkan, 1985

Tekken Namco, 1994

Tekken 5 Namco, 2005

Temple Run Imangi Studios, 2011

Terraria Re-Logic, 2011

Tetris Alexey Pajitnov, 1984

Tetris Beat N3TWORK, 2021

Tetris DS Nintendo, 2006

Tetris Effect Monstars/
Resonair, 2019
Tetris Party Deluxe Blue Planet
Software, 2010
Tom Clancy's Rainbow Six Siege
Ubisoft, 2015
Torment: Tides of Numenera inXile
Entertainment, 2017
Toss-Up Nintendo, 1980
Tower of Hell YXCeptional
Studios, 2024

Ultima Online Origin Systems, 1997
Ultra Street Fighter IV
Capcom, 2014
Uncharted 3: Drake's Deception
Naughty Dog, 2011
Uncharted 4: A Thief's End
Naughty Dog, 2016
Undertale Toby Fox, 2015

Valheim Iron Gate Studio, 2021
Valorant Riot Games, 2020
VCTR-SCTR Atari, 2022
Venba Visai Games, 2023

Video Olympics Atari, 1977
Viewfinder Sad Owl Studios, 2023
Virtua Striker Sega, 1994

What the Car? Triband, 2024
Wii Sports Nintendo, 2006
The Witcher 3: Wild Hunt CD
Prokekt Red, 2015
*The Witcher 3: Wild Hunt: Blood
and Wine* CD Projekt Red, 2016
Wolfenstein Raven Software, 2009
*World Soccer Winning Eleven
7 International* KCET/
Konami, 2004
World of Warcraft Blizzard, 2004
World of Warcraft: Dragonflight
Blizzard, 2022
World of Warcraft: Shadowlands
Blizzard, 2023

Yars' Revenge Reimagined
Atari, 2022

Zelda II: The Adventure of Link
Nintendo, 1987

ACKNOWLEDGEMENTS

Guinness World Records would like to thank the following for their help in compiling *Gamer's Edition 2025*:

Laura Adkins (AWR Music), Rob Barefoot (R. Talsorian games), Claire Beard (KAP toys), Jason Blagman (Rotten Tomatoes), David Bull (Crystal Dynamics), Madelyn Burr (JSA+Partners), Michael Cisneros (Sega of America, Inc.), Ellen Clark (The Walt Disney Company), Vince Clemente (Classic Tetris World Championship), Hannah Cook (Nintendo), Jeff Cork (Games Done Quick), Dana Cowley (Epic Games), Tom Goldberger (Square Enix), Tadeja Irmančnik (Outfit7), Sarah Jones (Epic Games), Daria

R Licausi (Mattel, Inc.), Michael Moccio (Innersloth), Stephanie Ngo (Nvidia), Dylan Quintero (The Walt Disney Company), Adrian Page-Mitchell (Computing History. org), Massimo Petrozzi (Computer History Museum), Shane Rhinewald (Museum of Play), Whitney Smith (AssemblyInc), Team Blue Scuti, Victoria Tran (Innersloth), Patrick Walker (Mattel, Inc.), Luke Wakeham, Ariel West (Riot Games), Colette Vignocchi (Zebra Partners).

LEGO builders: Frederick Lazell, Thomas Waugh, James Waugh, Grace Wild, Sam Wild, Theodore Maskell, Juliet Dawson, William Sinden, Henry Jones, Catherine Pearce, Caitlin Hyem

COUNTRY CODES

ABW	Aruba	GIN	Guinea	PAN	Panama
AFG	Afghanistan	GMB	Gambia	PER	Peru
AGO	Angola	GNB	Guinea-Bissau	PHL	Philippines
AIA	Anguilla	GNQ	Equatorial Guinea	PLW	Palau
ALB	Albania	GRC	Greece	PNG	Papua New Guinea
AND	Andorra	GRD	Grenada	POL	Poland
ANT	Netherlands Antilles	GRL	Greenland	PRI	Puerto Rico
		GTM	Guatemala	PRK	Korea, DPRO
ARG	Argentina	GUM	Guam	PRT	Portugal
ARM	Armenia	GUY	Guyana	PRY	Paraguay
ASM	American Samoa	HND	Honduras	QAT	Qatar
ATG	Antigua and Barbuda	HRV	Croatia (Hrvatska)	ROM	Romania
		HTI	Haiti	RUS	Russian Federation
AUS	Australia	HUN	Hungary	RWA	Rwanda
AUT	Austria	IDN	Indonesia	SAU	Saudi Arabia
AZE	Azerbaijan	IND	India	SDN	Sudan
BDI	Burundi	IRL	Ireland	SEN	Senegal
BEL	Belgium	IRN	Iran	SGP	Singapore
BEN	Benin	IRQ	Iraq	SHN	Saint Helena
BFA	Burkina Faso	ISL	Iceland	SLB	Solomon Islands
BGD	Bangladesh	ISR	Israel	SLE	Sierra Leone
BGR	Bulgaria	ITA	Italy	SLV	El Salvador
BHR	Bahrain	JAM	Jamaica	SMR	San Marino
BHS	The Bahamas	JOR	Jordan	SOM	Somalia
BIH	Bosnia and Herzegovina	JPN	Japan	SRB	Serbia
		KAZ	Kazakhstan	SSD	South Sudan
BLR	Belarus	KEN	Kenya	STP	São Tomé and Príncipe
BLZ	Belize	KGZ	Kyrgyzstan		
BMU	Bermuda	KHM	Cambodia	SUR	Suriname
BOL	Bolivia	KIR	Kiribati	SVK	Slovakia
BRA	Brazil	KNA	Saint Kitts and Nevis	SVN	Slovenia
BRB	Barbados			SWE	Sweden
BRN	Brunei Darussalam	KOR	Korea, Republic of	SWZ	Eswatini
BTN	Bhutan	KWT	Kuwait	SYC	Seychelles
BWA	Botswana	LAO	Laos	SYR	Syrian Arab Republic
CAF	Central African Republic	LBN	Lebanon		
		LBR	Liberia	TCA	Turks and Caicos Islands
CAN	Canada	LBY	Libya		
CHE	Switzerland	LCA	Saint Lucia	TCD	Chad
CHL	Chile	LIE	Liechtenstein	TGO	Togo
CHN	China	LKA	Sri Lanka	THA	Thailand
CIV	Côte d'Ivoire	LSO	Lesotho	TJK	Tajikistan
CMR	Cameroon	LTU	Lithuania	TKM	Turkmenistan
COD	Congo, DR of the	LUX	Luxembourg	TMP	East Timor
		LVA	Latvia	TON	Tonga
COG	Congo	MAR	Morocco	TTO	Trinidad and Tobago
COK	Cook Islands	MCO	Monaco		
		MDA	Moldova	TUN	Tunisia
COL	Colombia	MDG	Madagascar	TUR	Türkiye
COM	Comoros	MDV	Maldives	TUV	Tuvalu
CPV	Cape Verde	MEX	Mexico	TZA	Tanzania
CRI	Costa Rica	MHL	Marshall Islands	UAE	United Arab Emirates
CUB	Cuba	MKD	North Macedonia		
CYM	Cayman Islands	MLI	Mali	UGA	Uganda
CYP	Cyprus	MLT	Malta	UK	United Kingdom
CZE	Czechia	MMR	Myanmar	UKR	Ukraine
DEU	Germany	MNE	Montenegro	UMI	US Minor Islands
DJI	Djibouti	MNG	Mongolia	URY	Uruguay
DMA	Dominica	MNP	Northern Mariana Islands	USA	United States of America
DNK	Denmark				
DOM	Dominican Republic	MOZ	Mozambique	UZB	Uzbekistan
		MRT	Mauritania	VAT	Vatican City
DZA	Algeria	MSR	Montserrat	VCT	Saint Vincent and the Grenadines
ECU	Ecuador	MUS	Mauritius		
EGY	Egypt	MWI	Malawi	VEN	Venezuela
ERI	Eritrea	MYS	Malaysia	VGB	Virgin Islands (British)
ESP	Spain	NAM	Namibia		
EST	Estonia	NER	Niger	VIR	Virgin Islands (US)
ETH	Ethiopia	NGA	Nigeria	VNM	Vietnam
FIN	Finland	NIC	Nicaragua	VUT	Vanuatu
FJI	Fiji	NIU	Niue	WSM	Samoa
FRA	France	NLD	Netherlands	YEM	Yemen
FSM	Micronesia, Federated States of	NOR	Norway	ZAF	South Africa
		NPL	Nepal	ZMB	Zambia
GAB	Gabon	NRU	Nauru	ZWE	Zimbabwe
GEO	Georgia	NZ	New Zealand		
GHA	Ghana	OMN	Oman		
GIB	Gibraltar	PAK	Pakistan		

MEET THE TEAM

WESLEY YIN-POOLE
Gaming Consultant

What's your current job when not advising GWR on its gaming records?
I'm IGN's UK news editor.

What was your first gaming experience?
Super Mario Bros. on the NES. I think I was around eight or nine when we got a NES and I loved it. I played *Super Mario Bros. 2* and then *Super Mario Bros. 3* for years, trying to unearth every secret before moving on to *Super Mario World* on the SNES.

What was your favourite game as a kid?
Street Fighter 2, both in arcades and on the SNES. It was my first proper competitive multiplayer gaming experience and I fell in love with it. I imported the Japanese version before it launched in the UK and tried to make sense of the Japanese game manual!

Do you have a favourite game developer?
Capcom has made some of my favourite games of all time, mainly the *Street Fighter* series, but I also love the *Resident Evil* games, *Devil May Cry* and *Marvel vs. Capcom*.

And what are you really enjoying playing right now?
Generally I play a lot of *Call of Duty*. But right now I'm obsessed with *HELLDIVERS 2*. I love how it takes one of my favourite films, *Starship Troopers*, and turns it into a super-fun co-op shooter about blowing up bugs and robots.

If you had to join an esports team, what game would be your first choice?
I'm not as good as I used to be, but I'm still handy at *Street Fighter*, particularly the various versions of *Street Fighter 2*, with Guile and his Sonic Booms my go-to. I have a backup, Zangief, for when I'm desperate!

What new launches are you particularly looking forward to playing next year?
I think everyone in the world is looking forward to *Grand Theft Auto VI*!

What excites you about gaming?
Other than world records, you mean?! The best thing about videogames is their ability to build a community and steer fans in interesting directions. Gaming can provide a safe space to make like-minded friends and socialize. And in the world of videogames, there's always something new and exciting around the corner...

THOMAS MARSHALL
Gaming Records Curator

Reliving *Ghost of Tsushima* with a vengeful spirit

PIERRE SALARD
Writer, Spaceships feature

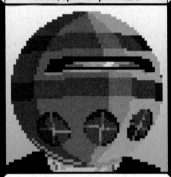

The Spaceshipper – curated by Pierre Salard – is on X, Threads, Bluesky, Mastodon and Instagram. The account is dedicated to the past, present and future of space sci-fi, highlighting the work of artists, keeping up with the latest news and looking back at the creation of classics. The Spaceshipper is also a series of threads, articles and deep dives into the making of sci-fi. And lots of spaceships!

Zangief from *Street Fighter*

CRAIG GLENDAY
Editor-in-Chief

Rediscovering the dark delights of *Inside* on the Switch

JANE BOATFIELD
Director of Publishing & Book Production

Cheating with Yoshi in *Super Mario Bros. Wonder* on the Switch!

RYAN GALE
Designer

Exploring *The Outer Worlds* again to achieve the Platinum trophy

CHRIS BRYANS
Layout Editor

Leading Preston NE to Champions League glory in *EA Sports FC 24*

EDDIE DE OLIVEIRA
Layout Editor

Fixing a failing marriage in *It Takes Two* on the PS5

LUCY TALAVERA
Picture Editor

Looking for Zelda in *The Legend of Zelda: Tears of the Kingdom*

BEN HOLLINGUM
Senior Editor

Getting distracted by Night City in *Cyberpunk 2077*

THOMAS MCCURDY
Production & Distribution Manager

Failing to meet the bar in *The Great Ace Attorney*

MATTHEW WHITE
Proofreader

On level 723 "Cardzilla" in MobilityWare's *Solitaire*

QUIZ ANSWERS

P.141: Female Characters
1. Aloy (*Horizon Zero Dawn*)
2. Ms. PAC-Man (*Ms. PAC-Man*)
3. Samus (*Metroid*)
4. Cereza (*Bayonetta*)
5. Princess Peach (*Mario*)
6. Yuna (*Resident Evil*)
7. Chun-Li (*Street Fighter*)
8. Ellie (*The Last of Us*)
9. Commander Shepard (*Mass Effect*)
10. Jill Valentine (*Resident Evil*)

How many iconic female characters can you name?

P.129: *EA Sports FC 24* stars
Front row (left to right): Alexander Isak, Selma Bacha, Alexia Putellas, Vinicius Júnior, Virgil van Dijk, Son Heung-min, Trinity Rodman, Federico Chiesa and Enzo Fernández.
Second row (left to right): Jude Bellingham, David Beckham, Vinicius Júnior, Erling Haaland, Sam Kerr, Leah Williamson, Marquinhos and Youssoufa Moukoko.
Third row (left to right): Mia Hamm, Johan Cruyff, Alex Scott, Ronaldinho, Alexandra Popp, Juan Román Riquelme, Didier Drogba and Leicy Santos.
Back row (left to right): Marta, Marcus Rashford, Rudi Völler, Pelé, Zinedine Zidane, Bukayo Saka and Andrea Pirlo.

SIDE QUEST UNLOCKED!

GUINNESS WORLD RECORDS 2025

OUT NOW!

GWR STORE

PLUS: HAVE YOU EVER PARTICIPATED IN A RECORD ATTEMPT?

Head over to the GWR Store now and grab your official, personalized certificate of participation!

Scan or vis
gwrstore.co